CW00402567

First Certificate

Masterclass

Student's Book

Simon Haines

Barbara Stewart

OXFORD UNIVERSITY PRESS

Exam factfile

Introduction

There are five papers in the Cambridge First Certificate exam. The papers are worth the same number of marks (40), except Paper 4, Listening, which is worth half as many marks as the others (20). The pass mark for the exam is about 100 out of 180. There are five grades: A, B and C are pass grades, D and E are fail grades.

Paper 1   Reading comprehension
(1 hour)

Section A

Vocabulary multiple-choice

Exam techniques, Unit 9, page 110

1 This consists of 25 sentences with single words or short phrases missing, for example:
   I never take much on holiday with me, just _____ clothes and a couple of books.
   A few   B little   C a few   D a little
2 You have to choose one of four possible words or phrases to fill the gaps. Only one of the four alternatives makes sense and is grammatically correct.
3 This part of the exam tests a wide range of grammar and vocabulary, including the following:
   a verb forms and tenses, including gerunds
   b phrasal verbs
   c appropriacy (the correct word in a particular context), e.g. *drive* a car, *ride* a motorbike
   d adjective-noun combinations, e.g. a *convenient* time, a *comfortable* chair
   e connectors, e.g. *because, and, despite, although*
   f word building, e.g. suffixes and prefixes
   g prepositions, especially after verbs.

Section B

Comprehension passages

Exam techniques, Unit 1, page 6

1 This section consists of at least three passages. Passage 1 is on a subject of *general interest*. Passage 2 is on a slightly more *specialist subject*, for example science or business. Passage 3 may be a *practical text* of some kind, for example a newspaper article or an advertisement.
2 Altogether there are 15 multiple-choice questions on the passages. You will have to choose answers or finish sentences, for example:
   The writer got to work late because
   A she always had a big breakfast.
   B she wasn't keen on her job.
   C she spent a long time getting ready.
   D she didn't get up in time.
3 Each answer in Section B is worth twice as many marks as each answer in Section A.
4 The questions test your general understanding of the passages, not a detailed understanding of every single word.
5 Only one of the suggested answers to multiple-choice questions is correct. However, the other answers may seem correct at first and may mislead you.

Paper 2   Composition
(1 hour 30 minutes)

Letter
formal Unit 6 page 72
informal Unit 9 page 112

Description
place Unit 1 page 12
object Unit 4 page 48
person Unit 7 page 86
event Unit 8 page 96

Narrative   Unit 5 page 56

Argument essay
Pros and cons Unit 2 page 22
Personal opinion Unit 3 page 36
                    Unit 13 page 158

Speech
formal speech Unit 11 page 134
informal talk Unit 10 page 118

Set book

1 This paper comprises six titles covering the above composition types.
2 You have to choose two titles and write a composition of 120 –180 words for each.
3 The composition tests your overall command of English, including the way you structure your

sentences and paragraphs, and the vocabulary you use. Grammar, punctuation and spelling are also important.

4 The overall impression is what counts. You do not lose marks for each mistake.

Paper 3 Use of English (2 hours)

Section A

Gap filling (Cloze)
Exam techniques, Unit 3, page 30

1 This is a passage of about 200 words with 20 words missing.

2 You have to fill each gap with one word, for example:
In the 1990s, _____ (1), the top players can earn twice as _____ (2) in a fortnight . . .

3 The missing words can be verbs, determiners, connectives, prepositions and parts of prepositional phrases, adjectives and adverbs, nouns or parts of idioms.

4 The gap filling passage tests several different abilities: how well you understand the general meaning of written English; how well you understand the links between parts of a text, and how well you know English grammar.

Sentence transformations
Exam techniques, Unit 7, page 80

1 This exercise consists of ten complete sentences and ten incomplete sentences.

2 You have to finish the incomplete sentences, using the word or words given, so that they mean the same as the original complete sentences, for example:
A holiday in Miami is cheaper than one in Bermuda.
A holiday in Bermuda . . .

3 Transformations test your understanding of how sentences are constructed, and your ability to recognize patterns of meaning.

Vocabulary exercises

1 These consist of ten questions, usually divided between two exercises.

2 The possible exercise types are:
a word building from a given root
My sister invited over a hundred people to her _____ party. ENGAGE

b filling gaps in sentences with various forms of one root
*Complete the sentences with a word or expression based on **child**.*
I spent most of my _____ in a village in the mountains.

c filling in various words associated with one topic
Fill the gaps in these sentences with one word connected with the sea.
In the evenings we often went for long walks along the sea _____ .

d filling in the collective noun for a group of given words
carrot, potato, pea, cabbage _____

e forming words which begin with a given word
*Complete the sentences with a word starting with **over**.*
Because my alarm clock didn't go off, I _____ and arrived at school nearly two hours late.

f phrasal verbs exercises.
*Complete these sentences with a phrase made from **take**.*
When my father retired, he _____ painting.

Dialogue completion
Exam techniques, Unit 5, page 62

1 Paper 3 includes either a dialogue completion or a letter expansion.

2 In the dialogue completion, you are given one part of a conversation. You have to write the other part.

3 You have to complete six or seven sentences, which are usually questions. You are generally given the first word of each sentence, for example:
Mike   What (1) _____ ?
Andy   I don't have very much, I'm afraid. But I play squash when I can.

4 The dialogue completion tests your understanding of how the parts of a conversation are linked, and your knowledge of grammar, especially question forms.

Letter expansion
Exam techniques, Unit 11, page 136

1 You are sometimes required to write a letter from notes, for example:
Dear Mr Stigwood,
I be/headmaster/Bradham Grammar/you study/1960−67
a) _____

2 This part of the exam tests your ability to recognize key words which give clues to verb tenses, and your knowledge of grammar.

Section B

Guided writing

Exam techniques, Unit 2, page 24; Unit 8, page 98; Unit 12, page 146

1 The final question in Paper 3 is a guided writing task which involves completing paragraphs which have been started for you.
2 This question tests a combination of different skills.
 a understanding and processing written information in various forms, such as texts, graphs, diagrams, etc.
 b organizing and summarizing information
 c writing clear, concise, fluent English
 d using correct grammar, spelling and punctuation
3 The Guided writing counts for about a quarter of the total marks for Paper 3.

Paper 4   Listening comprehension

(20–30 minutes)

Exam techniques, Unit 6, page 74; Unit 10, page 124

1 In this paper you will hear recordings of three, four or five pieces of natural spoken English. You will hear each piece twice with a short pause between each hearing. The whole test lasts about half an hour. All instructions are given on the cassette.
2 Your understanding will be tested in a number of ways. You may have to answer multiple-choice questions, identify true or false statements, fill gaps, re-order information or identify a picture.
3 The pieces you hear may be telephone conversations, radio broadcasts, conversations, discussions or announcements. You will have to extract information and interpret the opinions or the intentions of the people talking.
4 This is a test of understanding not writing, so you will have to tick boxes or write single words and phrases rather than whole sentences.
5 There is time at the end of the test for you to transfer your answers to the answer sheet.

Paper 5   Interview

(15–20 minutes)

Introduction

1 The oral part of the First Certificate exam is an interview lasting about 15 minutes.
2 The examiner may interview candidates individually or in groups of two or three.
3 To start with, the examiner will ask you a few questions about yourself to put you at ease.

Picture discussion

Exam techniques, Unit 4, page 46; Unit 13, page 160

1 You will be given one or more pictures to talk about. These pictures are usually photographs, but they could be other kinds of visuals like cartoons.
2 The examiner will ask you to talk about what you can see in the photos, and will then move on to more general questions about the subject of the picture.
3 The examiner wants to hear how fluent you are, so it is more important for you to keep talking about the general subject than to worry about details in the photos.

Passages for comment

As part of the oral interview you will be given one or more short texts to read. The texts follow the theme of the photographs in the *Picture discussion*. You will have to discuss the texts with the examiner who may ask you
• what the text is about
• whether you would read it or hear it
• where it is from
• who the speaker/writer is
• who would hear or read it
• why it was written.

Communication activity

1 You will be given a piece of printed information, for example an advertisement, a map or a timetable.
2 The information will be on a similar subject to the rest of the interview.
3 You may be asked to explain the information, make a choice and discuss it, act out a situation or describe something. If you do the interview in a pair or a group you may have to discuss the information, come to an agreement together, or give each other missing information.

1 Description

Old habits die hard

Introduction

A Both these people have unusual skills. The man on the left is Stevie Starr, a professional entertainer. What do you think he does?

B Make a list of all the objects you can see in the photograph of Stevie. What are these objects normally used for?

C The woman on the right is using a traditional skill for doing something. Do you know what she is doing? What are the modern scientific techniques for doing this?

D Do you know of any other traditional skills which are still practised today? Do you think these kinds of skill still have a place in 20th century life?

E Do you, or does anyone you know, have unusual skills or abilities?

Reading

1 Think ahead

You are going to read about Stevie Starr. Look at the title of the article. Does this help you to guess what his stage act consists of? If you have already made a guess, are you still confident that you are correct?

2 Reading

Read the article to find out if your guess is correct. How many of the objects in the photograph on page 1 are mentioned in the text?

A hard act to swallow

STEVIE grew up in a children's home in Scotland. Every week, the staff took a proportion of the children's pocket money to pay for holidays. Little Stevie developed a
5 daring strategy to hang on to what little money he had. He laughs about it now. 'I used to swallow all my coins. That got them really furious, so they'd put me in a room on my own as a punishment. After a few minutes in there, I'd hit myself on
10 the chest and cough the money back up.'

Since then, Stevie has turned into Stevie Starr, a professional regurgitator who does up to four shows a day, and can demand fees of £500 – £2000 a show.

Everything Stevie swallows comes back dry, except for
15 the goldfish. They swim about in his stomach in the water that he swallows for them first. After ten minutes they resume their normal lives in a goldfish bowl. 'They never die,' says Stevie.

Medical experts might have a few worries about Stevie.
20 The sight and sound of him swallowing and bringing back a snooker ball sometimes causes even normally calm people to panic. He also smokes a cigarette, retains the smoke in his stomach, then swallows some butane gas and mixes the two. Next he swallows some washing-up liquid,
25 blows a huge bubble, brings up the smoke and gas inside the bubble, cuts the bubble off, gets someone to set light to it, and BANG!

He enjoys watching audience reactions. 'I tend to start by swallowing a light bulb. There might be a thousand
30 people watching, but once I've done that, you can hear a pin drop.' He loves performing off-stage as well. 'I often go into a pub, order a couple of drinks and then cough up the money to pay for them.'

Watching his routine is an uncomfortable experience. 'I
35 can feel my stomach moving around while I talk to you,' says Stevie. He swallows some sugar, followed by a glass of water, and brings the sugar back dry.

He swallows a locked padlock, followed by the key, opens it in his stomach and returns the padlock.

40 He changes the pattern of a Rubik cube inside his stomach, and regurgitates piles of money selectively. When members of the audience, who have checked the dates of coins beforehand, ask for a 1978 10p or a 1988 20p, he extracts it from the pile of coins in his stomach and brings
45 it up.

Physically, Stevie doesn't believe he is any different from the rest of the human race, who use their stomachs simply to digest food. 'It's all done by muscle control,' he says. 'I imagine a little pair of hands in there doing everything, controlled by my brain. I'm sure I could teach anyone to do what I do.' ●
50

3 Points of view

1 What is your first reaction to reading about Stevie's act?
2 Do you think he really does what he says, or do you think he cheats in some way?
3 Would you go and see Stevie's act? Why? Why not?

4 Comprehension

A Answer these questions about the text.
1 Why was Stevie punished in the children's home?
2 What is the connection between his life in the home and his job now?
3 Why does the bubble go bang when someone sets light to it?
4 What effect does Stevie's swallowing the light bulb have on his audiences?
5 Why are the members of the audience important to Stevie's trick with the coins?
6 What, according to Stevie, is the secret of his skill?

B Vocabulary
Find words, phrases or expressions in the text which mean:
1 group of people who work somewhere together (1 word)
2 brave plan (2 words)
3 keep (3 words)
4 very angry (1 word)
5 payment for a service or job (1 word)
6 continue, carry on with (1 word)
7 doctors (2 words)
8 react in a frightened or alarmed way (1 word)
9 behaviour of people watching the show (2 words)
10 take out, select (1 word)

C Reading between the lines
When you read, you will often need to understand more than is actually written down. These questions will help you to read between the lines.
1 'Stevie grew up in a children's home.' What does this sentence tell you about Stevie's early childhood?
2 'They'd put me in a room on my own as a punishment.' What does this sentence tell you about the children's home?
3 Why do you think Stevie can ask for such a lot of money for a performance?
4 How do you think Stevie would try to teach other people his skill?
5 Choose one word from each of these pairs to best describe Stevie. What evidence is there in the text that your choices are appropriate?
stupid, clever   brave, cowardly   rich, poor

5 The show's over

Imagine you have just been to Stevie's show, or have seen it on television. Write 40–60 words to a friend, describing the show and your reactions to it.

7th May 1994

Dear Tom,

    I'm glad you enjoyed the weekend. It's a pity you couldn't stay longer – I've just seen an incredible performance by a professional regurgitator called Stevie Starr

Grammar and practice

1 Habitual actions and events

A Do these sentences from the article refer to Stevie's life now or to his life in the past?

1 Every week, the staff took a proportion of the children's pocket money.
2 'I used to swallow all my coins.'
3 'They'd put me in a room on my own as a punishment.'
4 'I'd hit myself on the chest and cough the money back up.'
5 'The goldfish never die.'
6 The sight and sound of him swallowing and bringing back a snooker ball sometimes causes even normally calm people to panic.
7 'I tend to start by swallowing a light bulb.'
8 'I often go into a pub, order a couple of drinks and then cough up the money to pay for them.'

B Now or past?

1 How did you decide that a particular sentence referred to the past or the present? Was it the form of the verb, or another word in the sentence, or something else?
2 How can you tell that all the sentences refer to actions or events that are habitual or repeated?

C Now read sections 1 and 2 in the Grammar reference on page 179.

2 Practice

A Finish each of the following sentences so that it means the same as the sentence printed before it.

Example   When I was six, I spent all my spare time with my friends.
           I used *to spend all my spare time with my friends when I was six.*

1 In the winter we played football.
   We used _____ .
2 I hardly ever play football these days.
   Now I don't _____ .
3 Every Saturday afternoon I'd go to a football match with my father.
   My father and I always _____ .
4 When I was eight, I used to go to school with my best friend.
   At the age of eight I always _____ .

5 We walked or ran to the bus-stop to catch our bus.
   We'd _____ .
6 These days I tend to travel everywhere by car.
   I usually _____ .
7 If the weather was bad, the bus was always late.
   Whenever the weather was bad, the bus used _____ .
8 On Saturday mornings my brother and I used to go into town to spend our pocket money.
   My brother and I would _____ .

B Now and then

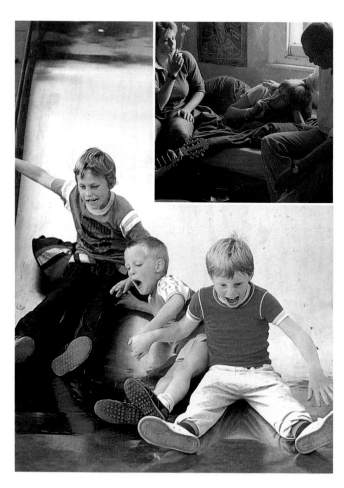

Compare aspects of your life as a child of six or seven with the same aspects of your life now. Think about these situations and make brief notes.

1 your favourite way of spending free time, like a public holiday or a day off school or work

   Example   then – *got up early, played with friends*
              now – *stay in bed, get up late, listen to music*

2 your attitude to money and buying things
3 favourite food and drinks
4 tastes in music and fashion

Compare your ideas in pairs or small groups.

C Think of at least three different ways of answering these questions about the way people behave in certain circumstances. The first one has been done for you.

How do people behave in these situations?

1 when they are tired
   They tend to forget things, fall asleep, and get bad-tempered. Sometimes they drop things or lose things.
2 when they are in a hurry
3 when they are nervous or embarrassed
4 when they want to impress someone

How do you react in these circumstances?

3 Fluency

You and your partner are going on a three-week trekking holiday in the Himalayas. One person has had to drop out of the party at the last minute and you need to find a suitable replacement. The trek is for people of average fitness, and involves no climbing.

The group will walk for six hours each day, which will mean an early start every morning. You'll share a tent at night. There will be a local guide, who speaks English, and Sherpas to carry your equipment.

A Before you read about the people who applied to join your expedition, decide what kind of person you are looking for. Write a list of important personal qualities.

B Student A, read the notes on page 174.
Student B, read these notes about the good and bad points of three applicants. Choose who you would most like to join the expedition. It is up to you to decide whether these people are male or female.

WM Peters

+ Physically fit, experienced climber. Works hard and is completely reliable. Speaks the local language.
− Talks a lot and is not a good listener.

L Palmer

+ Fit and physically strong. A trainee nurse who gets on very well with other people, and is not easily offended.
− Has a tendency to be rather forgetful. Quite lazy and likes to lie in in the morning.

F Trueman

+ Is very enthusiastic about joining the group despite lack of experience. Never complains about anything and always keeps a cool head in emergencies. Good at keeping secrets.
− Has no sense of humour and is not good at relaxing.

C Explain and justify your choice of new team member to your partner. Discuss each other's preferences and try to come to an agreement.

D Finally, compare choices with other pairs.

Exam techniques

Reading comprehension

1 Guidelines

Do	Don't
● Skim the passage quickly from beginning to end.	▶ Don't stop to think about the meaning of individual words you may not understand.
● Read the questions very carefully to find out exactly what they are asking.	▶ Don't rush this process or guess the answers at this stage.
● Read the passage again, this time very carefully. Look for the parts of the passage that contain the information you need.	▶ Don't hurry this second reading. The meanings of individual words may be important now.
● Choose the answer or sentence ending (A, B, C or D) that you think is correct and mark that letter.	▶ Don't guess. Look for evidence.
● Try to eliminate the other three answers, by finding logical reasons why they are wrong. If you can't find these reasons, think again about your choice of correct answer.	▶ Don't be too confident about your choice of answer until you have evidence that the other three cannot be correct.

2 Practice

A Try out the guidelines on the passage opposite. As you read through the text for the first time, decide what sort of passage it is and where it might be from.

B Choose the correct endings to these sentences. When you are confident about your choice, make a note of why the other three endings are wrong.

1   The writer of the passage wished
    A she had Sam's job.   C she looked like Sam.
    B she was called Sam.   D she was an art student.

2   In the mornings Sam used to
    A take a long time to put on her make-up.   C choose her clothes carefully.
    B get ready for work very quickly.   D lie around before going to work.

3   The writer went back to sleep in the mornings because
    A she couldn't face the day ahead.   C she didn't have a job.
    B she was always tired.   D she had no reason to get up.

4   The writer got to work late because
    A she always had a big breakfast.   C she wasn't keen on her job.
    B she spent a long time getting ready.   D she didn't get up in time.

5   Eventually the writer left her job because
    A she didn't want to do it any more.   C she couldn't get to work on time.
    B her employer dismissed her.   D she had got married.

3 Checking

In pairs, compare your choice of correct endings and your reasons for eliminating the wrong endings.

The Perfect Flatmate

When I was 21, I came to live in London. I shared a damp basement flat with a beautiful ex-art student from Brighton. Her name was Sam. She had long brown hair and a slim figure that I was madly jealous of. She ate three chocolate bars for breakfast every morning.

I used to lie in bed looking at her eating and getting dressed, wondering how she could possibly consume so much sugar without losing her teeth, her figure or her complexion. She'd put on her make-up in under a minute, throw on whatever clothes happened to be lying around the room, and rush off to work looking like a model on the cover of a fashion magazine. Like me, she was just an art teacher in a secondary school.

I, on the other hand, used to put on weight if I even smiled at a bar of chocolate. I'd already lost several upper teeth, my face was spotty and I looked like a heavyweight boxer whatever I wore.

My morning reaction to Sam was always the same. I'd shut my eyes, pull the blankets over my head and force myself back to sleep. I knew that I really ought to get up too, and make use of the early start to have a shower, iron my blouse, polish my shoes, paint my nails and eat something for breakfast.

But I have never been what you'd call a morning person. The teaching job I was doing at the time was the only period of my life, thank goodness, that I've had to be anywhere by 8.30 a.m. Anyway, I needed a few extra comforting dreams after the shock of seeing Sam looking so beautiful. Going back to sleep to shut everything out, and using my bed as a favourite means of retreat, became an addiction – my worst habit.

Of course, I overslept and was late for work every single day of the week. Eventually I was told if things didn't improve I might be given the sack. So I gave up my job and got married instead. I blame it all on Sam and her beauty.

4 Key words

Some words are more important than others to your understanding of a text. What are the key words in the story you have just read? Choose three words from each of these lists and be prepared to justify your choices in the light of the whole story.

Paragraph 1   London / flat / beautiful / slim / jealous / chocolate
Paragraph 2   bed / teeth / complexion / make-up / rush / model / teacher
Paragraph 3   weight / smiled / teeth / spotty / heavyweight boxer
Paragraph 4   morning / blankets / sleep / shower / blouse / breakfast

Choose your own key words from paragraphs 5 and 6 and compare your choices with other students.

1

Where on earth?

Introduction

A Which countries or parts of the world do you think these places are in? Look at the photographs and describe each place.

Example

This looks like the centre of a largish town or city. It's probably in a modern western country. Places like this are very busy because almost everyone has their own car. Too much traffic makes cities like this noisy and polluted.

B Which of these places is most like the place where you live? Have you ever lived in or visited places like the others?

C If you had to move, which of the places would you most like to live in, and which would you least like to live in? Give your reasons.

Listening

1 Think ahead

People go to new places for many different reasons. How many can you think of?

2 Listening

You are going to hear three people describing places they've lived in or visited on holiday. Listen to each speaker to find out why they went to the place they describe.

3 Comprehension

A Read the questions below, then listen to the first speaker again and choose the best answer or ending.

1 What did the speaker notice when she first arrived in Australia?
   A the temporary shops and houses
   B that everybody was in their garden
   C the American-style buildings
   D the single-storey wooden buildings

2 From the speaker's point of view, what made Sydney such a spectacular city?
   A a combination of natural and man-made features
   B the attractive modern architecture
   C all the old places and buildings
   D the fact that the Opera House overlooked the bay

3 Which is the most popular seaside resort for the people of Sydney?
   A Sydney Harbour   B The Gold Coast   C Manly Beach   D Darling Harbour

4 Why wouldn't the speaker want to live in Sydney?
   A The cost of living in the suburbs of Sydney is very high.
   B She dislikes living in city centres.
   C The roads are always busy with traffic.
   D She couldn't afford to live in a nice part of the city.

B Read these sentences, then listen to the second speaker again and decide whether they are true or false.

1 The speaker started working in Thailand in 1969.
2 The restaurant was especially popular with people who worked for the government.
3 The speaker thinks that Number One was a good name for the restaurant.
4 The cooking was done in a small room behind the restaurant.
5 The cooks wore very few clothes.
6 None of the cooks was a woman.
7 The food was cooked in advance and then reheated before being served.
8 The owner of Number One and his family lived in a house next to the restaurant.

C Listen to the third speaker again and complete these sentences in your own words. What you write must make sense and be grammatically correct.

1 The speaker works at . . .
2 He lives about a minute's walk away from . . .
3 Before they moved to their chalet, the speaker and his family lived in . . .
4 According to the speaker, people get coughs and colds because of the difference between the . . .
5 Some people compare the climate of Zimbabwe with . . .
6 The fact that it isn't too hot at night helps . . .

4 Over to you

Discuss these questions and give reasons for your opinions.

1 Which of the three places would you most like to visit for a holiday?
2 Which place would you most like to live and work in?
3 What is your idea of the perfect climate?

Grammar and practice

Used to

A What are the different meanings of *used to* in these three sentences from the listening?

1 You get *used to* seeing the sun every day.
2 We're already *used to* living here.
3 This is about a restaurant which I *used to* go to when I was working in north-east Thailand.

B Which sentence:
a refers to a past situation?
b refers to a present situation?
c refers to a change of situation?

C Now read the Grammar reference on page 179.

D *Be* and *get used to* are followed by -*ing* when *used* means accustomed. Do you know any other verbs like this? There is a list in section 1D3 in the Grammar reference on page 181.

E Practice
Complete these sentences in two different ways.

1 No matter how hard I try, I'll never get used . . .
2 When I was ten, I used . . .
3 People who have just retired are not used . . .
4 When my parents were young, they didn't use . . .
5 When foreigners visit my country, they aren't used . . .
6 When people get married, they have to get used . . .
7 When you were a child, where did you . . .
8 I'm absolutely exhausted. I'm just not . . .

Vocabulary

1 Describing places

Vocabulary reference p.196

A The place of my dreams

This illustration is the view from a building showing the immediate neighbourhood, the community, and the wider geographical region. Read these three descriptions and choose the one which most closely matches the illustration.

My dream home would be a large flat on the top floor of a luxury apartment block in a quiet residential area of a large city. There would be parks and other open spaces around, and it would be quite close to mountains. I wouldn't want it to be a seaside resort, but it shouldn't be too far from the coast.

If I could live anywhere I liked, I'd choose an old house in the centre of a medium-sized town. The town would have all the normal modern facilities like banks, cinemas and supermarkets. Ideally it would also be of historical interest with a castle or an old church, but it shouldn't be too popular with tourists. It would be close to water of some kind – perhaps a river or a lake.

If I could choose, I'd live in a small cottage in a country lane on the outskirts of a village. The village would have a few small shops and a friendly pub. It would be surrounded by countryside and be about ten miles from the nearest town. Ideally, it would be in a hilly area close to a forest.

B Scan the three descriptions and underline all the place words you can find. List the words under the following headings.

housing, e.g. *flat*
communities, e.g. *town*
natural features, e.g. *mountain*

facilities, e.g. *shop*
parts of a community, e.g. *outskirts*

Add any other words you know, then compare your lists with those on page 196.

C Think about your dream or nightmare home, and describe it to your partner.

D Write 60–70 words about the place you have been describing.

E Wordsearch

Find the ten place words in this wordsearch. There are definitions to help you.

```
P  S  U  B  U  R  B  A  L  T
O  H  O  A  U  R  B  A  N  O
R  Y  E  L  L  A  V  N  I  S
T  I  B  U  N  G  A  L  O  W
O  S  S  B  J  P  F  E  L  I
H  B  E  D  S  I  T  C  A  E
P  I  N  E  D  R  A  G  R  T
E  S  L  A  R  W  E  D  U  P
E  T  B  L  D  R  P  L  R  M
R  E  P  A  R  C  S  Y  K  S
```

1 residential area outside the centre of a town or city
2 adjective used to describe a built-up area like a town
3 area of land between two hills or mountains, often with a river running along it
4 town on the coast with a harbour
5 single-storey house
6 room used for sleeping and living in; a very small apartment
7 area of land belonging to a house, often used for growing flowers or vegetables
8 a low mountain
9 adjective used to describe a country area away from towns
10 very tall, modern, city building

F The sea

Fill the gaps in these sentences with one word connected with the sea.

1 When we were children, my brother and I spent our summer holidays in Torremolinos, a famous _____ town in Spain.
2 I remember having a wonderful week in Deauville, which is a popular holiday _____ on the north _____ of France.
3 We spent most of our time swimming in the _____ or building castles on the _____.
4 In the evenings we often went for long walks along the sea_____.

2 Phrasal verbs

A Phrasal verbs are two- or three-part verbs which are frequently used in natural, conversational English, for example, *Stevie **grew up** in a children's home*. Read these snippets of conversation and fill each gap with the correct form of one of the phrasal verbs from the list below.

go on	grow up	hurry up	turn into
put up	settle down	touch down	

1 If you don't _____, we'll miss the beginning of the film.
2 Look at all those people over there. I wonder what's _____.
3 Hi, it's me. I'm sorry, but I'm still at the airport. We only _____ ten minutes ago.
4 My parents can't understand why I keep changing jobs. They'd really like me to _____.
5 Have you seen that new office building they _____ in the town centre? It's really ugly.
6 It took me years to get used to living in London – probably because I _____ in a quiet country area.
7 What started as a slight disagreement quickly _____ a full-scale argument.

B The grammar of phrasal verbs is explained on page 194, followed by a list of the most useful phrasal verbs on page 195.

Writing

Describing places

> **My least favourite place**
>
> Croydon is a largish town on the outskirts of London. It's a popular shopping centre and several large businesses have their headquarters there. Many of the people who live there work in
> ₅ London, which is about half an hour away by train.
>
> I went to school in Croydon for six years and I never liked it. In the first place, there are hardly any historical buildings, so it is a rather dull town. Secondly, it is full of unfriendly people who are too busy to stop and chat. Lastly, because it is on a main road into
> ₁₀ London, the streets are always full of traffic and sometimes the air is so polluted that it's almost impossible to breathe.
>
> As far as I'm concerned, I wouldn't mind if I never went to Croydon again.

1 Writing in paragraphs

A Read this description of Croydon. Do you know any towns like this?

B When you write compositions, it is important to divide what you write into paragraphs. Each time you change the subject, or your focus of attention, you should start a new paragraph. What is the subject or focus of each of the three paragraphs in the text above? Choose one of these titles.

1 The reasons I don't like Croydon   4 The future of Croydon
2 The reasons for Croydon's popularity   5 A description of Croydon
3 Final thoughts

2 Punctuation

A Read this unpunctuated description of a small town in Brittany. As you read it, divide it into three paragraphs.

My favourite place

chateauneuf is in the centre of brittany in north-west france and is on a hill overlooking a river most of the inhabitants are farmers or shopkeepers but there are a few businessmen who work in quimper which is 22 kilometres away everybody lives in stone houses or cottages with whitewashed walls ive visited chateauneuf every easter for six years now because i love the atmosphere and the friendly people chateauneuf is not on the coast so it hasnt been spoilt by tourists there are two small hotels where you can eat traditional french food quite cheaply at easter chateauneuf has a festival of traditional breton music if youre in brittany book into the gai logis hotel try the local food and then go for a walk along the river bank you wont regret it

B Read the text again and add the necessary punctuation. The missing punctuation marks are capital letters, full stops, commas and apostrophes.
Check how these punctuation marks are used by looking at the Grammar reference on page 178.

3 Think, plan, write

Write a description of 120–180 words with the title *My favourite place* or *My least favourite place*. Follow this paragraph plan. Paragraph 1: a physical description of the place. Paragraph 2: reasons for liking or disliking the place. Paragraph 3: final comments. When you have finished, check your punctuation carefully.

2 Future

Cruiseliner

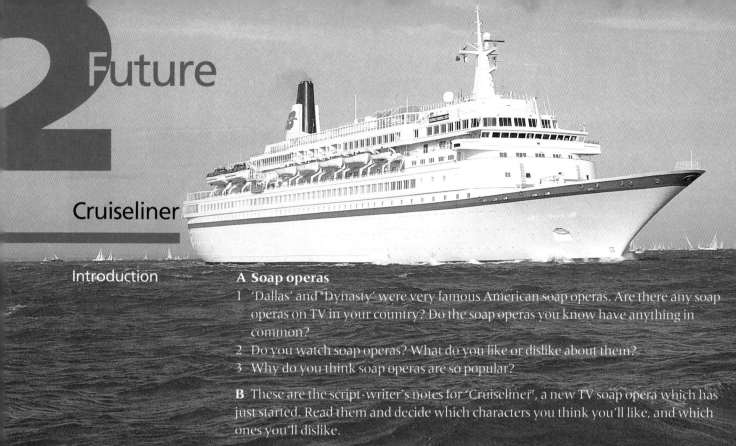

Introduction

A Soap operas

1 'Dallas' and 'Dynasty' were very famous American soap operas. Are there any soap operas on TV in your country? Do the soap operas you know have anything in common?

2 Do you watch soap operas? What do you like or dislike about them?

3 Why do you think soap operas are so popular?

B These are the script-writer's notes for 'Cruiseliner', a new TV soap opera which has just started. Read them and decide which characters you think you'll like, and which ones you'll dislike.

SETTING — The Niagara, liner used for 4-week cruises in Mediterranean and Caribbean.

SERIES — 12 episodes about one 4-week cruise

MAIN CHARACTERS

THE CREW

Captain Charles Ogilvie, 48
Marriage broke up last year. Spends lots of time in ship's bar.

George Armstrong, 46
Chief Engineer. Married with 3 children. Well-paid, but short of money. Envious of Ogilvie's position.

Jason Matthews, 29
Head barman, single. Has worked on ship since age of 16. No qualifications but good at job. Reputation for being honest.

Paula and Patti Pink, 40 and 45
Cabaret singers. Not real sisters. Had hit record in 1975. Now only work in clubs and on ships. Patti has illness. Needs operation soon or will have to give up work.

Ed Green and Mick Blade, 19 and 21
Waiters. Popular. Get lots of tips from passengers. Neither is married. Ed has steady girlfriend who works on ship as chambermaid. Last year Ed accused of stealing money from cabin. Found not guilty.

THE PASSENGERS

Barbara Brown and Stuart Lodge, 49 and 51
Barbara — romantic novelist, Stuart — film producer, well-known for violent temper. Barbara's 4th husband. Doesn't like wife being centre of press attention. Couple met 2 months ago, married after whirlwind romance. Cruise is honeymoon.

Nick Flynn, 47
Divorced, no children. Rich — money from gambling. Now lives in lonely luxury. Few friends, no family.

Bill Speare, 41
Gossip columnist for _Daily Post_. Writes about rich and famous. Is covering Barbara's wedding. Has arranged interview with Barbara — doesn't know Stuart will try to make difficulties.

Gilbert and Betty Gable, 65 and 62
Gilbert retired bank clerk. Cruise is present from colleagues. The couple have never had such a luxurious holiday.

Virginia Dorado, 19
Photographer from very rich family. Alone on cruise — getting over love affair that recently ended.

STORYLINE — EPISODE 1

Crew and passengers introduced. Background details given. Passengers boarded ship and settled into routine. Lodge warned Speare to keep away from Barbara.

C Now read these notes describing what happened in Episode 2 of 'Cruiseliner' and match four of the events with the pictures.

STORYLINE – EPISODE 2

• Ogilvie, Lodge and Flynn met in bar. Jason heard Flynn boasting about wealth.
• Ogilvie and Armstrong had row because Armstrong missed important meeting.
• Paula did show alone because Patti ill. Spent rest of evening with Flynn. Told him about Patti's illness.
• Gables discovered £1000 missing from cabin.
• Ogilvie invited honeymoon couple to dinner.
• Virginia Dorado took photos on ship. Took one of Ed leaving Gables' cabin.
• Speare and Barbara Brown arranged secret interview.

Listening

1 Think ahead

What do you think will happen in Episode 3? Think of ideas in pairs, groups or as a whole class.

2 Conversations

You are going to hear three short conversations which are connected in some way with Episode 3 of the soap opera 'Cruiseliner'. Listen to them all, work out what is happening in each, and see if anybody mentions any of the events you predicted.

3 Comprehension

A Read the questions below, then listen to the conversations again. Choose the correct answer or finish the sentences in the best way.

1 How does one of the speakers in the first conversation think Stuart Lodge will find out about the secret interview?
   A Barbara Brown will tell him herself.
   B Bill Speare will tell him after the interview is over.
   ✗ C He will interrupt his wife and Bill Speare.
   D Virginia Dorado will show him a photo of the interview.

2 How does the other speaker think the argument between Lodge and Speare will end?
   ✗ A Speare will die.   C Speare will be saved from drowning.
   B Lodge will fall overboard.   D Speare will fall down after Lodge hits him.

3 Mandy Ryman, who plays the part of Virginia, says that at the end of Episode 3
   A people are going to dislike Virginia even more.
   B people are going to change their minds about Virginia.
   C Virginia is going to help one of the other passengers.
   D one of the other characters is going to fall in love with Virginia.

4 According to Paula, how is Patti this morning?
   A She is feeling much better.   C Her condition has not changed.
   B She has had an operation.   D Her condition has improved.

5 What definite arrangements do Paula and Nick make for this evening?
   A They arrange to meet in Paula's cabin after the show.
   B They arrange to meet in Nick's cabin after the show.
   C They don't arrange anything because Nick has some business to do.
   D Nick promises to come and see the show as soon as his business is finished.

B Vocabulary

Read these extracts from the conversations and match the words in *italics* with their meanings. There are two more meanings than you need.

1 Speare will fall overboard and *drown* b	a honest, sincere
2 she'll *accidentally* take a photo e	b die in water because it is impossible to breathe
3 she'll *blackmail* Lodge d	c damaged, destroyed
4 I've got to *dash* now h	d demand money by threatening something unpleasant
5 the *spoilt* daughter of a property tycoon g	e by chance, not deliberately
6 a *fair* description of Virginia a	f approximate, rough
	g given too much attention or praise
	h hurry, rush

C Listening between the lines

1 Virginia Dorado is already very rich, so why would she be interested in blackmailing Stuart Lodge?

2 Why do you think Paula Pink thanks Nick for being 'such a good listener'?

4 Listening

A It is the day after Episode 3 of 'Cruiseliner' was shown on TV. You are going to hear another conversation between the two office workers. Listen and check how many of your predictions were correct.

B Guess the meanings of the expressions in *italics* in these extracts from the conversation.

1 Come on then, don't *keep me in suspense*.
2 I was right about Stuart Lodge *catching his wife* with Bill Speare.
3 *It all came out* when the Captain interviewed him.
4 Yes, completely *out of the blue*.
5 No, I think *that's about it*.
6 Don't worry – *I'm really hooked* now.

5 Over to you

1 This soap opera is set on a liner. If you were writing a soap opera where would you set it? Why?

2 Do you think people are more interested in soap operas which reflect everyday life, or those which show a glamorous, film-star type of existence?

Grammar and practice

1 The future

A As you know, there are several different ways of talking about the future in English. Five of these ways are used in these sentences from the listening section.

1 I'm going to watch 'Cruiseliner'.
2 It starts at half-past seven.
3 Lodge will hit Speare and Speare will rush out of the cabin.
4 Virginia Dorado will be wandering round the ship taking photos.
5 I'm rehearsing in ten minutes.

Match the sentences with the kind of future they refer to.

a a future event that has already been arranged
b a prediction or expectation
c an intention or plan to do something
d a scheduled or timetabled event
e an event or action that will be in progress at a specific time in the future

B Before continuing, check your understanding of the future tenses in the Grammar reference on pages 179–80.

2 Practice

A Read this newspaper article about the actor John Miner. Put the verbs in *italics* in the correct future form, and explain your answers.

B An audition

'Cruiseliner' needs several new actors for the next series, and the producer is trying to arrange auditions. Work in pairs.

Student A, turn to page 174 and read your instructions.
Student B, read these instructions.

You are the producer of 'Cruiseliner'. Student A is one of the actors you are especially keen to get for a part in the new series. You are going to phone to arrange a suitable time for an audition, on Monday, Tuesday or Wednesday of next week. Before you phone, work out how to start the conversation.

C Predictions

Going to usually expresses intentions.

Example   *I'm going to watch 'Cruiseliner' this evening.*
            This is what I intend to do.

Sometimes, if the speaker has evidence for a future event, *going to* is used instead of *will* for predictions.

Example   *By the end of the episode everyone's going to love Virginia!*
            Mandy knows this because she has already filmed this episode.

Fill the gaps in these sentences with *will* or *going to*.

1 Virginia's going into the captain's cabin. I'm sure she _____ show him the photo she took of Ed.
2 I should think more and more people _____ watch 'Cruiseliner'.
3 Barbara Brown _____ have a baby in about four months.
4 Patti's illness is getting worse and worse. I think she _____ die.
5 I imagine Barbara and Stuart _____ split up pretty soon.

Miner to leave cruise

John Miner, who plays George Armstrong in TV5's new soap, **Cruiseliner**, *leave* (1) the show at the end of the current series. It is understood that Mr Miner has had serious disagreements with the production team. In a recent interview he said, 'As soon as we've finished filming, I'm off to the States. My flight *leave* (2) on June 27th. Quite honestly I can't wait. This time next year I *appear* (3) regularly on American TV, if everything goes according to plan.' Other members of the **Cruiseliner** cast *not be* (4) sorry to see the back of Miner, who is apparently arrogant and unsociable. Producer, Barbara Scott, was more diplomatic. 'I expect the public *miss* (5) John – he always gets tons of fan mail, mainly from middle-aged women. We *film* (6) the next series in June and July, so we *look* (7) for a replacement pretty soon.'

T...
y...
targe... ...ea, a ne...
sat in his flat for five hours   armed officers surrou... ...nis fla...

D Look at this cartoon and make predictions using *will* and *going to*.

E What'll happen to me?

Write 40–60 words about your own future. Choose one of the following subjects.

• things that are already arranged for the next year or two
• intentions and predictions for the next five years
• personal and career ambitions

3 Articles

A Look at these extracts from the recordings and fill the gaps with the definite article *the* or the indefinite article *a / an*.

1 I really like _____ bloke that plays Nick Flynn.
2 Speare and Lodge will have _____ fight. Perhaps while they're having _____ fight Virginia Dorado will be wandering around.
3 I'm just ringing to say how much I enjoyed _____ show.
4 Please give _____ warm welcome to Mandy Ryman, or, as you know her better, _____ spoilt daughter of _____ property tycoon.
5 Armstrong is blackmailing _____ Captain.

B Look at the gaps you filled with *the*. Why did you decide to use *the* in each case? Choose one of these reasons:

a because this is not the first time this person or thing is mentioned.

b because the speaker and the listener know what or who is being referred to.

c because there is only one of these things or people in this context.

C Now complete these sentences with *the* or Ø (no article). A few gaps have been filled for you.

1 *The* Niagara takes _____ passengers on _____ cruises around *the* Mediterranean.
2 Stuart Lodge was born in _____ England but now lives in _____ United States. He met Barbara in _____ New York.
3 _____ journalists like Bill Speare spend most of their time mixing with _____ rich and famous.
4 The Captain spends his evenings in _____ bar drinking _____ whisky.
5 On _____ last evening of _____ cruise, Stuart and Barbara went on _____ deck. They looked at _____ moon and talked about _____ love.

D Compare answers with a partner. Work out some rules which explain when no article is used.

E Check your understanding of articles in the Grammar reference on page 180.

F Turn back to page 13 and expand the notes about the Niagara's crew or passengers, adding articles where necessary.

Congratulations! You're 130 today.

Introduction

A What is your personal definition of the age expressions *middle-aged, elderly, old* and *very old*? When do each of these ages start and finish? At what age are people regarded as old in your country?

B How are old people treated in your country?

Reading

1 Think ahead

What would be the best thing and the worst thing about living to be 130 years old?

2 Reading

Read this article and decide if you would like to live to the age of 130.

LONG LIFE

Scientists are finally beginning to unlock the secret everyone has been dying to know: just how long can we live? They confidently predict that in the 21st century people will be living to the incredible age of 130. And this is just the start. Experts studying the [5] process of ageing believe it is possible that people will live long enough to have great-great-great-great-great-grandchildren. This prediction [10] is based on research and on the fact that the centenarian population is mushrooming as our general health improves. There are around 4000 people of over 100 in Britain – ten times more than 30 years ago. [15]

Dr Vijg, a Dutch biologist, is the co-ordinator of a project which is studying the growing senior citizen population. Dr Vijg and his colleagues are looking at our genes, which, they believe, hold the key to what kills us, early or late in life.

A century ago average life expectancy in Europe was 45. [20] Today, providing we look after ourselves, drive our cars carefully, and cut down on things like butter, alcohol and cigarettes, we can add nearly 30 years to that figure. Dr Vijg reckons that by the year 2000 we will all have added a couple more years to our lives. [25]

But that is nothing compared to what will happen once scientists have cracked the secret of our genes. Some of the problem genes have already been tracked down, like those that cause haemophilia and muscular dystrophy. Dr Vijg says, 'Nobody dies from old age – just from diseases that [30] affect people as they get older.' And he forecasts that within 30 years, science will be preparing people for a longer life. 'Already the killer diseases are being eradicated,' he says. 'About 50% of cancers are curable, and I really believe that this will increase to 80%.' [35]

There are also encouraging developments in the fight against Aids, and although a vaccine will not be available for some time, the experts are cautiously hopeful that by early in the next century the disease will have been brought under control. Doctors believe that the death rate from the [40] biggest killers – diseases of the circulatory system – will decline as man comes to his senses by giving up smoking and eating more healthily. Dr Vijg points to experiments with animals in laboratories. 'Those given less food, but of a higher quality, lived to the human equivalent of 150 [45] years.'

Dr Vijg believes that as life span increases, so will other expectations. Women will be having babies at an older age. 'More and more women are having their first child when they are over 30,' he says. 'In another ten years people might [50] think it normal for a woman of 50 to be having her first child.'

What about living forever? Will eternal life ever become a reality? 'So far, that is science fiction,' says Dr Vijg. 'Theoretically it is possible, but it will be another hundred, perhaps two hundred years before we know all the secrets [55] of our genes.'

3 Points of view

Conduct a brief class survey. How many students would like to live to the age of 130? How many would not?

4 Comprehension

A Read the questions, then read the passage again and choose the best answer for each question.

1 One of the results of improvements in people's general health is that
   A the total population is decreasing.
   B the number of people living to be 100 is increasing.
   C people are having more great-grandchildren.
   D the population of large cities is increasing.

2 In the text, haemophilia is used as an example of
   A a disease common a century ago.
   B one of the most serious killer-diseases.
   C a disease which affects people in old age.
   D a disease which is caused by a defect in our genes.

3 Animal experiments have shown that
   A diseases of the circulatory system are declining.
   B long life depends on eating well.
   C women could have babies at an older age.
   D Aids is being brought under control.

4 What does Dr Vijg say about eternal life?
   A He has written stories about it.   C He has a theory about it.
   B It isn't impossible.   D It'll be a reality in 200 years.

B Text references

What do the words and phrases in *italics* in these extracts from the text refer to? You will need to look back at the text to check. The first one has been done as an example.

1 *they* confidently predict (line 2)   *they* = scientists
2 and *this* is just the start (line 4)
3 *this prediction* is based on research (line 10)
4 we can add nearly 30 years to *that figure* (line 23)
5 like *those* that cause haemophilia (line 28)
6 I really believe that *this* will increase to 80% (line 35)
7 *those* given less food (line 44)
8 so far *that* is science fiction (line 53)

C Vocabulary

The words in this table are from the text. Fill as many of the gaps as you can with related words.

	Noun	Verb	Adjective	Adverb
1	_____	0	_____	confidently
2	_____	predict	_____	_____
3	health	0	_____	_____
4	_____	improve	0	0
5	_____	_____	(in)curable	0
6	_____	0	_____	cautiously
7	expectation	_____	_____	0
8	reality	0	_____	_____

Grammar and practice

1 The future continuous

In the first part of the unit the future continuous was used to talk about actions or events which will be in progress at a specific time in the future.

Example   *Virginia Dorado **will be wandering** around the ship taking photos.*

This tense can also be used to predict future trends, developments or tendencies.

Example   *In the 21st century people **will be living** to the incredible age of 130.*
*Women **will be having** babies at an older age.*

2 The future perfect

Another way of expressing predictions about the future is to talk about actions or events which will be completed by a particular time in the future. The future perfect tense is used for this purpose.

Example   *Dr Vijg reckons that **by** the year 2000 **we will all have added** a couple more years to our lives.*
***By** early in the next century the disease **will have been brought** under control.*

3 Practice

A Predict some possible 21st century trends. Here are some subjects to think about.

- education   number of years at school, university

Example   *In the 21st century, more students will be going to university.*

- employment   working hours, holidays, retirement age
- leisure   facilities, hobbies, TV, sports
- diet   meat, cost, health, convenience

B Look into your own future. Think about this time tomorrow, this time next week and this time next year. Think about all the things you will or won't do in the period between now and these times. Now talk to a partner about what you will or won't have done by these times.

Example   *What will you have done by this time next year? By this time next year, I'll have left school, but I won't have started work.*

If you are not sure about the future, use the word *probably*.

Example   *I'll **probably** have left school, but I **probably** won't have started work.*

4 Fluency

New Year's Eve 1999 will be a momentous occasion. It will be a thousand years since the start of the last new millennium.

A Make some predictions about your life in the year 2000. Think about things you will have done by this time, and things you'll still be doing. Compare ideas with other students.

B What do you think your country or town will do, or should do, to celebrate this occasion? How do you intend to celebrate?

Vocabulary

1 Jobs

Vocabulary reference p.196

A Word building

Scientist and *biologist* are two occupations mentioned in the reading text. Some other common endings for the names of occupations are *-er*, *-or*, *-ian*, and *-ant*.

Choose one of the five endings to form the occupations associated with these subjects.

1 electricity	3 journalism	5 economics	7 jewellery
2 law	4 music	6 sailing	8 accountancy

B Who's who?

The answers to all these questions are words for people's jobs. There is a list of jobs to help you on page 196.

What do you call someone who . . .

1 plays a part in a play or a film?
2 designs or builds bridges, etc?
3 is elected to be part of a government?
4 works underground digging coal?
5 collects rubbish from people's houses?
6 constructs houses and other buildings?
7 cooks meals in a restaurant?
8 makes bread?
9 sells meat?
10 teaches at a university?

C Hotels

Fill the gaps in these sentences with the names of jobs in a hotel.

1 When I checked into the hotel the _____ asked me to fill in a registration card.
2 The _____ carried my suitcases to my room for me.
3 Half an hour later I went down to the restaurant for a meal, but the _____ told me very politely that he couldn't serve me because the _____ had already finished cooking for the day.
4 I decided to complain to the _____, but when I rang his number his secretary told me he was on holiday.

2 Phrasal verbs

In the Introduction on page 13, we are told that Charles Ogilvie's 'marriage *broke up* last year'. Like many phrasal verbs, *break up* has an obvious, literal meaning and several idiomatic meanings. It means break into pieces, come to an end, separate, finish school for the holidays. *Put up* means raise, increase, provide accommodation for, display, build, tolerate (*put up* **with**).

Fill the gaps in these sentences with the correct form of either *break up* or *put up*.

1 Over the last six months garages _____ the price of petrol three times.
2 A group of American students are coming to stay next year. We've offered _____ three of them.
3 Although the meeting lasted nearly six hours, it _____ without agreement.
4 To get the teacher's attention, you've got to _____ your hand.
5 Last night I went round to complain about my neighbour's TV. I just couldn't _____ the noise any longer.
6 When does your school _____ for the Christmas holidays?
7 It was lucky that the pilot jumped out when he did – the plane _____ and burst into flames as soon as it hit the ground.
8 Mark's really fed up. He and his girlfriend _____ last night.

Writing

Advantages and disadvantages

1 Read and discuss

A Suggest a suitable title for this composition by reading just the first paragraph.

> People have always dreamed of living forever, and although we all know this will never happen, we still want to live as long as possible. Naturally, there are advantages and disadvantages to a long life.
>
> In the first place, people who live longer can spend more time with
> 5 their family and friends. Secondly, people who have busy working lives look forward to a long, relaxing retirement, when they can do all the things they have never had time for.
>
> On the other hand, there are some serious disadvantages. Firstly, many people become ill and consequently have to spend time in hospital
> 10 or become dependent on their children and friends. Many of them find this dependence annoying or embarrassing. In addition to this, the older people get, the fewer friends they seem to have because old friends die or become ill and it's often difficult to make new friends.
>
> To sum up, it seems that living to a very old age is worthwhile for
> 15 people who stay healthy enough to remain independent and enjoy life.

B Before you read the rest of the composition, think of as many advantages and disadvantages of a long life as you can.

C Read the composition and see how many of your ideas are mentioned. How many of your ideas are not mentioned? Why didn't the writer use more ideas?

2 Analysis

A What is each of the four paragraphs in the above composition about?

B How many advantages and disadvantages did you find in the second and third paragraphs? Although the third paragraph is longer than the second, it doesn't contain any more ideas, but the writer has decided to explain the ideas. This makes the composition more interesting.

3 Language study

A Read carefully through the composition again and circle all the words and phrases which are used to introduce the main points in the writer's argument, e.g. *In the first place*.

B The words and phrases below are all used for one of the following purposes:
1 to introduce additional information.
2 to introduce information which contrasts with what has come before.
3 to summarize or conclude an argument.
Group them according to their purpose.

on balance	besides (this)	however
to conclude	in conclusion	in contrast
nevertheless	in short	to summarize
as well as (that)	what is more	on the whole

C Add any more words and phrases you know to these lists.

4 Think, plan, write

A You are going to write a composition of 120–180 words to answer the question *What are the advantages and disadvantages of old people living with younger members of their families?* In groups, or as a class, think of as many ideas as you can in five minutes to add to these:

Advantages *grandparents and grandchildren get to know each other well*
Disadvantages *children are noisy and old people often like peace and quiet*

B You won't have room to include all your ideas, so choose two advantages and two disadvantages. Now plan your composition and make notes as shown below.

1 Introduction What general information could you start your composition with? How will you finish the paragraph?

many old people can't look after themselves – have to live with families – naturally, advantages and disadvantages

2 Advantages Note down your advantages, and add an explanation if there's room.

grandchildren and grandparents get to know each other well – learn to understand people of different generations

3 Disadvantages Now note down your disadvantages, and add an explanation if there's room.

children often noisy, old people like peace – could be disagreements

4 Conclusion Summarize your ideas. You could add your own opinion.

can be good if people are happy to make compromises

C Expand your notes into a composition. Use the words and phrases from the Language study to help you. Write the composition out in full, using 120–180 words. When you have finished, check your grammar, spelling and punctuation carefully.

Exam techniques

Guided writing – matching information

1 Guidelines

Do	Don't
• Read the instructions very carefully.	▶ Don't start writing until you have read the instructions, the paragraph beginnings and all the information.
• Read the beginning of the paragraphs you have to finish.	
• Read all the information you are given.	
• Decide and make notes on how to finish the paragraphs.	▶ Don't panic if you can't see how to organize the information you have read. Decide on your answer and justify it.
• Work through the paragraphs one by one, using clear report-style language.	▶ Don't finish any of the paragraphs until you have decided how to finish them all.

2 Exam task and practice

Use the information from the Entertainment programme and the notes about the passengers to continue each of these three paragraphs with about 50 words of your own. Give reasons for your choices.
1 Nick Flynn will probably start by . . .
2 During the early part of the evening I think Bill Speare will . . .
3 There isn't much for someone like Virginia Dorado to do, but I think . . .

Find the most suitable entertainments for each passenger by thinking about the questions below. Then complete the paragraphs, giving all your reasons.

Nick Flynn 47, divorced, gambler
• is falling in love with Paula Pink ◀ *Where would he go?*
• prefers doing things to watching other people ◀ *Which activities is he more likely to enjoy?*
• wealthy, and needs no more money ◀ *Where won't he go?*

Bill Speare 41, journalist
• well-educated ◀ *Where could he show how clever he is?*
• good sense of humour ◀ *Where could he go for a good laugh?*
• doesn't drink or gamble ◀ *Where wouldn't he go?*

Virginia Dorado 19, photographer, from wealthy family
• getting over a love affair ◀ *What mood do you think she is in?*
• doesn't like being alone ◀ *Where won't she go?*
• likes music and dancing ◀ *Where might she go?*

THE NIAGARA PRESENTS

CINEMA DELUXE
Raiders of the Lost Ark
8.15–10.00
Harrison Ford stars in this brilliant 1981 adventure. Ford plays Indiana Jones, an archaeologist who travels the world in search of priceless treasure. He faces terrifying danger every step of the way.

LOUNGE BAR
Quiz night
8.00–10.00
The crew take on the passengers in this nightly test of general knowledge.

Casino
10.00–4.00

CLEOPATRA'S NIGHT SPOT
Paula Pink sings
9.00–10.00

The Needle Disco
10.00–2.00
Nostalgia night with the Niagara's very own DJ Ed Eden.

THE FALLS THEATRE
Bingo 8.30–10.00
Tonight's star prize is £100 plus dinner at the Captain's table.

Late night comedy
10.00–Midnight
On board comedian Harry Chivers will make sure you go to bed laughing.

opinion

The rich and famous

Introduction

A In your opinion, what are the advantages and disadvantages of being famous? Make two lists.

B Do you think the lives of all famous people are affected by the points on your lists? Name some people who are, or have been, most affected.

Reading

1 Think ahead   What do you know about Elton John? Do you think he is happy with his life? Why? Why not?

2 Reading   Read the text as quickly as you can to find out if you were right.

Talking to . . .
Elton John

Q Do you miss doing the ordinary things in life?

I like plodding round the kitchen doing the things everybody else
5 does. I love going to the supermarket to do the shopping. I come back with far more stuff than I need. When I am on holiday in St. Tropez, I love to get up at six in the morning to get
10 the fresh bread. People often see me wheeling my trolley round the supermarkets in the town.

Q Do you mind being recognized?

I've tried going out in disguise, but in
15 the end most people recognize me. Ninety-nine per cent are very pleasant, very polite. But it's frustrating if you get out of bed on the wrong side – and you do some
20 days – and someone asks you for an autograph and they haven't got a pen or a piece of paper. But I enjoy my popularity; I don't see the point in being a recluse.

25 **Q You once said that you're a bit of a loner.**

Yeah, I always have been. By that I don't mean that I'm lonely. It's just that I like to be my own boss all
30 the time. Don't confuse that with being lonely because I'm not. I've lots of great friends around me. But I'm terribly set in my ways and, at my age, it's very hard to change.
35 I don't particularly want to, either. Being successful has given me the confidence to do things I wouldn't have had the courage to do otherwise. But I still retain that
40 shyness when I first meet people. I'm never going to get rid of that.

Q You like your food, don't you?

I'm one of those people who only
45 has to look at a doughnut and I immediately put on two pounds* without even eating it. I've always had a problem with my weight. It doesn't bother me too much,
50 although I get depressed when I'm very overweight. I dieted once and I became so obsessed that I nearly made myself ill. But I'm happy with the way I am at the moment.
55 If you exercise at least three or four times a week and play tennis, then it's no problem, but you have to keep at it.

_____
* about 1 kg

Q Do you follow any special fitness regime?
60

When I get up in the morning, I go on this exercise machine I've got and walk four or five miles in an hour. That burns off the calories for the
65 rest of the day. When I'm on tour, I eat three meals a day and don't snack. I can't eat before or after a show so that helps. It's when I'm at home – the worst thing is the fridge
70 and snacking. I'm a terrible snacker. I'm a big bread fan and I love curry.

Q Do you think you will still be touring and making records in another ten years' time?

75 I can't keep touring and making records for the rest of my life – I've got to try something different now and then. One thing I am interested in doing is writing a musical.

80 **Q So do you think we will see you on stage in your own musical one day?**

I doubt it. I'm not interested in going into a theatre and
85 performing every night. You may find that strange but if you're on tour, you're changing cities. I played at the Hammersmith Odeon once for fourteen nights and by the end
90 of it I was going crazy. It was like going to the office. So people who actually appear in plays and musicals for two to three years have my greatest sympathy and
95 admiration. I never consider what I do as work.

3 Comprehension

A Read the text again carefully, and choose the best answer for each question.

1 When Elton John goes out, he
   A is recognized by 99% of the population. C gets annoyed if he is recognized.
   B wears a disguise.   D accepts he will probably be recognized.

2 How has fame changed Elton John?
   A He has become very bossy.   C He feels more confident.
   B He doesn't like to be on his own.   D He has become shy.

3 What does Elton John say about his weight?
   A He is obsessed with his weight.   C He has learnt to control his weight.
   B He gets depressed when he diets.   D He wishes he were thin.

4 What is his future ambition?
   A to appear in a play or musical   C to do a world tour
   B to break with his present routine   D to play at the Hammersmith Odeon

B Vocabulary

Choose the correct definitions for these words and expressions from the text.

1 a recluse (line 24)   3 set in one's ways (line 33)
   A an ordinary person   A used to living with other people
   B a celebrity   B bad-tempered and difficult
   C a person who avoids other people   C having fixed habits

2 a loner (line 26)   4 to get out of bed on the wrong side
   A a person who likes being alone   (line 18)
   B a bossy person   A to wake up in a bad mood
   C a person who is unhappy without   B to wake up in a good mood
      other people around   C to be away from home

C Reading between the lines

1 'I've tried going out in disguise' (line 14). In your own words say how you think Elton John did this.
2 'You like your food, don't you?' (line 42). What question is the interviewer really asking?
3 Why do you think Elton John 'can't eat before or after a show' (line 67)?
4 Elton compares playing at the Hammersmith Odeon to working in an office (line 90). What does this tell us about his attitude to work?
5 Find evidence in the text which suggests that Elton John is basically happy with himself and his lifestyle.

4 Over to you

A Have you ever met a famous person or received a letter from someone famous? Tell the class about it.

B If you saw someone famous in a public place like a restaurant, what would you do?

C What would you most like and most dislike about being famous?

5 A night out

You have won first prize in a competition – an evening out in a place of your choice with the celebrity of your choice. Write a paragraph explaining who you have chosen and where you have chosen to go.

Grammar and practice

1 Gerunds

A Form and use

Gerunds are verbs which behave like nouns. They can be used in different ways. Look at these sentences from the interview with Elton John. Underline the gerunds.

1 The worst thing is the fridge and snacking.
2 I can't keep touring and making records for the rest of my life.
3 Being successful has given me the confidence to do things I wouldn't have had the courage to do otherwise.
4 One thing I am interested in doing is writing a musical.

Match the gerunds with their uses, a–d, below.

a after prepositions (verbs and adjectives can be followed by a preposition + gerund)
b as the object or complement of a clause or sentence
c after certain verbs
d as the subject of a clause or sentence

B Find more examples of these uses of the gerund in the interview and underline them. Are there any other -ing words which are not gerunds? What are they?

C Subject and object

Complete the sentences by adding a verb in the gerund form and some more words. Finish each sentence in two different ways. Look back at the reading text and the Introduction for ideas. The first one has been done for you.

1 *Being a well-known pop star* means you are recognized wherever you go.
   Being a celebrity means you are recognized wherever you go.
2 _____ is a trick used by many stars to try to avoid recognition.
3 When you are rich and famous, _____ becomes an ordinary everyday activity.
4 Most famous people find _____ an extremely boring, but unavoidable part of being famous.
5 _____ is another disadvantage.
6 But for the majority, _____ more than compensates for any disadvantages fame brings.

2 Gerunds after prepositions

Match the sentence beginnings (1–12) with their endings (a–l). Then complete each sentence by choosing the correct preposition from the box. There is sometimes more than one possible ending.

1 He was arrested . . .
2 I'm terrified . . .
3 The children are responsible . . .
4 You've been warned . . .
5 I'm sorry . . .
6 My parents congratulated me . . .
7 I'm bored . . .
8 I'm very indecisive. I'm really bad . . .
9 I'm worried . . .
10 You need some help. I insist . . .
11 She's a brilliant athlete and is capable . . .
12 He's asked me to make a speech at his wedding but I get very nervous . . .

| about | at | for | of | on | with |

a doing the same thing all the time; I need a change.
b eating fruit which hasn't been washed.
c taking decisions.
d winning the gold medal.
e giving you a hand.
f leaving such a young girl to look after the children.
g being in the house on my own.
h passing my exams.
i cleaning their own rooms.
j not writing back sooner.
k speaking in public.
l driving dangerously.

3 Verbs followed by gerunds

A The verbs in the following exercise can be followed by a noun or a gerund verb form.
Example
She couldn't resist **the chocolate cake**.
She couldn't resist **having** *another slice*.

Use verbs from the list below to fill the gaps in these sentences. You will need to put the verb in the correct tense. There are four extra verbs.

1 I've decided that I really must _____ smoking. I just can't get rid of this cough.
2 I'll never get this finished if you _____ interrupting me!
3 I know Paul didn't take it. Sara has _____ stealing it.
4 I'm getting so fed up with my job that I'm seriously _____ handing in my notice.
5 Would you _____ repeating that? I didn't catch what you said.
6 You can't _____ going to the dentist forever. You'll have to go sometime.
7 Being a nurse _____ always being cheerful, working unsocial hours, and coming home smelling of disinfectant.
8 You _____ losing your job if your boss finds out you weren't really ill.
9 Adrian's doctor has _____ cutting down on fatty foods and taking gentle exercise.
10 You can go home as soon as you've _____ typing those letters.

admit	give up	keep	prevent	risk
consider	imagine	mind	put off	suggest
finish	involve	miss	report	

B Now read section 1 in the Grammar reference on page 180.

4 Gerunds after verbs of liking and disliking

A There are several verbs and expressions in English which express how much or how little we like something, e.g. *enjoy*, *can't stand*. How many others do you know? Make a list, then put them in order from extreme liking to extreme disliking.

B Tell the person sitting next to you about your likes and dislikes, using as many of these verbs and expressions as you can. Think about films and TV, music, sports and games, travel, food, other people, duties and obligations.

Example   *I enjoy watching horror films.*
            I can't stand people smoking while I'm eating.

Do you share any likes and dislikes with your partner?

5 Fluency

Changing places

Work with a partner. Decide which of you is Student A and which is Student B and read your instructions.

Student A

Imagine you can change places with anyone you like for a week. This person can be famous or ordinary, a man or a woman. Choose someone but don't tell your partner who you have chosen. Now imagine yourself in this person's shoes. Think about what you do, where you live, what you do in your spare time, what you like/dislike about your new lifestyle, and make notes. Your partner will interview you and will try to guess who you have changed places with.

Student B

You are a reporter and you are going to interview Student A. Student A has changed places with another person for a week. This person may be famous or not. Prepare the list of questions you will ask Student A to find out what they like and dislike about their lifestyle. Here are some ideas to help you. Ask about:
• where they live.
• what they do in their spare time.
• what they can do now that they couldn't do before.
• what they do in their job.
You cannot ask who they have changed places with. You must guess this at the end of the interview.

Exam techniques

Gap filling

1 Guidelines

Do	Don't
• Read the whole passage through quickly first.	▶ Don't read the text too slowly.
• Read the text again. Try summarizing it in your head. Then think what kinds of word are missing, e.g. nouns, prepositions, etc.	▶ Don't worry yet about what the missing words are.
• Read the text one sentence at a time, filling the gaps you are confident about first. Remember to add one word only.	▶ Don't panic if you can't fill all the gaps immediately.
• Read the text again and fill the remaining gaps. If you aren't sure, make sensible guesses.	▶ Don't leave any gaps empty.
• Check for accuracy of grammar and spelling.	

2 Practice

A Read the text through quickly once and decide which of these three titles best describes what the text is about.
1 Men still at top of earnings league
2 Monica Seles: a profile
3 Million dollar kids

B Now try out the guidelines on the text and use the questions and clues opposite to help you decide your answers.

In the 1960s women tennis players received little or no prize money at all. In the 1990s, _____ (1), the top players can earn twice as _____ (2) in a fortnight as a successful company director does in a whole year.

And _____ (3) most young people their age were still _____ (4) for exams, players _____ (5) Monica Seles and Jennifer Capriati were earning thousands of pounds a week. When she was _____ (6) sixteen, Seles was rich _____ (7) to buy any car she _____ (8).

Nowadays, most of a _____ (9) tennis player's income comes from sponsorship contracts with fashion _____ (10) sportswear companies rather than from major championships. Players are _____ (11) huge sums of money to wear anything from tennis shoes _____ (12) a wristwatch. Official prize _____ (13), in fact, only accounts for a fraction of total earnings.

But _____ (14) so much money in the bank, and the world at their _____ (15), it will be _____ (16) if these young stars _____ (17) not affected by success. Both Seles and Capriati are coached by their fathers, _____ (18) do their best to protect their daughters _____ (19) the pressure fame _____ (20) brought. Only time will tell whether this is enough.

Questions and clues

1 The writer is contrasting the situation of women tennis players in the 60s and in the 90s. Which conjunction introduces a contrast and can come between commas?

2 When you see one *as*, look for another *as*. What kind of construction do they indicate? The word *earn* gives you another clue to the missing word.

3 Look ahead to 4 and the end of the sentence. The missing word, together with the tense of the verbs, indicates that both actions were happening at the same time.

4 It is part of the verb which is missing. What tense is the verb which follows? Is this the same tense? What verb is followed by *for* in connection with exams?

5 Seles and Capriati are examples of women players who earn thousands a week. Which word indicates that an example will follow?

6 Sixteen is young to be able to buy a car. Which word can emphasize that sixteen is young?

7 Which word means *sufficiently* and comes after adjectives but before nouns?

8 There is a subject *she*, so there must be a verb. What tense is the verb? Look at the tense of the previous verb.

9 What clues are there that tell you the missing word is an adjective? What kind of tennis players is the writer talking about?

10 This word joins words or phrases together.

11 Part of the verb is missing. Which part? *Money* is another clue.

12 Which preposition frequently occurs after *from*?

13 *Prize* is a noun. What other noun can combine with it to make a compound noun? *Earnings* gives you a clue.

14 This preposition means 'because they have'.

15 A possessive adjective must be followed by a noun. Here the missing word completes an idiom. If you don't know the idiom, have a guess. Perhaps you have a similar idiom in your language.

16 What's the missing adjective? Can you think of more than one possibility?

17 What tense is the missing part of the verb? *If* and *will* are clues.

18 This word refers to *fathers*. The comma tells us that what follows is extra information.

19 Which preposition comes after *protect*?

20 Which tense is this? Which part of the verb is missing?

Art for art's sake

canvas   carving   charcoal   clay   cloth   drawing   knitting   painting
papier-mâché   pottery   sculpture   sewing   steel   stone   wood   wool

Introduction

A Match the materials and the names of the arts and crafts with the drawings.

B Have you ever made anything? What did you make it from? Was it useful or decorative or both? Were you pleased with the result?

Listening

1 Think ahead

Look at these photos of sculptures made by two young British sculptors. Which sculptures do you think were made by the same sculptor? Why? What materials do you think the sculptors used?

2 Listening

You are going to hear the sculptors talking about two of the sculptures in the photos above. As you listen to part one for the first time, decide which two sculptures they are talking about.

3 Comprehension

A Listen to part one again and for questions 1–3 choose the best answer, A, B, C or D.

1 The sculptor intended the first sculpture to represent
  A the creation of the world.   C nature.
  B war and peace.   D the human mind.

2 The first sculpture is made from
  A wood and papier-mâché.   C wood, plaster and string.
  B wood and plaster.   D metal, wood and plaster.

3 What does the second artist say about her use of colour?
  A She likes bright colours because she used to live in Africa.
  B She almost always makes use of colour in her sculptures.
  C Every colour means something different.
  D She always knows in advance what colours she will use.

B As you listen to part two, decide whether the following sentences are true, false, or not known (the information is not given).

Sculpture 1   1 The man thinks the name of the sculpture is appropriate.
              2 The sculpture is over six metres high.
              3 Both of them like the colours.
Sculpture 2   4 The man compares the sculpture to rubbish.
              5 The man doesn't like anything about the sculpture.
Sculpture 3   6 The man thinks 'The Giant' is more realistic than this piece.
              7 The man thinks art is about beauty.

4 Points of view

What do you think of the sculptures?

Grammar and practice

Gerunds and infinitives

A Change or no change of meaning?
Look at these two sentences from the listening texts.
1 I tried *to give* the idea of what a woman is for me.
2 And I like *working* with papier-mâché.
Can the gerund form be used instead of the infinitive, and vice-versa, without changing the meaning of the sentences?

B Change of meaning
Look at the five pairs of sentences or clauses in *italics*. First try to match the sentences (a and b) with their definitions (c and d). Then choose the best sentence or clause (e and f) to follow.
Example   1 – a, c, f and b, d, e
1 a *I don't remember inviting him . . .*
  b *Sorry, I didn't remember to invite him . . .*
  c I have no recollection of the event.
  d I didn't do something I intended to do.
  e I've had such a busy day.
  f In fact, I've never even seen him before.
2 a *I've tried taking the pills the doctor prescribed . . .*
  b *I've tried to take the pills the doctor prescribed . . .*
  c I've done the action as an experiment.
  d I've made an effort to do the action.
  e but I just can't swallow them.
  f but I still can't sleep.

3 a *I stopped to speak to Richard . . .*
  b *I stopped speaking to Richard . . .*
  c I interrupted one activity in order to do another.
  d I finished an activity.
  e after he lied to me.
  f to ask him about the weekend.
4 a *I regret to tell you . . .*
  b *I regret telling her . . .*
  c I am sorry about something I did in the past.
  d I am sorry about something I am doing now or am about to do.
  e that I am unable to offer you the job.
  f I was sacked from my last job.
5 a *He went on talking . . .*
  b *He went on to talk . . .*
  c He finished one activity and started another.
  d He continued to do the action.
  e even after he'd been told to keep quiet.
  f about his solutions after he'd outlined the problems.

C Now read section 2 in the Grammar reference on page 181 before you do the practice exercise.

D Practice
Fill the spaces with an appropriate verb in the correct form.
1 I hope he's remembered _____ the tickets.
2 UK Air regrets _____ the late arrival of flight UA127.
3 He's tried _____ the window but it's stuck.
4 Will you stop _____ while I'm talking!
5 Shall we go on _____ the next item on the agenda?

Vocabulary

1 The arts

Vocabulary reference p.196

aisle
audience
circle
conductor
curtain
drummer
footlight
gallery

guitarist
loudspeaker
microphone
orchestra pit
screen
set
stage
stalls

A Venues

Match the words in the box with the correct features in the illustrations.

B Choose the word which best completes each sentence.

1 The group played for two hours and then came back for a(n) _____ .
   A encore   B extra   C performance   D ending
2 There was a twenty-minute _____ after the third act.
   A break   B pause   C rest   D interval
3 The _____ of the jealous husband was played by Paul Newman.
   A paper   B part   C interpretation   D acting
4 The _____ applauded warmly when the curtain dropped.
   A observers   B crowd   C spectators   D audience
5 The play is _____ in 18th century England.
   A set   B situated   C cast   D held

C A memorable event

Complete the dialogue by filling in the missing questions.

Anne   Have you ever seen 'Dire Straits'?
Rob   Yes, I have, actually.
Anne   So have I. (1) _____ ?
Rob   In London. At Earls Court. In May 1992, I think.
Anne   Oh, I saw that concert too. (2) _____ ?
Rob   In the front row of the gallery. What about you?
Anne   Near the back of the circle. (3) _____ ?
Rob   Quite well. Not all the stage, though. What about you?
Anne   Not bad. Those big screens at the side of the stage made a difference.
    (4) _____ ?
Rob   Well, I thought the atmosphere and the lighting were excellent. And Mark
    Knopfler was brilliant too. But the acoustics were awful!
Anne   They were, weren't they? They're always bad at Earls Court. But then it was
    built for exhibitions not concerts. (5) _____ ?
Rob   Yes, in Madrid. At an open-air concert. I mean, I enjoyed this concert but
    their concert in Spain was sheer magic!

2 Word combinations

A *See* **and** *watch*

When do you use *see* and when do you use *watch* ? Fill in the table with a tick (√) or a cross (×).

	TV	any programme on TV	a film, play, ballet, exhibition	a(n) (sports) event
see				
watch				

B Practice

Complete the following sentences with the correct form of *see* or *watch* and make any other necessary changes.

1 The average teenager in Europe now spends more time playing computer games than _____ TV.
2 One of the funniest films I've ever _____ is 'Mr Hulot's Holiday' by Jacques Tati.
3 Millions of people all over the world _____ the opening ceremony of the Olympic Games.
4 I first _____ 'Swan Lake' performed by the Bolshoi Ballet.
5 He rarely misses _____ his team play whether they're at home or away.

3 Word building

Noun suffixes

Four of the most common noun endings in English are *-tion*, *-ence*, *-ness* and *-ity*.

1 Find an example of nouns with each of these endings in the interview with Elton John on page 26. What are the corresponding adjectives?
2 Make these adjectives into nouns: intelligent, lonely, educated, secure, sincere, dark. Remember that getting a feel for what is right is important; try saying them to yourself and see how they sound. Then check your answers in a dictionary.

4 Phrasal verbs

A Elton John says, 'I only have to look at a doughnut and I immediately *put on* two pounds.' Phrasal verbs with *put* have many different meanings. Fill in the gaps in the following sentences with *put on* or *put off* in the correct tense and make any other necessary changes.

1 He quickly _____ his clothes and rushed out.
2 She _____ all the lights if she is in the house on her own.
3 When you get toothache, you can't _____ going to the dentist any longer.
4 He can't concentrate if people talk to him while he's driving. It really _____ .
5 He _____ at least seven kilos since he got married.
6 She thought of becoming a nurse but she changed her mind. She _____ by the long hours and poor pay.

B Match the phrasal verbs in each of the sentences above with their definitions.

delay	get dressed in	increase weight
discourage	switch on	distract

C Which uses of *put on* can you find opposites for?

Writing

Expressing an opinion

1 'Outraged'

The photo shows a new sculpture which has been added to a building in the centre of a small town. As soon as it was finished, the council started receiving letters from local residents giving their opinions. Read this extract from one of the letters.

I am writing to tell you what I think of the 'sculpture' which has recently appeared in George Street. I believe that this is just one of several examples of 'art' which we, the taxpayer, have paid for to 'brighten up' the streets of our town.

5 Personally, I find this 'sculpture' extremely unattractive. I feel that it does nothing to improve the appearance of the street; quite the contrary, in fact. The scaffolding, which I presume is part of the 'sculpture', is not only ugly but an obstruction for pedestrians, who either have to walk under it or risk their lives 10 by walking on the road.

It really makes me angry that taxpayers' money has been spent on what can only be called junk. As far as I'm concerned, this would not even brighten up a scrap-yard!

2 Language of opinion

A Underline the words and phrases in the letter which show that the writer is going to tell you their opinion. Do you know any other words and phrases which could replace them? What changes, if any, would you need to make to the grammatical structure of the sentences which follow?

B Now find examples of words and phrases in the text which express the writer's opinion and underline them, e.g. *extremely unattractive*.

C Think of words and phrases you would use to describe the sculpture. Compare your ideas with another student.

3 Writing

While you and your family were away on holiday, the owners of the house opposite yours 'did up' the outside of their house. Write a short letter to a friend (about 120 words) giving your opinion of the changes. Describe briefly what the house used to look like and what it looks like now, and say what you think about it.

4 Comparison

Power games

Introduction

A Television

1 How many hours of television do you watch a day or a week?
2 What do you like most and least about television in your country?

B Reading

The British TV schedule below is for a typical weekday evening.

1 Which channel seems to
  a be the most serious?
  b be the most light-hearted?
  c be the most varied?
  d have the most news and current affairs programmes?
2 Are there any programmes that are on TV in your country?

C Plan and discuss

1 Imagine that you have decided to spend the evening at home watching TV. Look through the schedule again and note down the programmes you would watch.
  Example   *7.30 BBC 2 Young Musician of the Year*
2 Work with two or three other students. You are spending the evening at home together. Say which programmes you each want to watch. Try to agree about the evening's viewing. There is only one television and no video recorder.
3 Which programmes have you agreed to watch? Are you going to watch more or less TV than you originally intended?

BBC 1	BBC 2	ITV	CHANNEL 4
7.30 Telly Addicts Weekly TV quiz show.	**7.30 Young Musician of the Year** Five young performers compete for this year's top prize.	**7.30 Coronation Street** Will Don leave Ivy? Don't miss this moving episode of the ever-popular Manchester soap opera.	**7.30 Channel 4 News** Comment and current affairs.
8.30 2 point 4 children A new situation comedy.			**8.00 Brookside** Who is the father of Sammy's baby? All is revealed tonight in Liverpool's soap.
9.00 News	**8.10 Rembrandt** A programme to mark a new exhibition of the master's portraits.	**8.00 Inspector Morse** Private eye in Crete.	
9.30 QED: Pisa Tonight's documentary asks 'How long will the tower last?'		**10.00 News at Ten**	**8.30 The Food File** An investigation into supermarket prices.
	9.00 Film: Casablanca (1942) Bogart and Bergman making magic in wartime romance. (B/W)	**10.40 Spitting Image** Political satire with your favourite puppet friends.	**9.00 Anderson's People** Chat show with a difference.
	**10.40 Newsnight**	**11.10 Film: Green Card (1991)** Depardieu hits the USA in gentle comedy.	**10.00 The Golden Girls** Comedy American style.
	11.25 The Late Show Arts round-up. The latest and best in theatre and literature.		**10.30 Film: Psycho (1960)** Classic Hitchcock thriller. (B/W)
10.20 Sportsnight Athletics – a profile of Carl Lewis. Golf – the US Masters.			**12.20 Midnight Special** A last look at the day's news.
11.30 Weather			

Reading

1 Think ahead   Look at the title and the picture below and then guess what the article is about.

2 Reading   Read the article through once, quickly, to see if you guessed correctly.

Whose finger is on the button in your house?

Imagine the scene: you and your family are relaxing after a hard day's work. You've just watched the news on TV. What are you going to watch next? Or, perhaps more importantly, who decides what you are going to watch next? Whose finger is on the button?

Deciding what to watch on TV is a battle of wills that is fought in homes all over the world. According to psychologists, it is much more serious than simply deciding between a soap opera and a sports programme, or between pop music and politics. This television conflict is part of a bigger power game which goes on in homes, even though most of the players are unaware that they are playing a game at all. The game is called, *Who's Boss?*

'It's such a subtle game,' says psychologist Dr David Lewis, 'that many people don't even know they're playing it. It's all about the balance of power in the home, and who's in control.'

Unconsciously, people begin to play the game as soon as they meet their future husband or wife. By the time the couple get married, the rules of the game are already well-established. The big decisions, like where to live and which school to send the children to, are usually joint decisions. When it comes to less important things, like deciding where to go on holiday, or what sort of car to buy, it's a different matter. Here's just one example of this process at work. He looks through a pile of holiday brochures and announces his preference: 'The South of France'. She quickly agrees before he realizes that the only brochures she gave him were those for the South of France. Similarly, she may decide what time the children should go to bed, and on how the home should be decorated, but he chooses the new car and decides what the family does at weekends.

'Family power struggles are fascinating,' says Dr Lewis. 'Of course, some people are naturally more dominant than others, and the most dominant personality in a family tries to lead. These days, even though so many couples make a conscious effort to have a true and equal partnership, men generally have a greater need to appear to be in physical control. Women, on the other hand, are not as interested in physical control as in emotional control. On the whole, they're more manipulative and can make the man think something was his idea in the first place.'

The tussle over what to watch on TV is a good example of this fight for control. Recently, research psychologists persuaded 400 families to have a 'C-Box' installed in their living rooms. This is a video machine which watches you as you watch TV. They found that 80% of the time it was the man in the house who had his finger on the button, followed by the eldest child, then the youngest child, and only then the woman of the house.

'A child with a strong personality can totally dominate a family,' says Dr Lewis. 'Most kids are far less innocent, far more knowing than their parents realize. Many of them are so sensitive to non-verbal communication that they can pick up atmospheres and sense the strengths and weaknesses of the adults around them. They can be very stubborn and they soon realize that the more stubborn they are, the more quickly they get their own way. When the 'C-Box' was used to study groups of children on their own watching television, the researchers found that the children who had the remote control liked to show off their power by irritating everyone and changing channels every two or three minutes.'

So, next time you've got your finger on the button ready to ZAP the rest of the family with your assertiveness, think about the power game you're playing. ◄

3 Points of view

1 Who decides which TV programmes you and your family watch?
2 Which of these statements about the article do you agree with?
In my experience, the ideas in the article are true to life.
The ideas in the article are gross generalizations.
The families referred to in the article are not like any families I know.
The article presents a stereotyped, sexist view of the world.
3 The families mentioned in the article had remote control devices to change TV channels. Do you think the research findings would have been different if the people had not had remote controls?

4 Comprehension

A True or false?
According to the article, are these statements true or false? Rephrase the false sentences to make them true.
1 Deciding what to watch on television is only one aspect of a larger power game played by families.
2 Most people pretend they are not involved in these family power games.
3 The rules of the power game are fixed soon after couples get married.
4 The majority of married couples take really important decisions together.
5 Men want people to think they are in charge in their families.
6 The C-Box is a device which records people's television watching habits.
7 In 80 per cent of cases it was the eldest child who decided what the family watched on TV.
8 Parents don't realize how sensitive their children are to the power relationships in their families.

B Vocabulary
Guess the meanings of these words and phrases from the article.
1 a battle of wills (paragraph 2)
2 the balance of power (paragraph 3)
3 a joint decision (paragraph 4)
4 a power struggle (paragraph 5)
5 the tussle (paragraph 6)
6 non-verbal communication (paragraph 7). Give examples of this kind of communication.
7 to get your own way (paragraph 7)
8 to zap (paragraph 8)

C Reading between the lines
1 What do you think is the average size of the families in the experiment?
2 What else does the article imply about the lifestyle of these families?
3 Which members of your family would watch these programmes mentioned in the article?
soap opera   sports programmes   pop music   politics
4 Do you think that the women in the families in the C-Box experiment were really the least influential people in their families?

5 Over to you

Do you think that television has an influence on the way you behave or think?

6 Stop that!

You are watching TV with two small children who keep changing channels every two minutes while you are trying to watch your favourite programme. In about 60 words, write what you say to persuade them to stop.

Grammar and practice

1 Comparisons

The reading text includes a number of comparison phrases. Without looking back at the text, try to fill the gaps in these extracts. The first one has been done for you.

1 When it comes to *less* important things, like deciding where to go on holiday, it's a different matter.
2 The battle of wills is _____ more serious _____ simply deciding between a soap opera and a sports programme.
3 Some people are naturally _____ dominant _____ others.
4 The _____ dominant person in the family tries to lead.
5 Men generally have a g_____ need to appear to be in physical control.
6 Women are not _____ interested in physical control _____ in emotional control.
7 Most kids are far _____ innocent, far _____ knowing than their parents realize.

Now look back at the text and check your answers.

2 Comparative and superlative adjectives

A What are the comparative and superlative forms of these adjectives?

bad   common*   far   friendly*   good
high*   important*   old   strange*   thin*

* Think of two or three more adjectives which have comparative and superlative forms like these.

B Here are some phrases which are used with comparative adjectives.

a bit   far   a little   much   a lot   slightly

Which phrases are used to compare two things which are very different from each other, and which are used to compare things which are almost the same?

C Before continuing, check your understanding of comparative and superlative adjectives in the Grammar reference on pages 181–182.

3 Practice

A Compare these famous partners using comparative adjectives and some of the phrases from 2B.

1 Laurel and Hardy   2 Tom and Jerry   3 Popeye and Olive Oyl

B Compare these sets using comparative and superlative adjectives. Make comparisons according to the ways suggested or any other ways you can think of.

1 size, price, taste

2 size, price, comfort

3 any way you like

4 Family likenesses

A Look at this photograph of the Addams family and answer the questions.
1 How many of the characters in this famous film and TV family can you name? Match these names with the numbers in the photograph.
Gomez   Grandma   Lurch   Morticia   Pugsley
Uncle Fester   Wednesday
2 How are these characters related to each other?

B Now look for similarities and differences between the members of the family. Compare grandparents and grandchildren, parents and children, brothers and sisters, etc.
Example   *Wednesday is much shorter than Morticia.*

5 *The . . . the . . .*

A Look at this sentence from the reading text.
   The more stubborn they are, the more quickly they get their own way.
The comparative phrase in the first part of the sentence is balanced by a comparative phrase in the second part. How are the two parts of this sentence related to each other in meaning? Here are some more examples of sentences with double comparatives.

The harder he worked, the more money he earned.
The richer he became, the more food he ate.
The more he ate, the fatter he got.
The fatter he got, the more slowly he worked.
The more slowly he worked, the less he earned.
The less he earned, the less food he could afford.
The less food he bought, the thinner he got.

B Notice how many different kinds of words can follow *the*. There are notes on these comparative expressions in the Grammar reference on page 182.

C Make up your own sequences starting with these sentences.
1 The later she became, the faster she ran.
2 The less work he did, the more free time he had.
3 The more worried he was, the more cigarettes he smoked.

6 *So* and *such*

A What do these extracts from this unit show about the use of *so* and *such*?
1 It's *such* a subtle game that many people don't even know they're playing it.
2 Many children are *so* sensitive to non-verbal communication that they can pick up atmospheres . . .
How else can *so* and *such* be used? Think of what types of words can follow *so* and *such*. Compare ideas with a partner.

B Before continuing, check your understanding of *so* and *such* in the Grammar reference on page 183.

7 Practice

Rewrite these sentences starting with the words provided. In each case your answers should include *so* instead of *such* and *such* instead of *so*.
1 Maria works so hard that she's always top of her class.
   Maria is _____ .
2 John's got such a high IQ that he got into university when he was only 14.
   John's IQ _____ .
3 Claudia is such a fast writer that she always finishes first.
   Claudia writes _____ .
4 I know so many people who wish they hadn't left school.
   I know _____ .
5 Some people have such boring jobs that they can't wait to retire.
   Some people have jobs that are _____ .

Just for fun

Introduction

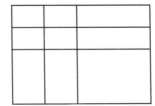

Working with a partner, time yourselves to see how long you take to solve these problems.

1 How many rectangles are there in this figure?

2 'The day before yesterday I was 18, but next year I'll be 21.' Can you work out the date of the speaker's birthday and the date on which this statement was made?

3 Two friends on the beach are sharing a personal stereo. They work out that they will be able to listen for exactly 48 minutes each in the time they have. Suddenly, four more of their friends arrive. They all want an equal go at listening to the stereo in the same amount of time as the first two had already agreed. How long will each one be able to listen for?

Listening

1 Think ahead

You are going to hear about a TV programme called 'Just for Fun' in which contestants have to solve mathematical problems and puzzles like the ones above. Do you think men or women are better at mathematical puzzles like this? Make lists of things that you think women are better at than men, and that men are better at than women. Think of a range of abilities and skills, for example, music, sports, scientific experiments, politics, languages, cookery, child-rearing, teaching, magic, painting. Compare and discuss ideas in pairs.

2 Listening

Read these six statements. Which of them do you think refer to men and which to women? Predict the answers and write M or W in the spaces.

1 On the TV programme 'Just for Fun' *they*'ve got more confidence. ___

2 On 'Just for Fun', *they* get more problems right. ___

3 *They* don't show as much self-confidence. ___

4 When people are watching them, *they* panic. ___

5 *They* don't like to take risks. ___

6 'Just for Fun' suggests that *they* may be naturally better at maths. ___

As you listen for the first time, check your predictions.

3 Comprehension

A Read the questions below then listen again. For each question choose the answer which you think fits best.

1 In answer to the question, 'Who's better at maths: boys or girls?' the teacher says,
   A Boys are always better than girls.
   B Boys are better than girls when they are young.
   C Boys and girls are about the same when they are young.
   D Girls are better than boys at polytechnic or university.

2 The accepted theory about what men and women are good at seems to be
   A questioned by the TV programme 'Just for Fun'.
   B explained by the TV programme 'Just for Fun'.
   C ignored by the TV programme 'Just for Fun'.
   D proved by the TV programme 'Just for Fun'.

3 One of the purposes of the programme 'Just for Fun' is to show that
   A maths is a difficult subject for most people.
   B maths is not as difficult as many people think.
   C maths has to be explained by specialists.
   D you have to be clever to be good at maths.

4 Kathy thinks that the saying 'behind every successful man there is a successful woman' may mean that
   A women provide support for men.
   B women always stay in the background.
   C women organize everything for men.
   D women take decisions for men.

5 How do men react when they are in competition with women on the programme?
   A They are put off by the lights.
   B They want more time to answer questions.
   C They remain very calm.
   D They get very agitated.

B Vocabulary

Guess or work out the meanings of the words or phrases in *italics* in these extracts from the recording. Then answer any questions that follow.

1 'On "Just for Fun" we're trying to bring maths to a *non-specialist audience*.'
   What other kinds of audience could there be?

2 'The strange thing is that, on public display, the *macho image* begins to *crack*.'
   How do men with a *macho image* behave? Think of some examples of typical *macho* behaviour.

3 '*In the limelight* the men become so nervous: *blind panic* crosses their faces and their minds seem to turn *blank*.'
   What kinds of people spend most of their life *in the limelight*?
   On what occasions do people's minds *turn blank*?

4 Over to you

Discuss the following questions.

1 At what age are the abilities of men and women, or of boys and girls, the most similar? At what age are they the most different? Why?

2 Boys and girls behave in different ways at school. Do you think they should be taught in separate classes? What benefits and problems would there be? Who would benefit most?

Vocabulary

1 Relationships

Vocabulary reference p.196

A Families

1 Go through the members of the British Royal Family in turn and say what relation they are to Prince Charles.

Example   *Captain Mark Phillips is his* **ex-brother-in-law.**

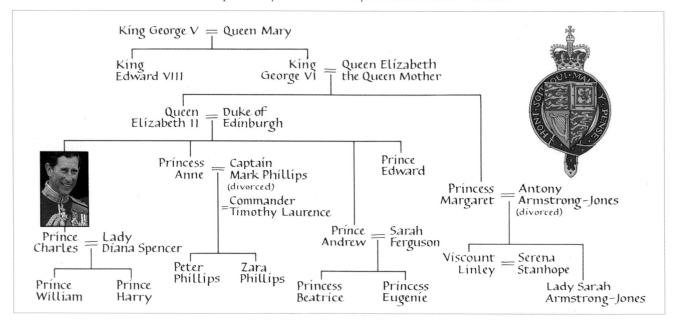

2 Now say what relationship these pairs of people are or were to each other.

Example   King George VI and Queen Elizabeth the Queen Mother
They were **husband** *and* **wife.** *Now she is his* **widow.**

a Mark Phillips and Princess Anne
b Queen Elizabeth and Prince William
c Prince Philip and Princess Diana
d Princess Diana and Princess Anne
e Queen Elizabeth the Queen Mother and Princess Eugenie

3 Work in pairs or small groups.
Find out about each other's families.

a brothers and sisters   How many? How old?
b cousins   How many? How old? Boys or girls?
c grandparents   How many? How old?

B Other relationships

Complete this puzzle with words which fit the ten definitions.

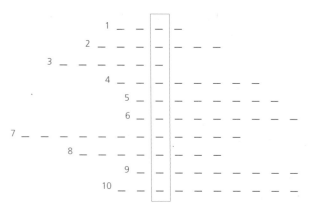

1 your superior at work
2 person you have a legal business relationship with
3 man engaged to be married to a woman
4 person who gives you work
5 person you give work to
6 person you work with
7 person you know but are not especially friendly with
8 female child
9 person who lives next door
10 man or boy's romantic partner

What does the vertical word that you have made mean?

C The word in capital letters at the end of each of these sentences can be used in a form that fits suitably in the blank space. Fill each blank in this way.

1 The problem of _____ is growing as more and more businesses close down. EMPLOY
2 I've known Sue for nearly three years now. Our _____ started when we met at a railway station. FRIEND
3 Most of the people who live round here are elderly, so it's a very quiet _____ . NEIGHBOUR
4 Even though the divorce rate is increasing, _____ is still very popular among young people. MARRY
5 My sister invited over a hundred people to her _____ party. ENGAGE

2 Word building

Compound nouns

In English, compound nouns can be made from various word combinations. Some are written as single words, some are joined by hyphens, and some are separate words. You will need to check them in a dictionary.

Examples   single words: *birthday, weekend*
              two words joined by a hyphen: *round-up, half-time, self-confidence*
              two separate words: *video recorder, soap opera, power game*

A What are the compound nouns (single words) which match these definitions?
1 a schedule which tells you when a train leaves or arrives
2 safety strap worn in a car or aircraft to prevent passengers being thrown forward
3 total amount of rain which has fallen in a particular area over a particular time
4 road junction in the form of a circle
5 part of a radio, record player, etc. which changes electrical impulses into sounds

B Think of more two-word compound nouns joined by hyphens in these categories.
1 nouns from phrasal verbs, e.g. *round-up*
2 words starting with *half*, e.g. *half-time*
3 words starting with *self*, e.g. *self-confidence*

C How many compound nouns can you think of using these words?
hand   foot   day   night   sun   star   head   heart   water   air
For example, *handbag, tap-water*. In pairs or groups, brainstorm ideas and write lists. Say whether you think each compound should be a single word, two words joined by a hyphen, or two separate words. Finally, check your lists of words in a dictionary.

3 Phrasal verbs

Read this sentence from the listening. 'The old saying "behind every successful man there is a successful woman" may have taken on a new meaning.' Here *take on* means *assume* or *develop*. *Take* can be used with other particles to express different meanings. Replace the verbs in *italics* in these sentences with the correct form of *take* and one of the particles from this list.

     after   back   down   over   to   up

1 Within the last year Japanese corporations *have gained control of* more than a hundred European companies.
2 I *retracted* everything I said as soon as I realized that none of it was true.
3 The reporter *wrote* everything I said in his notebook.
4 I didn't start playing basketball until I was 15, but I *liked* it immediately.
5 When my father retired he *started* painting.
6 He's very quick to lose his temper. In that respect he *resembles* his father.

Exam techniques

Picture discussion

1 Guidelines

Do	Don't
• Look carefully at the photos. Think about how to describe what you can see.	▶ Don't worry if you don't understand immediately what is going on in the picture. You will not lose marks for not knowing exactly what is happening.
• Be as precise as you can when you describe the photo itself. Use some 'position' language (see below) if it helps.	▶ Don't worry if you don't know the precise words for what you can see; use alternatives. Remember you will be given marks for fluency as well as for accuracy.
• Use present continuous verbs to describe what is happening.	▶ Don't use the present simple to describe what is happening.
• Answer questions as fully as possible. This will help you to keep talking.	▶ Don't give too many one- or two-word answers.
• Direct the conversation towards something you are interested in and can talk about easily.	▶ Don't feel you have to stick rigidly to subjects raised by the examiner.

2 Picture description language

Location
Match the phrases on the left with the appropriate places in this photograph.

at the bottom

at the top

on the right-hand side

on the left-hand side

in the top left-hand corner

in the bottom right-hand corner

in the foreground

in the background

on the left

on the right

in the middle

3 Picture discussion

Look carefully at the photograph and then answer the questions on page 47. If you are not certain what is happening, use these expressions to make suggestions.

they seem to be   maybe they're   I think they're   it could/might be

I'm not quite sure, but   it looks as if they're   it looks like a

A Description

1 What can you see in the photograph?
2 How are the eight people in this photograph related?
3 What else could you describe to the examiner?

B General questions

1 How many people are there in your family? Would you like to be a twin, a triplet or even a sextuplet? Why? Why not?
2 Why do you think parents often dress twins in the same clothes?
3 From a child's point of view, what are the pros and cons of being part of a big family?
4 From the parents' point of view, what are the advantages and disadvantages of having only one child?

4 Practice

Work with a partner. You are going to take it in turns to ask each other questions about two more photographs.

Student A

You are the oral examiner. Think of some questions to ask your partner about the photo on the left. There are brief notes on this photograph and some general question ideas on page 174. First, ask one or two questions about what is happening in the photo, and then ask some more general questions about the subject.

Student B

You are a student at the FCE oral interview. Spend a few minutes thinking about what is happening in the photo on the left. Answer the examiner's (your partner's) questions.

Now exchange roles and repeat the sequence of activities with the photo on the right. Student B is now the examiner. There are brief notes on this photograph and some general question ideas on page 174.

Writing

Describing objects

In one of the compositions you write for Paper 2, you may need to describe an object.

1 Theft!

Read this newspaper report of a theft.

Thieves strike while bride dances

Two men posing as wedding guests strolled into the Mill Hotel last Saturday and stole items from a display of wedding presents.

The theft occurred while the bride and groom were dancing and chatting to guests. No one realized that anything was wrong until the end of the evening when the bride's mother, Mrs Pamela Hill, found a number of empty boxes.

The police were called and after they had arrived, some of the guests were asked to write descriptions of their wedding gifts. Read these descriptions of three of the missing presents.

They're a matching pair of candlesticks – about two hundred years old, according to the dealer I bought them from. They're solid silver and extremely heavy. The main part – the stem – is made of three pieces of metal woven together. The two arms each have a candle holder at the end. They were very expensive.

It's quite a small travel alarm clock – about eight centimetres high and six wide. The knobs are all on the back, which is round. It's made of black plastic but, of course, the face is clear. The numbers and the two hands are white and the alarm hand is black. All the hands have luminous green tips which glow in the dark. It cost about £10, as far as I can remember.

It's a medium-sized table lamp, about 50 centimetres tall, I suppose. It's got a plain blue pottery base and a wide shade, which is dark blue with a pretty, flowery pattern. It hasn't got a plug on the end or a bulb in it. The on-off switch is just below the bulb holder. I can't remember exactly how much it cost, but I know it was more than £40.

2 What to include in a description

A Look at the descriptions again and for each present find the words or phrases which describe the features listed below.

Size/measurements   Shape   Weight   Colour
Material   Position of parts in relation to each other
Purpose   Price/value

B Now add other words which you might use in a description.

3 Expanding notes

Write a description of a personal stereo using these notes.

14 cm x 8 cm, lightweight, black metal and plastic, see-through lid, buttons on long edge, microphone at end, headphone socket and volume on short edge

4 Writing

Write your own description of something that is of great value to you. Include the features listed in 2A above.

R1 Revision

This section gives you extra practice in the grammar and vocabulary covered in Units 1–4. Before you begin, remind yourself of this language by reading the Grammar reference notes on pages 179–183 and the Vocabulary reference on pages 196–197. This is not a test so you should refer to Units 1–4 and the reference sections as you work through these exercises.

1 Vocabulary multiple-choice

Choose the word or phrase which best completes these sentences. Look up any words you don't know when you've finished.

1 When British people go abroad, it takes them several days to get used to _____ on the right-hand side of the road.
   A drive B driven C driving D drove

2 Many old people don't like change. They are very set in their _____ .
   A life B habits C routines D ways

3 By the year 2000, many people currently employed _____ their jobs.
   A have lost   C will be losing
   B will have lost   D are losing

4 Many young people travel all over the world, and do all kinds of jobs before they _____ .
   A lie down   C settle down
   B touch down   D put down

5 Brighton is a famous _____ town on the south coast of England.
   A resort B port C coast D seaside

6 My friends have just moved to a new flat in a residential area on the _____ of Paris.
   A suburbs B outside C outskirts D side

7 Even though Alan didn't have much money, he insisted _____ everybody a drink.
   A to buy   C buying
   B in buying   D on buying

8 I couldn't concentrate on my homework, because my brother kept _____ me with silly questions.
   A interrupting   C to interrupt
   B interrupted   D interruption

9 I'm terrified _____ breaking down on a motorway at night.
   A for B with C from D of

10 I've never _____ very well with my brother. We've got completely different personalities.
   A got off B got on C got away D got up

11 The more a car costs, _____ it goes.
   A faster   C so faster
   B the faster   D the fastest

12 Children should not be allowed to get their own _____ all the time. If they do, they can become spoilt.
   A way B wishes C desires D path

13 The noise of the typewriter really _____ me off. I just couldn't concentrate.
   A put B pulled C set D took

14 My neighbours made _____ noise last night that I couldn't get to sleep.
   A so many B so much C such D so

15 _____ a famous personality has its advantages and its disadvantages.
   A To be B Been C Be D Being

16 These days British people _____ to book their summer holidays in December or January.
   A usually B often C will D tend

17 My parents always _____ of me smoking. They even told me once it would stop me growing taller.
   A disapproved   C disproved
   B approved   D proved

18 I find my boss difficult to work with – she is always _____ my ideas.
   A criticize   C criticized
   B criticizes   D criticizing

19 That bag looks very heavy. _____ carry it for you?
   A Am I going to   C Shall I
   B Will I   D Would I

20 I'm much fitter than _____ .
   A she is B her is C she's D she

2 Word building

Use the word in capitals at the end of each of these sentences to form a word that fits in the blank space.

1 Sam works as a _____ in an office in the town centre. TELEPHONE

2 Switzerland and Austria are both _____ countries. MOUNTAIN

3 My brother lives in an attractive _____ part of Paris. RESIDE

4 We brought back several carved _____ statues from our holiday in Africa. WOOD

5 We were lucky enough to get tickets for the first _____ of the hit musical *Cats*. PERFORM

6 Our journey took nearly five hours. It was much _____ than I'd thought. FAR

7 Jeremy has just got _____ to a girl he's known since he was a boy. ENGAGE

8 More and more young people want a university _____ . EDUCATE

3 Gap filling

Look back at the Exam techniques section pages 30–31 to remind yourself how to work through gap filling exercises. Then fill each gap with one word.

The state of California in the United States is famous for its traffic problems. We've all seen television pictures of Los Angeles during the evening rush hour. Too _____(1) cars want to use the roads and motorways _____(2) the same time. Scientists, who have been trying to solve these problems _____(3) several years now, have suggested various solutions, such _____(4) two-storey motorways. Not surprisingly, people rejected this idea _____(5) of the damage it would cause _____(6) the environment.

Now the scientists have _____(7) of another solution: they want cars on motorways to be controlled _____(8) computers instead _____(9) human beings. If their plan goes ahead, cars _____(10) travel on special lanes at 100 kilometres an hour, just one metre from _____(11) other. Because the cars are _____(12) the control of a computer, drivers will be able to take _____(13) hands off the steering _____(14) and sit back and _____(15) the newspaper. They won't even need to look _____(16) they are going.

The cars will travel along the motorways in groups of twenty and _____(17) will be a gap of 100 metres _____(18) these groups. It might sound dangerous, _____(19) apparently, if there is a crash or if the computer fails, it will actually be safer for the cars to be close together.

Although the technology is ready, the system will _____(20) start operating on public roads until the year 2000.

4 Transformations

Complete each unfinished sentence so that it means the same as the sentence printed before it.

Example   Mike doesn't play tennis as well as Julia.
          Julia plays *tennis better than Mike.*

1 It was such a cold day yesterday that I wore my winter coat.
  I felt _____

2 After a hard day's work, he usually falls asleep on the train.
  He tends _____

3 As Elton John became more famous, it was more difficult for him to avoid newspaper reporters.
  The more famous _____

4 My last exam is on Thursday afternoon.
  By Friday morning I _____

5 I'm on the point of losing my temper!
  I'm about _____

6 I'm sorry I sent you that letter. It was very rude of me.
  I regret _____

7 When I was a child we lived in Bristol.
  We used _____

8 Our house is older than all the other houses in the road.
  Our house is the _____

9 Six cars were stolen from the car park. A teenage boy is responsible.
  A teenage boy is responsible _____

10 It was two years ago at the end of this week that I started working here.
   At the end of this week I'll _____

You are now ready to do Progress test 1.

5 Narrative

It happened to me

Introduction

Describe what is happening in these pictures. Has anything similar happened to you while travelling? Or to someone you know? What other things can go wrong? Make lists for air, sea, road and rail travel, and discuss your ideas with another student.

Reading

1 Think ahead

You are going to read the true story of how Nigel Hughes flew to Brazil by accident. How do you think this could have happened?

2 Reading

Now read the text through quickly and check whether your prediction was right.

I FLEW TO BRAZIL BY ACCIDENT

Settling into my seat on the plane, I felt tired, ready for a drink and looking forward to getting home. As I sipped a gin and tonic and pushed my seat back, I remember thinking, 'Only a couple of hours and I'll be home.' I'd phoned my girlfriend, Georgina, from Copenhagen before the plane took off, to tell her I was on my way. She'd said she'd pick me up at Heathrow Airport but I told her not to bother. After another drink, I snoozed until I heard a flight attendant announce, 'We will shortly be landing at Heathrow.' 'Better get my things together,' I thought. And that was it. I honestly don't remember another thing until I woke up again later on. For a couple of minutes I sat wondering sleepily if we were still on our way down to Heathrow. Then I began to realize something funny was going on. The two seats next to me had been empty when I fell asleep. Now a man was lying across them sleeping. There'd been a little girl in front, who'd kept grinning at me over the back of her seat. She had gone. And, weirdest of all, all the lights were off and everyone seemed to be asleep.

Slowly it began to dawn on me what had happened. I simply couldn't believe it and felt increasingly horrified. The plane must have landed at Heathrow, let off some passengers, taken on others and set off on the next part of its journey. And I knew where that was to – Rio de Janeiro, in Brazil.

What on earth was I going to do? Poor Georgina would be wondering what had happened to me, and by now she was probably frantic with worry. And I was stuck on the plane with no ticket. Would they believe it was an accident? Had I really fallen so deeply asleep that I'd completely missed the plane landing and taking off again? I'd certainly been tired but this was ridiculous!

Not knowing what else to do, I went to look for a flight attendant and told her what had happened. I found out it was about 3 a.m. and we were several hours into the 11-hour flight to Brazil. The flight attendant thought it was very funny and told me not to worry. There wasn't much anyone could do, anyway.

We landed in Rio at lunchtime on the Saturday. I was slightly worried that I might be hauled off the plane and locked up as an illegal immigrant. In fact, they took me straight to the departure lounge and told me that I had to sit and wait for the next flight to London, which was at 10 o'clock.

The first thing I did was call Georgina. She was furious because she had convinced herself that I'd been in a plane crash which she'd heard about on the news. Once I'd made the call, I decided it would be a shame to be in Rio and not see any of it. So, slipping out of the airport, I jumped into a passing taxi. It was surprisingly easy! The driver took me round Rio and down to Copacabana beach. It was great! There I was, sitting on one of the most exotic beaches in the world instead of being back in gloomy England, hard at work. The thought of work and the valuable contract I knew I had now lost depressed me for a moment. But then I decided that since I couldn't do a thing about it, I might as well take in the sights.

In the late afternoon I headed back to the airport. I had to confess that I'd sneaked out. The airline staff were not at all pleased and gave me an escort to watch my every move. However, I wasn't planning on going anywhere else – I wasn't going to miss that plane home. Fortunately, there were no problems or delays and we landed at Heathrow at lunchtime on the Sunday. I'd set off from Denmark 48 hours earlier and had spent most of that time in the air. I'd travelled an unbelievable 11,000 miles across the world and back, had a quick paddle in Brazil and landed back home again, tired, fed-up but none the worse for the experience.

Georgina recovered from the shock and was able to see the funny side of it, eventually. As for me, I still haven't worked out how I slept through a whole landing and take-off.

3 Points of view

If you flew somewhere by accident, where would you like it to be? If you only had time to do one thing there, what would you do?

4 Comprehension

A Read the questions, then read the passage again and choose the correct answer or ending.

1 What did Nigel do during the Copenhagen to London Heathrow part of the flight?
   A He had something to eat and drink.　C He had a couple of drinks and a sleep.
   B He talked, drank and slept.　D He slept the whole time.

2 How did he first feel when he realized they had left Heathrow?
   A amused　C excited
   B shocked　D frightened

3 When he arrived in Rio, he was
   A arrested for illegal entry.　C ordered to stay in the departure lounge.
   B fined because he hadn't got a ticket.　D offered a flight home the next day.

4 He spent his time in Rio
   A sightseeing.　C worrying about work.
   B sunbathing.　D taking photos.

B Vocabulary

Find a word or phrase in the text which means:
1 drink in small quantities (paragraph 1)　5 I realized (paragraph 2)
2 have a short, light sleep (paragraph 1)　6 dark and depressing (paragraph 6)
3 soon (paragraph 1)　7 walk with bare feet in shallow
4 smile from ear to ear (paragraph 1)　water (paragraph 7)

C Reading between the lines

1 What had probably happened to the little girl who had been sitting in front of him? (line 17)
2 Why did he have to confess that he'd sneaked out? (line 60)
3 Why do you think the airline staff 'were not at all pleased' that he had left the airport? (line 61)

5 Over to you

If something similar happened to you, would you do the same as Nigel Hughes did? Or would you do something different?

Grammar and practice

1 The past

A Form and use of tenses

The following four sentences from the reading text contain examples of the past simple, past continuous, present perfect and past perfect. Name the tenses in each sentence.

1 I*'d phoned* my girlfriend, Georgina, from Copenhagen before the plane took off.
2 Now a man *was lying* across the seats, sleeping.
3 We *landed* in Rio at lunchtime on the Saturday.
4 I still *haven't worked out* how I slept through a whole landing and take-off.

Which of the above verb tenses do we use to describe a past event or situation that:

a happened before another past event or situation?
b happened at an unspecified time and is relevant to the present?
c happened at a specific time in the past? A time reference is given or understood from the context.
d continued over a period of time?

B Differences in meaning

Name the verb tenses in the following pairs of sentences. What is the difference in meaning between the sentences in each pair?

1 a When Dave arrived, Emma left.
  b When Dave arrived, Emma had left.
2 a I've decorated the hall.
  b I've been decorating the hall.
3 a I was crossing the road when I saw Michelle.
  b I crossed the road when I saw Michelle.
4 a Linda did her homework last night.
  b Linda was doing her homework last night.
5 a He played for the local football team for two seasons.
  b He's played for the local football team for two seasons.

C Before going on to the following practice exercises, check your understanding of past verb forms in the Grammar reference on page 183.

2 Practice

A Read the following newspaper article and choose the most appropriate verb form from the three alternatives given.

Three hurt in crash

Three people were injured in a crash involving two lorries and a van on the A45 near Bury St Edmunds on Saturday. The accident _____ (1) in heavy rain at approximately 2.45 p.m. when a lorry, which _____ (2) grain, _____ (3) on the wet surface of the dual carriageway, spilling its load across both lanes. According to a police spokesperson, the driver of the lorry _____ (4) suddenly to avoid hitting a dog which had run out into the road in front of him. The drivers of the two other vehicles involved, Darren Holmes, aged 21, and Brendan Murphy, aged 37, _____ (5) too close behind to be able to stop in time. Ambulances, which _____ (6) on the scene within minutes, _____ (7) the injured to the nearby Royal Infirmary. Holmes, of Stanway near Colchester, has three broken ribs and is still under observation. The drivers of the lorries, John Peters, 52, of Ipswich, and Brendan Murphy, of Clacton-on-Sea, were treated for minor injuries and later sent home. The police _____ (8) all three drivers with dangerous driving.

1 A has been happening
  B had happened
  C happened

2 A carried
  B was carrying
  C has been carrying

3 A skidded
  B was skidding
  C has skidded

4 A had braked
  B has braked
  C was braking

5 A drove
  B had driven
  C had been driving

6 A have been arriving
  B arrived
  C have arrived

7 A took
  B were taking
  C had taken

8 A had charged
  B have charged
  C were charging

B Fill in the gaps with one of the following time expressions and put the verbs in *italics* in an appropriate past tense form, making any other necessary changes. Try to use all the time expressions.

after	as	as soon as	before
then	when	whenever	

I travel all over the country in my job and _____ (1) I take the train to Scotland, I remember the story about the man whose wife just *have* (2) a baby. He *work* (3) in London at the time but he *live* (4) in Newcastle, which is in the north-east of England, not far from the Scottish border. _____ (5) he *hear* (6) the news, he *rush* (7) to King's Cross Station. He bought his ticket and _____ (8), just _____ (9) he *jump* (10) on the first train north, he *ring* (11) his wife to say he would soon be with her. He *be* (12) so excited at the news that he *tell* (13) the woman who *sit* (14) in the same compartment. She *ask* (15) him if he lived in Edinburgh, as that was where the train *go* (16), and was surprised to hear that he lived in Newcastle. 'But this train doesn't stop at Newcastle,' she *reply* (17). 'It goes straight to Edinburgh.' _____ (18) the man *hear* (19) this, he *run* (20) to the front of the train to speak to the driver. _____ (21) telling him his story, he *beg* (22) him to stop the train at Newcastle. He even *offer* (23) him money, but the driver still *refuse* (24). However, he *agree* (25) to slow the train down to 15 m.p.h. so that the man could jump off. An hour later, _____ (26) the train *approach* (27) Newcastle Station, the ticket-collector *hold* (28) the man out of the window and he *begin* (29) running in mid-air. _____ (30) they *reach* (31) the station, the ticket-collector gently *drop* (32) the man onto the platform and he *run* (33) very fast along it. The guard, at the back of the train, *see* (34) a man running along the platform. He *put out* (35) his hand and *pull* (36) the man onto the train. 'Lucky I *see* (37) you,' *say* (38) the guard. 'You almost *miss* (39) the train.'

3 Pronunciation of regular verbs

The *-ed* ending of past tense regular verbs can be pronounced in three different ways:
- like *d* after a voiced sound, e.g. *b, n*.
- like *t* after a voiceless sound, e.g. *p, s*.
- like *id* after *t* or *d*.

A Look back at the regular verbs in exercise 2B and decide how they are pronounced in the past simple. Write them in the order in which they occur in the text under the headings *d, t, id*. Listen to the cassette to check your pronunciation.

B Do the same with *wash, shave, brush, cook, wait, push, arrive, shout*. Listen to the cassette to check your pronunciation.

C Now make up a story starting with the words *It was eight o'clock when Ian woke up. He was late as usual. He quickly washed his face . . .*
Try to use ten regular verbs. Read your story aloud, paying particular attention to your pronunciation.

4 Fluency

A Listen to Michael talking about something that happened to him when he was in Germany. During the recording there will be five pauses. In groups, guess the next part of the story. Again, pay attention to your pronunciation of past tenses.

B Tell your partner or your group about something that has happened to you or to someone you know. Choose something sad, funny, embarrassing, or exciting. As you listen to other students' stories, ask questions to encourage the story-teller to give more details. Interrupt if you think you can guess what happened.

Writing

The narrative composition

1 Model

A As you read the following story, number the drawings below in order.

Who? Lisa and Alex
Where?
When?
Situation?

> It was seven o'clock when Lisa and Alex arrived home after spending the day with friends. While Alex was parking the car, Lisa walked towards the front door, feeling in her bag for her keys.
> 'Oh no!' she cried.
> 5 'What's the matter?' shouted Alex.
> 'I've left the keys inside. We're locked out!'
> 'Don't worry. I can get in with the ladder,' said Alex, spotting the open bathroom window.
>
> 'You will be careful, won't you?' said Lisa anxiously as Alex
> 10 climbed up the ladder and in through the bathroom window.
> 'Yes,' replied Alex, his words drowned by a loud crash and the sound of breaking glass.
>
> Just then a policeman appeared. It took Lisa some time to explain but finally he was satisfied, and left.
> 15 'Are you all right?' Lisa asked as Alex walked towards her.
> 'No broken bones! Come on, let's go in!'
>
> They walked up the path but just as they reached the door it blew shut. 'Oh, dear!' said Alex, looking up at the bathroom window, which he had carefully closed. 'Not so easy this time!'

What happened?

(1)

(2) Alex crashed into something.

(3)

(4)

(5)

Conclusion

B Note down answers to the questions in the margin. Two have been done for you.

C Underline any time sequence expressions in the text, e.g. *While Alex was parking the car*. Think of alternatives for each of these expressions.

2 Focus on direct speech

A How is direct speech punctuated? Look back at the text, then read the Grammar reference notes on page 178.

B How many words can you find in the text that refer to ways of talking, e.g. *cried.* How many others do you know?

C Rewrite the following text. First decide which parts to put in direct speech, then add all the necessary punctuation, not forgetting speech marks.

An embarrassing incident

one summer job i had as a student was in a rather exclusive restaurant in glasgow on this particular day we were expecting forty members of a football club for lunch i had to peel the potatoes i thought i was managing quite well with my small knife until the owner appeared are those all the potatoes youve peeled she complained why didnt you use the potato peeler i had no idea what a potato peeler was so she led me into a small room behind the main kitchen and showed me a small machine which looked rather like the rubbish bins some people have in their bathrooms you put the potatoes in close the lid press the button and thats all she explained as if to a small child ten minutes later she came back i really think its quicker to do them by hand i said what do you mean she asked well they arent ready yet you can imagine how i felt when she lifted the lid and took out the potatoes the size of peas the potato peeler was not automatic

3 Think, plan, write

A You are going to write a story of between 120 and 180 words which ends with the words *That's the last time I go there on holiday.* With a partner, spend five minutes talking about all the things which can spoil a holiday. Use the pictures on the left and your own personal experiences to help you note down some ideas.

B Make notes for your composition, following this plan.

Paragraph 1	Introduction	Who was involved? Where did the story happen? When did it happen? Why were you there? What were you doing at the beginning of the story?
Paragraph 2	Story	List the things that happened, in the order that they happened. Think of time expressions you can use to join your ideas together. Be careful to use the right tenses. Check your tenses in the Grammar reference on page 183.
Paragraph 3	Conclusion	What happened in the end? Remember to finish with *That's the last time I go there on holiday.*

C Write out the composition in full. If you use direct speech, make sure you punctuate it correctly.

A close shave

Introduction

These people are cavers. They explore underground caves as a sport. What sort of people go caving? What things can go wrong? What precautions should cavers take?

Listening

1 Think ahead

You are going to hear a news report about a caving expedition to the Baliem River caves. The caves are in the Trikora Mountains of Irian Jaya, New Guinea. Before you listen, study the four diagrams below carefully.

2 Listening

As you listen for the first time, decide which diagram best represents the place and the incident you hear about. Put a tick (√) in the appropriate box.

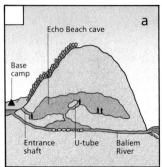
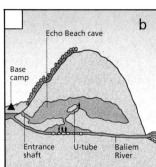
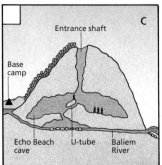
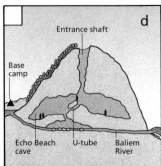

3 Comprehension

A True or false?

As you listen for the second time, decide if the following information is true or false. Write T or F in the box next to each statement.

1 The caving incident happened yesterday.
2 The mountains are difficult to reach.
3 This was the group's second visit to the area.
4 They descended to the river-bed on their first trip.
5 The team are all shocked by the incident.
6 The cavers explored together.
7 They were expecting it to rain.
8 Tony realized the danger before the others.
9 The caves were flooded in about 45 minutes.
10 The team are impatient to continue the expedition.

B Listening between the lines

1 Why did the cavers develop techniques for moving along the roof of the cave?
2 The reporter says, 'They've all gone back to the base camp to check their equipment and see what the situation is.' What situation is he referring to? How can they check the situation from the base camp?

4 Over to you

1 Have you ever been caving or done any other sport which involves taking risks, like parachuting, mountaineering or hang-gliding? What do you like about the sport? Have you ever been in a dangerous situation? What happened?
2 Would you like to do one of these sports or a similar one? Why? Why not?

Grammar and practice

Participle clauses

A Form and use

These extracts from the reading and listening texts in this unit all contain a participle clause in *italics*. Each extract is followed by a sentence with the same meaning, but in which the participle clause has been rephrased.

1 *Settling into my seat*, I felt tired.
   As I settled into my seat, I felt tired.
2 *Not knowing what else to do*, I went to look for a stewardess.
   Because / As / Since I didn't know what else to do, I went to look for a stewardess.
3 So, *slipping out of the airport*, I jumped into a passing taxi.
   So I slipped out of the airport **and** jumped into a passing taxi.
4 *Having spent so much time getting the trip under way*, they don't want it all to go to waste.

Because / As / Since they have spent *so much time getting the trip under way*, they don't want it all to go to waste.

B Read the Grammar reference on page 184 before you do the practice exercise.

C Practice

Rewrite every sentence in this story in an alternative way, as in the examples above, making all necessary changes. The first sentence has been done for you.

Opening the living room door, Michael went inside.
Michael opened the living room door and went inside.

But because he didn't recollect the man's face immediately, he said nothing. Then, opening his mouth to ask him what he wanted, Michael realized who the man was. As he hadn't seen him for over twenty years, he hadn't recognized him earlier. His brother, having grown a beard, looked quite different. Michael threw his arms around him and hugged him tightly.

Now finish the story in your own words. Where had Michael's brother been for the last twenty years? Was he as happy to see Michael?

Vocabulary

1 Sports
Vocabulary reference p.197

A Sports and personalities

1 Which sports are these people famous for? Match them with the symbols.

Gary Lineker   Monica Seles   Michael Jordan   Seve Ballesteros
Alain Prost   Merlene Ottey   Miguel Indurain   Jahangir Khan

2 Write the name of the sport under each symbol. Use the Vocabulary reference on page 197 to help you.

a _____   b _____   c _____   d _____   e _____   f _____

g _____

3 What is the name for the person who does each of the sports, e.g. athletics, *athlete*?

4 Which are the most popular sports in your country? Which sports are not very popular? Why? Who are your favourite sports personalities? Why?

B What do you know?

1 Where do sporting activities take place?

Example   motor-racing, *on a circuit* or *race-track*

Fill in the missing letters to give you the names of the places where the following activities take place. You can use a dictionary and the Vocabulary reference on page 197 to help you.

h _____

football	P _ _ _ H	diving	_ _ _ _
tennis	_ _ _ R T	gymnastics	_ _ M
ice-skating	R _ _ _	horse-racing	C _ _ R _ _

i _____

2 How many other sports do you know which take place in or on each of these places? Make a list.

C Choose three sports you have either played or watched. Working with two or three other students, compare the sports on your lists from these points of view.
1 How dangerous are they?
2 How energetic do you have to be?
3 Are they expensive to play?
4 How competitive are they?

j _____

D Complete the following sentences with one appropriate word connected with the subject of sport.
1 Paul Gascoigne _____ the first of England's three goals against Turkey.
2 Top athletes _____ for months before an important event, both on and off the track.
3 To win the gold medal you have to _____ all the other competitors.
4 In Britain, most football _____ are still played on Saturdays.
5 You cannot compete in the Olympics if you are a _____ . You must be an amateur.

k _____

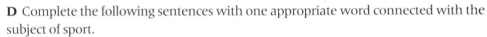

l _____

E Over to you

What is your least favourite sport? Why do you dislike it so much? Tell the rest of the class and see who agrees with you and who disagrees.

m _____

2 Compound adjectives

Compound adjectives are often joined by hyphens. One of the commonest types is formed with a number and a singular noun. 'I found out it was about 3 a.m. and we were several hours into the *11-hour flight* to Brazil.' This kind of compound adjective gives information about age, weight, duration, etc.

Match the compound adjectives in Box A with the nouns in Box B. Then fill in the gaps in the following sentences with an appropriate adjective + noun combination from the ones you have just matched.

Box A

| one-egg | one-litre | three-course | five-minute | ten-ton |
| twelve-man | fifteen-piece | thirty-five-hour | ninety-year-old | 2,000-word |

Box B

| bottle of whisky | essay | grandmother | jury | lorry |
| meal | omelette | orchestra | walk | week |

1 It's excellent value for money. You get a _____ and coffee for under £10 per person.
2 A _____ is getting married for the fourth time.
3 He was convicted of murder by the _____ .
4 They are on strike for better pay and a _____ .
5 Their new house is very handy for the shops and only a _____ from Lisa's school.
6 Joe's cat was run over by a _____ .
7 I didn't have a big lunch. Just a _____ and some salad.
8 The price of a _____ has gone up by 60p.
9 I can't go out. I have to write a _____ by tomorrow.
10 The concert was performed by a _____ .

3 Phrasal verbs

The phrasal verbs which fill the gaps in the following sentences mean the opposite of the verbs in *italics*. Put the missing verb in the correct tense and make any other necessary changes.
1 The plane _____ on time but *landed* 20 minutes late.
2 I _____ the end of term but I *dread* the end-of-term exams.
3 Simon always _____ on his way to work and *drops* me *off* outside my office.
4 Although they _____ in the early morning, they didn't *get to* Manchester until almost midnight.
5 She *fell asleep* immediately but _____ shortly afterwards by the sound of someone knocking at the door.
6 Sally _____ every single letter Bill ever wrote to her. She hasn't *kept* one.

Exam techniques

Dialogue completion

1 Guidelines

Do	Don't
• Read the whole dialogue through once quickly.	▶ Don't try to fill any gaps until you have read the whole conversation.
• Try to complete the dialogue sentence by sentence.	▶ Don't panic if you can't complete a particular sentence. Go on to the next one.
• Check to see if the sentence required is a question or an exclamation.	▶ Don't assume you must always write a question.
• Look for clues. The first part of the following sentence will probably be the answer to the question, while the rest of the sentence will give more information.	▶ Don't be confused by the extra information. It is there to help, not to put you off.
• Be careful if you are given the first word of the sentence. With *how*, the question could be *how*, *how much*, or *how long*, for example.	• Don't repeat too many of the words that you are given. This isn't normal in conversation, and means you are probably writing the wrong sentence.
• If you are not sure what the sentence is, make a sensible guess.	▶ Don't leave any empty spaces.
• Check for accuracy of grammar and spelling and read it through to see if it sounds natural.	

2 Practice

Follow the guidelines and use the clues and questions on the left to help you complete the gaps in the following conversation.

The TV chat show host Mike Frost is interviewing Andy Marsh, a well-known footballer.

(1) What tense is the verb? Does *much* refer to a countable or an uncountable noun? What doesn't Andy have very much of?

(2) *Better* is the comparative of which adjective?

(3) *Ago* is used with a particular verb tense.

(4) Andy's answer gives a reason why he likes squash.

(5) What kind of sentence is *Why don't you?* e.g. invitation, request, etc.

(6) Andy disagrees with the statement. *Age* is a clue. You need an adjective.

Mike   What (1)_____?
Andy   I don't have very much, I'm afraid. But I play squash when I can.
Mike   Are (2)_____?
Andy   Not really. I haven't been playing very long. I'm much better at football.
Mike   When (3)_____?
Andy   About two years ago. My brother needed a partner and he persuaded me to try it.
Mike   What (4)_____?
Andy   Above all, the fact that it's an individual sport. It makes a change from playing in a team.
Mike   The doctor's told me I'm not getting enough exercise. Which
        (5)_____?
Andy   Why don't you try tennis?
Mike   (6) _____!
Andy   Nonsense! There's no age limit. You do it at your own pace.
Mike   Well, we'll have to leave it there. Thanks, Andy, for coming along this evening. Ladies and gentlemen, Andy Marsh.

Conditions

What if...?

Introduction

	Food and Drink	Gift-giving time	Cost per family	Holidays	Customs
Britain	Turkey, cranberry sauce, Christmas pudding, sherry, port and wine	Christmas Day	£358	Bank holidays: Christmas Day, Boxing Day, New Year's Day	Carol singing, Boxing Day sport
France	Oysters, foie gras, turkey, cheeses, white wine and champagne	Before Christmas meal	£550	A long break of five days	Big family meal on Christmas Eve, cards at New Year
Germany	Carp or herring on Christmas Eve, roast goose on Christmas Day	Christmas Day	£385	Dec 25, 26 and Jan 1 are national holidays	Christmas Eve, parents decorate the tree for the children
Italy	Christmas dinner served on 24th, steamed fish, cod or bass, white wine	Not before midnight on Christmas Eve	£275	Christmas Day and St. Stephen's (Boxing Day)	Mistletoe given by guests visiting another family for luck
Netherlands	Rabbit, game and venison, served on Christmas Day and Boxing Day	Christmas morning	£132	Christmas Eve to the first week of January	Fir trees, holly and Father Christmas
Belgium	Veal sausage stuffed with truffles, wild boar, hot wine, traditional cake	St. Nicholas, Dec 6, and Christmas Day	£275	Two days off work – Dec 25 and 26	Chocolate and marzipan
Luxembourg	Blood sausage, apples, sparkling Luxembourg wine	St. Nicholas, Dec 6, and Christmas Day	£220	Two days off work – Dec 25 and 26	Colourful outdoor street markets on Christmas Eve
Denmark	Duck, goose stuffed with fruit, rice pudding with cinnamon	After dinner on Christmas Eve	£440	Dec 24, 25 and 26, most people take time off until after New Year	Children put out rice pudding and almonds for the Christmas pixies
Ireland	Turkey and ham on Christmas Day	Christmas morning	£550	Bank holidays are Dec 25, 26 and 27	Ceilidh (traditional dance), going to pubs, visiting with home-made food
Spain	Shellfish, roast lamb, turkey, suckling pig	Small presents on Christmas Day, big presents on Epiphany, Jan 6th	£900	Holidays are Dec 24, 25 and 26, Jan 1 and 6	Eating turron, a sweet almond toffee
Portugal	Salt cod eaten at a meal called the Consoada, sweet port wine	Christmas Eve	£275	Christmas Eve and Christmas Day	Most families put up a manger and a Christmas tree
Greece	Turkey served with wine	Christmas morning	£220	Christmas Day, Boxing Day, New Year's Day and Epiphany	A traditional gamble

A Christmas in Europe quiz

Before looking at the chart, answer as many of these questions as you can. If you don't know the answers, have a guess.

1 How many days off work do French people have at Christmas?
2 What do we call the religious songs sung in Britain at Christmas?
3 When do Greek children open their Christmas presents?
4 Name three nationalities who eat turkey at Christmas.
5 Which nationality spends the most money at Christmas?
6 In which country is *turron* eaten at Christmas?

Compare answers with a partner, and then check your answers by reading the chart.

B Make your own chart

What are your family's Christmas customs? Write notes under the five headings used in the chart. If Christmas is not celebrated in your country, write about another popular festival.

C Talking points

These questions are about Christmas, but you could talk about any traditional festival.

1 Do you think people spend too much money at Christmas time?
2 What is your favourite Christmas custom or activity?
3 Is there anything you don't like about Christmas?

1 Think ahead

People complain that festivals like Christmas are losing their meaning and becoming over-commercialized. How are festivals like Christmas changing? Do you think it matters? Can anything be done to stop these changes?

2 Reading

Read the text quickly. Do you think that, if he had the choice, the writer would keep Christmas or abolish it?

The couple in front of me in the supermarket queue paid for the umpteen bottles of booze in their basket and announced that if they didn't have children, they wouldn't bother at all.

5 The woman behind me said that, when she saw what was in store on the box this year, she wondered why she paid her licence fee.

The festival of hope

The girl on the till said it was the same every year – regular as clockwork. Come Christmas Eve, she
10 started a cold.

And the man who loaded my shopping into the car just shook his head and told me categorically that it wasn't a bit like Christmas. Which made me wonder yet again, as I drove home, what
15 Christmas was meant to be like.

Why, indeed, do we still bother, children or no children? Particularly nowadays, when there is so much to concern us abroad and at home. How can we sit and stuff ourselves silly when famine
20 and genocide are so widespread?

We should be driving mercy missions to war zones, not playing with remote control racing cars. And filling parcels with food for refugees, not unwrapping boxes of chocolates.

25 Good heavens, hundreds of people are sleeping in cardboard boxes hardly bigger than the ones which carried our food mountain back from the supermarket. So, with all that on our collective conscience, how can we possibly support
30 Christmas any more?

Charity

In fact, we should support Christmas even more and even louder. Because, if it weren't for Christmas, I doubt very much if those in need would hear from anyone at all.

35 And that is why, particularly in these ever-worsening times, we are right to celebrate the festival. After all, if we actually stopped bothering and did away with Christmas altogether, we would think even less of each
40 other than ever.

And as for the people who say they are disappointed by Christmas, they have only themselves to blame. If they over-indulge and end up feeling they want to murder their nearest
45 and dearest, that's down to them, not Christmas.

Yet it's impossible to gather exactly what it is these people expect: Father Christmas really coming down their chimneys? Little robins hopping around in the snow?

Childhood

50 Some claim that what's missing is something more intangible, something that's gone from Christmas, something that's long been lost. I think what they are looking for is something they never had in the first place. They never had it, not because
55 it wasn't there, but because they didn't know where to look for it.

Christmas isn't to be found under the tree or in a stocking or on a groaning table. It's in us, in ourselves. It's what we put into it, not what we
60 can get out of it.

Imagine what life would be like without Christmas. Imagine your childhood and that of your own children, imagine all the missed excitement and the shared joys. You can't, can you? I certainly
65 can't imagine what each year would be like without Christmas – because it simply isn't imaginable. So, perhaps we should think, instead, of the good it brings: of the good it brings out in people and the good it brings to them.

3 Points of view

1 Why do you think people still celebrate Christmas?
2 Should we help poor and disadvantaged people at Christmas instead of spending a lot of money on ourselves?

4 Comprehension

A Vocabulary

Match these informal words and phrases from the text with their correct meanings.

don't be such a nuisance
don't bother me
nagging

1	umpteen e	(paragraph 1)	a	television
2	booze h	(paragraph 1)	b	family members
3	box a	(paragraph 2)	c	understand
4	bother f	(paragraph 5)	d	their fault
5	stuff ourselves silly	(paragraph 5)	e	too many to count, lots
6	down to them	(paragraph 10)	f	take the trouble to do something
7	nearest and dearest	(paragraph 10)	g	eat too much
8	gather c	(paragraph 11)	h	alcoholic drink

B Text references

What do the words and phrases in italics in these extracts from the text refer to? You will need to look back at the text to check.

1 . . . hardly bigger than *the ones* which carried our shopping . . . (paragraph 7)
2 So, with *all that* on our collective conscience . . . (paragraph 7)
3 And *that* is why, particularly in these ever-worsening times . . . (paragraph 9)
4 . . . that's down to *them*, not Christmas. (paragraph 10)
5 . . . they didn't know where to look for *it*. (paragraph 12)
6 Imagine your childhood and *that* of your children . . . (paragraph 14)

C Reading between the lines

1 Is the woman mentioned in paragraph 2 looking forward to watching television at Christmas or not?
2 What did the man who loaded the writer's shopping mean by 'it wasn't a bit like Christmas'?
3 What does the writer think is wrong with remote control racing cars and boxes of chocolates?
4 Who are the hundreds of people sleeping in cardboard boxes?
5 Why might people want to murder their nearest and dearest at Christmas time?

5 Alternative Christmas

You have decided to spend Christmas helping other people. Write a brief description (about 80 words) of how you will spend your money and time.

6 Over to you

A How do you decide what presents to give to your friends and family? Are the presents you give and receive always surprises?

B Have you got any present suggestions for 'someone who has everything'? Compare your ideas in groups.

Grammar and practice

1 Conditional sentences, types 0, 1 and 2

A In what ways are these three conditional sentences different?
1 If I *get* a present I don't like, I *give* it away.
2 If I *get* a present I don't like, I *'ll give* it away.
3 If I *got* a present I didn't like, I *'d give* it away.

Which verb tenses are used in the two parts of each of these sentences? How do the tense differences affect the meaning of the sentences? Which sentence:
a refers to an imaginary or unreal event or situation?
b refers to a general rule that's always true?
c refers to a possible or likely future event or situation?

B Here are some more conditional sentences. Which type are they – 0, 1 or 2?
1 If they didn't have children, they wouldn't bother.
2 If we stopped bothering and did away with Christmas, we would think even less of each other.
3 If they over-indulge and end up wanting to murder their nearest and dearest, that's down to them.
4 If someone forgets to send me a Christmas card, I take them off my list.
5 I'll certainly see Santa Claus if I stay awake all night.
6 If you stay awake, Santa Claus won't leave you any presents.
7 If you can't sleep, count sheep or read a book.

C What is the difference in meaning between these two sentences?
If you stay awake, Santa Claus won't leave you any presents.
If you stay awake, Santa Claus might not leave you any presents.

D How could this sentence be rewritten using the word *unless*?
If you don't go to sleep, Santa Claus won't come.

E Before continuing with the practice exercises, read sections 1–3 in the Grammar reference on page 184.

2 Practice

A What do you do?
People have their own cures for minor problems, such as headaches, colds, etc. Finish these conditional sentences (type 0) with your own favourite cures. The first one has been done as an example.

1 If I have a headache, *I go to bed and sleep for an hour.*
2 If I have hiccups,   4 If I catch a cold,
3 If my nose bleeds,   5 If I can't get to sleep,

B Type 1 conditional sentences are often used to persuade or warn. Here are the first parts of sentences spoken by adults trying to persuade or warn children. Finish each of these sentences in different ways.
1 If you watch too much television,
2 If you don't go to bed earlier,
3 Unless you work harder at school,
4 Unless you tidy your room this weekend,
Make up some more sentences of your own like these. Think about things your parents or your teachers used to say to you when you were young.

C Types 1 and 2 conditional sentences can also be used in bargaining or negotiating situations. For example, children might say to their mother or father:
'I'll do the washing up if you let me watch the late film.'
'I'd do the shopping if my friend could come for the day.'
Make up some more sentences of your own like these.

D Fill the gaps in these conditional sentences about health and safety with the correct form of one of these verbs. You may have to use negative verbs.

break   catch   have   smoke   stay   take   walk

1 If I _____ a headache, I usually _____ a tablet.
2 If you _____ your leg, you wouldn't be able to _____ for several weeks.
3 If you _____ flu, you'll have to _____ in bed.
4 If you _____ so much, you wouldn't have such a bad cough.

3 What would you do if . . .?

What would you do if the building you are in now caught fire?
1 How would you escape from the fire? Work out your best route.
2 What things would you try and take with you?
3 If you could get back into the building, what other things would you try to save?

Conditions

6

If only . . .

Introduction

How would you react in these situations?

1 A friend gives you an expensive present. Unfortunately, you have recently bought the same thing for yourself. Your friend asks you if you like it. What do you say?

2 A friend visits you at Christmas and brings you a present. Unfortunately, you've been so busy that you've forgotten to buy a present for your friend. What do you do or say?

Listening

1 Think ahead

Can you remember an occasion when you told a deliberate lie? If you can, answer these questions.

1 Was it a serious lie or just a bit of fun?
2 Did you lie for your own benefit or for someone else's?
3 Did anyone find out about the lie?

2 Listening

A You are going to hear ten people talking about lying. As you listen, match the speakers with their reasons for lying. Write the number of the speaker in the space provided.

Which speaker lies:

1 for fun? __
2 to get themselves out of trouble? __
3 to stop themselves being embarrassed? __
4 to prevent other people's embarrassment? __
5 to prevent other people from being hurt? __
6 to avoid giving away information about a third person? __
7 to avoid having to see someone they don't like? __
8 for no particular reason? __
9 when telling the truth might be risky? __
10 to shock or surprise other people? __

B Now listen to five other people talking about situations in which they lied. Which of their lies is most like the one you discussed in Think ahead?

3 Points of view   Do you know anyone like the third speaker who lies for their own amusement?

4 Comprehension   **A** For each question choose the best answer. All the questions refer to the second part of the listening.

1 Why didn't the first speaker stay for lunch at his girlfriend's house?
   A Because someone was waiting for him at home.
   B Because he had already had his lunch.
   C Because he didn't feel at all hungry.
   D Because he couldn't stand her mother's cooking.

2 Why didn't the second speaker give her neighbour any information about her sister?
   A Because the rumour about her sister was not true.
   B Because she knew nothing about her sister's situation.
   C Because she didn't want everyone to know.
   D Because several other people were involved.

3 Why did the third speaker say her cousin had been a famous footballer?
   A Because she was getting bored with the conversation.
   B In order to impress the man she was talking to.
   C She couldn't stop herself from lying.
   D She was as keen on football as the man at the party.

4 Why did the fourth speaker answer the phone?
   A Because his brother was out.
   B Because he thought the phone call was for him.
   C Because his brother didn't want to answer it.
   D Because his brother had told him he didn't want to speak to Annie.

5 Why didn't the fifth speaker tell her sister her exam results?
   A She didn't want her to know she had opened her letter.
   B Because her sister wasn't interested in the result.
   C Because she didn't want to spoil her sister's holiday.
   D Because she didn't know where to contact her.

B Vocabulary

Match the words and phrases in *italics* with their correct meanings.

1 I was in town the other day and I *bumped into* one of my neighbours.
2 She's a well-known *busy-body*.
3 She'd heard that my sister and her husband had *split up*.
a 4 I *got stuck* talking to this really boring bloke.
d 5 I thought he was going to *pass out* with excitement.
6 He even asked for my *autograph*, of all things.
c 7 It was a *blatant* lie, of course.
8 Not *wicked* ones, you know, just white ones.

a became trapped
b separated
c obvious, unashamed
d faint, lose consciousness
e met by chance
f signature
g very bad
h person who interferes in other people's affairs

5 Over to you   1 Have you ever known anyone who is a compulsive liar?
2 What do you do when you don't know whether the person you are talking to is telling the truth or not?

Grammar and practice

1 Conditional sentences type 3

A Form and use

What verb forms are used in the two parts of these sentences from the listening?

1 *If I'd known it was Annie, I'd have spoken to her.*
2 *If I'd told her the result, it would have ruined her holiday.*

What is the difference in meaning between type 3 conditional sentences and the three types introduced earlier in the unit? Here are some examples to think about.

*My life **is** very dull if I **don't tell** lies.* (0)
*My life **will be** very dull if I **don't tell** lies.* (1)
*My life **would be** very dull if I **didn't tell** lies.* (2)
*My life **would have been** very dull if I **hadn't told** lies.* (3)

Discuss your ideas with a partner if you wish.

B Before going on with the practice exercises, read section 4 in the Grammar reference on page 185.

C Making excuses

Without changing their meanings, rewrite these sentences, starting with the words or phrases given.

1 I didn't answer the phone because I didn't know it was you.
  If I _____ .
2 I didn't know you were back from your holiday, so I didn't phone you.
  I would _____ .
3 She didn't send me a postcard because she didn't have my address with her.
  If she _____ .
4 He forgot to put his watch on – that's why he was late.
  He wouldn't _____ .
5 I didn't know it was your birthday or I'd have bought you a present.
  If _____ .
6 We got back from work really late – that's why we didn't come to your party.
  If _____ .

2 Moments of decision

What would you have done and what wouldn't you have done in the same situations as the people in these stories? Use some of these expressions.

If I'd been in X's situation,   If I'd been in X's shoes,
If it'd been me,   If that had been me,   If I'd been X,

Fishing trip scare

John and Ed Walker hired a boat for a day's fishing off the south coast last weekend. The brothers, aged 15 and 12, had a good day, but when it was time to head back to the shore, they couldn't restart the boat's engine.

Motorway nightmare

When Jill Frame broke down on the M1 at 2 a.m. last Tuesday, she got out of her Mini and went to find a telephone. The nearest one was on the opposite side of the six-lane motorway.

Supermarket Mum

Mother-to-be Sheila Sutton and her friend, Liz Curry, were doing their shopping in the local supermarket. It was a Friday evening and the shop was very busy. Suddenly Sheila realized that her baby was on its way.

3 On the spot

Have you ever been in a difficult situation where you had to make an important decision very quickly? What happened as a result of your quick decision? Think about what would and would not have happened if you had made a different decision. Write three paragraphs following this plan.

Paragraph 1   a brief description of the situation and your decision

Paragraph 2   what happened as a result of your decision

Paragraph 3   what would or would not have happened if you had made a different decision

Vocabulary

1 Body language
Vocabulary reference p.197

A Reactions
In the listening about lying, one of the speakers said 'His eyes nearly popped out of his head.' This is a description of how people react when they feel very surprised. How do people react when they are in these situations?

1 afraid, e.g. *they turn pale*
2 cold
3 angry
4 embarrassed

B Parts of the body
Label the parts of the body shown in these photos.

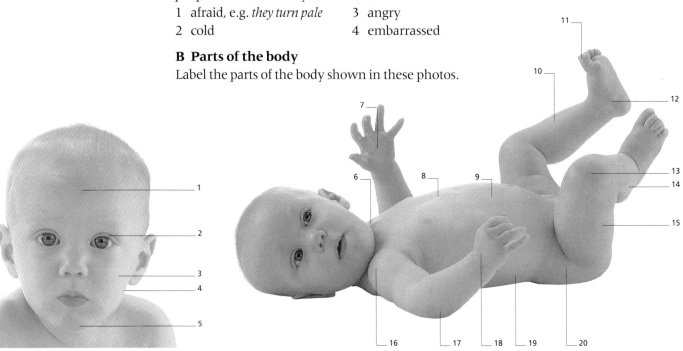

Now use eight of these words to fill the gaps in these sentences.
1 When I asked her the time, she just shrugged her _____ and said she didn't know.
2 As I went upstairs to bed last night, I stubbed my _____ on one of the stairs.
3 Some fortune-tellers read people's _____ .
4 I saw this really pretty girl at the party. I think she liked me because she fluttered her _____ at me.
5 I always wear my watch on my left _____ .
6 It was easy to see who the boss was – the woman standing with her hands on her _____ .
7 Babies crawl around on their hands and _____ .
8 He sat with his _____ on the table and his head in his hands.

C Body idioms
Can you guess the meaning of this idiom?
I **kept** an absolutely **straight face.**
Now choose the correct part of the body to fill the gaps in the idioms used in these sentences.
1 Her father says 'Yes' to everything she asks for. She can *twist him round her* _____ .
  A right arm   B left leg   C little finger   D big toe
2 Don't get too friendly with Matt. He may *stab you in the* _____ .
  A back   B chest   C arm   D leg
3 The film was so frightening it *made my* _____ *stand on end*.
  A head   B ears   C eyes   D hair

4 By the time children are 16 or 17 they've learnt *to stand on their own two* _____ .
  A legs　　　　B feet　　　　C hands　　　　D toes
5 *I'd give my right* _____ for a ticket to the Olympic Games.
  A hand　　　　B leg　　　　C foot　　　　D arm
6 The person behind me was a real *pain in the* _____ . He talked all through the concert.
  A head　　　　B ear　　　　C neck　　　　D back

2 Word building

Compound adjectives

We often use compound adjectives to describe people. They are formed by joining an adjective and a 'body noun' which looks like a past participle, e.g. *red-faced*, *long-haired*. Use compound adjectives like these to describe people you know well, perhaps another student in the class, a member of your family or a famous person. Think about these features.

shoulders	broad or narrow?	*legs*	long or short?
eyes	colour	*hair*	length and colour
skin	colour	*face*	shape
hands	which one do they write with?		

3 Word combinations

Say, speak, talk, tell

The verbs *say*, *speak*, *talk* and *tell* have similar and related meanings, but they are not interchangeable. So, for example, you can say **tell** *a lie*, but not **talk** *a lie*. Complete these phrases with the correct verbs. Occasionally more than one combination is possible.

_____ someone's fortune　　_____ hello and goodbye　　_____ a language

_____ a lie　　_____ your mind　　_____ your name

_____ a prayer　　_____ sense or nonsense　　_____ rubbish

_____ a story　　_____ a joke　　_____ the time

_____ the truth　　_____ 'yes' and 'no'

4 Phrasal verbs

It is often possible to form nouns from phrasal verbs. For example, in the story 'Motorway nightmare' on page 69, the first sentence 'Jill Frame *broke down* on the M1' could be rewritten as 'Jill Frame had a *breakdown* on the M1'.

A Fill the gaps in these sentences with phrasal verbs related to these nouns.

break-out　　give-away　　hold-up　　let-down　　turn-out

1 Three armed men _____ the main branch of Barclays Bank in Swindon last Tuesday morning.
2 Nearly 50,000 people _____ to see their team win the cup.
3 We tried to find out the exam results but our teacher _____ nothing _____ .
4 Six prisoners _____ of the high security prison last night.
5 You can rely on Paula. She'll never _____ you _____ .

B Now guess or work out the meanings of these nouns related to phrasal verbs.

1 a scientific *breakthrough*
2 children and *grown-ups*
3 a Chinese *takeaway*
4 my car was a *write-off*
5 a supermarket *checkout*
6 a *workout* in the gym
7 an *outbreak* of flu
8 a medical *check-up*

Writing

Formal letters

1 Letter of complaint

Imagine that you work in the Customer Relations Department of VGC Electronics. As you read this letter of complaint from a dissatisfied customer, complete this Complaint Record card.

Complaint Record   **VGC**

Customer's name _____

Date of letter _____

VGC Product _____

Date of purchase (if known) _____

Purchase price (if known) _____

Causes of complaint (summary) _____

_____

_____

_____

Your address without your name goes in the top right-hand corner.

Write the date under your address. The most common ways of writing the date are *2nd April 1994* or *April 2 1994*.

The name and address of the person you are writing to goes on the left side below the line the date is on. If you don't know the name of the person, write their position, e.g *Customer Relations Officer, The Personnel Manager*, etc.

If you do not know the name of the person you are writing to, start with *Dear Sir or Madam* , and end with *Yours faithfully.*

If you know the person by name, start with *Dear Mr / Mrs / Ms Smith* , etc. and end with *Yours sincerely.*

Show paragraphs clearly. Either leave space under the last line of a paragraph, or indent the first line of a new paragraph.

Finally, sign the letter with your signature, and below this print your name clearly.

17 Oxted Road
Hedge Green
Dorking
Surrey
RH12 3BT

2nd April 1994

Customer Relations Officer
VGC Electronics
Second Avenue
Millstone Keys
Bedfordshire
MK2 5TG

Dear Sir or Madam

Re : VGC Stereo Unit Z500

I am writing to complain about a VGC stereo which I gave my son for Christmas. Almost immediately, things started going wrong.

First of all, when we pressed the OPEN/CLOSE button on the CD player, the drawer opened and closed so quickly that we did not have time to put
5 a CD in. It took us nearly five minutes and my son trapped his fingers several times. The cassette player was even worse. Whenever we attempted to record music, it sounded distorted.

Because of these problems, I returned the stereo to the shop where I had purchased it. They said it would take a week to repair. Three weeks later,
10 when I telephoned to inquire what was happening, I was informed that they were waiting for spare parts. After nine weeks it was ready. When I tried it at home, I found that the CD problem had been rectified but the cassette player was no better.

I am not satisfied with the stereo unit itself or with the service we have
15 received, and I am now writing to ask for a full refund. I look forward to receiving your cheque for £537.50.

Yours faithfully

Philip Dean

PHILIP DEAN

2 Analysis

Discuss these questions about Philip Dean's letter with a partner.
1 What facts are included in Philip's letter? Write a list.
2 Why is it important for facts to be accurate in a letter like this?
3 What are the subjects of the paragraphs in the letter?
4 Which words or phrases are used to link the paragraphs?
5 What can you tell from the way Philip begins and ends his letter?

3 Language notes

We tend to write formal letters when we have a serious message to communicate. In informal personal letters, we write more or less as we speak, but in formal letters, more formal language is used.

* Full verbs, not contractions, are used.
  Example   **I am** *writing* not **I'm** *writing*
* Relative pronouns tend to be used, not omitted.
  Example   *a VGC stereo* **which** *I gave my son* not *a VGC stereo I gave my son*
* Choice of vocabulary is more formal.
  Example   *attempt* rather than *try*

Find the formal verbs in the model letter which have the same meanings as these informal verbs.

ask   buy   have   mend   put right   ring   take back   tell

4 Practice for writing

Expand these notes into a full letter of complaint. As you write it out, divide it into paragraphs.

Dear Sir,

Re: Holiday No. 231

I write / complain / recent skiing holiday / I book / your company. From the first day / go wrong. The hotel I stay / be very disappointing / there be no room service / nothing seem / work properly. What be worse be / the resort be not suitable / beginners / me. On the third day I bring my complaints / the attention / your representative / say he look into them. Nothing happen / the day before I leave / I give a special room. I not satisfy / the holiday / the service I receive / your representative. I now write / ask / full refund. I look forward / receive a cheque for £950 / you.

Yours faithfully,
Norman Bates

5 Think, plan, write

Write a letter of complaint to the manager of a restaurant where you went to celebrate a friend's birthday. The meal was poor and the service was very slow.

A Imagine the evening at the restaurant. Make notes of the words and phrases you can use to describe the meal and the service. Did you complain while you were there? Who did you speak to? What did they do?

B Plan your letter using the example letter opposite to help you. How many paragraphs will you need? What will each paragraph contain?

C Write up the letter in 120–180 words, taking care to set it out correctly.

Exam techniques

Listening

1 General guidelines

Do	Don't
• Read the instructions and the task before listening to the recording for the first time. In the exam itself, you will also hear the instructions. Ask yourself these questions: How many people am I going to hear? Where are they? What are they going to talk about? What have I got to do?	• Don't worry if you can't understand every word that you hear. It is more important to understand the gist of the piece.
• As you listen for the first time, try to understand the general meaning. If you feel confident, note down a few answers.	▶ Don't write answers during the first hearing if this means that you have to stop listening.
• In the pause between the two hearings, check the task again to make sure you know what to do.	
• As you listen for the second time, write your answers.	▶ Don't leave any empty spaces or unanswered questions. Make a sensible guess if necessary.

2 Practice

Now try out the guidelines on this practice exercise.
You are going to hear a street interview between a member of the public and a market researcher who is investigating people's Christmas shopping habits.
Fill in the missing information on the researcher's Interview record sheet.

Interview record sheet

Note: Tick the boxes or fill in the missing words.

A Interviewee profile

1 Age   ☐ 11–19   ☐ 20–29   ☐ 30–39   ☐ 40–49   ☐ 50+

2 Occupation _____

3 Marital status   ☐ single   ☐ married   ☐ separated   ☐ divorced   ☐ widowed

4 Children's ages _____

B Christmas spending

5 Main shopper in house _____

6 Total spent by the household at Christmas
   ☐ 0–£100   ☐ £100–£250   ☐ £250–£500   ☐ £500+

7 How was this money spent? (Tick items interviewee spent money on.)
   ☐ Cards   ☐ Cinema   ☐ Clothes   ☐ Decorations   ☐ Drinks
   ☐ Food   ☐ Presents   ☐ Theatre   ☐ Travelling   ☐ Other

C Attitudes

8 Richer or poorer than last year? _____

9 Optimistic or pessimistic about future? _____

7 Description

A woman's place

Introduction

A What occupations are shown above?

B The following adjectives can be used to describe a person's character or physical condition.

brave	creative	fair	hard-working	sociable
caring	energetic	fit	organized	strong
cheerful	enthusiastic	patient	well-educated	

Match each adjective with its definition. Write the adjective next to the definition. The first one has been done for you.

A person who is

a *well-educated*   has had a good education.

b _____ is always lively and doesn't tire easily.

c _____ is original, artistic and imaginative.

d _____ has well-developed muscles and can do hard, physical work.

e _____ is calm and does not get annoyed or frustrated.

f _____ is helpful and sympathetic to other people.

g _____ is not afraid of frightening or dangerous situations.

h _____ is friendly and enjoys being with other people.

i _____ treats everyone equally and is not influenced by personal feelings.

j _____ is efficient, and good at making and carrying out plans.

k _____ is healthy and in good physical condition.

l _____ is interested in and excited about something.

m _____ is not at all lazy.

n _____ is always happy and optimistic.

C With a partner, choose two of the jobs shown in the photos above. Decide on your own what qualities you think people need to do these jobs well, and why they need these particular qualities. Choose from the adjectives listed in B and add any other adjectives of your own. Then compare your ideas with your partner. Did you agree or disagree about the qualities needed?

Reading

1 Picture discussion

Study both pictures of this woman carefully and look for clues to the following questions.
1 What do you think she does for a living?
2 What kind of person do you think she is?
Discuss your ideas with a partner.

2 Reading

Read the text quickly. Did you guess her job correctly?

Living Dangerously

here's a joke going round at the moment: 'War's about to break out in Britain.' 'How do you know?' 'Because Kate Adie flew into Heathrow this morning.' No one's suggesting she's a trouble-maker. But it seems that no disaster, in any part of the world, is complete without the distinctive voice of the BBC's star reporter bringing the news to us from the middle of a danger zone.

Beirut, Libya – wherever the bombs fall and the bullets fly is where you'll find Kate Adie. And nearer home too, covering national tragedies such as the Zeebrugge and Hillsborough disasters. But it's her cool, objective reporting that people most praise. The reporter, whose sensible haircut and pearl ear-rings make her look more like a school prefect than a war correspondent, admits that her job rules her life. She's never off-duty. She recalls the time when the telephone rang in the middle of a dinner party. 'I had to turn to everyone and say, "Does anyone know how to cook trout?"' And she ran off to cover the Brixton riots.

There's a price to pay of course. Single at 43, she's described as being married to the BBC. Certainly, it would be a very tolerant man who would stay at home while Kate rushed off on an assignment. It's not a life that most people would choose. And it's one where you find few women.

Being the first woman to make it as a front-line TV reporter has its own problems, however. When she got her first foreign assignment she was terrified that the camera crew would think she was a 'silly, frilly girl'. That's the reason why she crammed everything she needed into a tiny bag which would fit underneath her plane seat. She was then amazed to see the cameraman stagger into the airport with a trunk. Now she knows that it's her appearance as well as her words that matter.

She used to get letters from viewers saying, 'You look a real mess. Haven't you got a hair-dresser?' So she decided to include a pair of curling tongs in a holdall that she now takes everywhere. But as she said, 'Can you imagine getting out a hairbrush when someone's pointing a rifle at you?'

She's often worked in dangerous situations but she says she's not a heroine. 'I don't get a buzz or wonderful feeling when I go into danger,' she says. 'I'm a 5'7" chicken and I run fast. You're not there to fight. You're there to report.'

However, despite all the drawbacks, she wouldn't change her life for the world. 'It's an incredible job. You go to places you'd never dream of going to.' So could she ever give it up? 'I don't tend to plan ahead,' she says. 'I just bump along from one story to another. But I suppose one of these days I'll have to stop climbing over walls when arthritis sets in!'

Heathrow – London's main airport.
Zeebrugge – A port in Belgium where 193 people, mainly British, were drowned when a ferry overturned in March 1987.
Hillsborough – The football ground of Sheffield Wednesday, where 95 Liverpool supporters were crushed to death in April 1989.
The Brixton Riots – Brixton is a district of London with heavy unemployment. The riots occurred in April 1981 and lasted 4 days.
5'7" – Five feet and seven inches is about 1.70 m.

3 Points of view

1 Would you do a job that took up as much of your life as Kate Adie's job does?

2 Who do you think does a more valuable job? Someone who works in the emergency services, e.g. a firefighter, ambulance driver, etc.? Or a reporter like Kate Adie? Give reasons for your answer.

4 Comprehension

A Read the questions, then read the article again carefully and choose the best answer.

1 People have a high opinion of Kate Adie because
A she works hard in her job.
B she is a newsreader for the BBC.
C she reports events in an unemotional way.
D she is an expert pilot.

2 Why didn't she take much luggage with her on her first foreign assignment?
A She only had a small bag.
B She wanted the camera crew to take her seriously.
C She wanted to travel light.
D She thought there were baggage restrictions.

3 In her view, how important is her appearance?
A It is more important than what she says.
B It is less important than what she says.
C It is as important as what she says.
D It is unimportant.

4 How does Kate summarize her feelings about her job?
A She is happy in her job although it has its disadvantages.
B It gives her the opportunity to visit places she has always wanted to.
C She would give up her job only if she got married.
D She wouldn't want to do the same job for the rest of her working life.

B Reading between the lines

1 What does the joke (line 2) tell you about Kate Adie?
2 How important is Kate Adie's job to her? Find evidence to support your answer.
3 She recalls the time when the telephone rang in the middle of a dinner party (line 26). Who do you think phoned her? What do you think they said?
4 'There's a price to pay, of course.' (line 32) What is the price she has to pay?

5 Over to you

'It is not enough to *read* about events, like famine and other natural or man-made disasters. It is important to be able to *see* these events too.'

Do you agree or disagree with the above statement? Before you begin your discussion, make a list of some disasters or tragedies you have seen reported in television news programmes. Then think about your own personal responses to these questions.

1 Did you learn anything that you could not have learnt from just reading about the event?

2 Did the report have any effect on you or on people you know? What kind of effect? Did you do anything as a result?

Grammar and practice

1 Relative clauses

Form and Use

Relative clauses can be introduced by the relative pronouns *who, which, that, whose* or no relative pronoun (Ø).

Look at the following sentences from the article about Kate Adie. Fill in the gaps with relative pronouns, giving as many alternatives for each answer as you can. Then check your answers with the article.

1 The reporter, _____ sensible haircut and pearl earrings make her look more like a school prefect than a war correspondent, admits that her job rules her life. (line 20)
2 It would be a very tolerant man _____ would stay at home while Kate rushed off on an assignment. (line 34)
3 It's not a life _____ most people would choose. (line 37)

2 Identifying and non-identifying clauses

A Difference in meaning

Look at these two sentences. How do the commas change the meaning?

1 My sister who lives in Melbourne has two children.
2 My sister, who lives in Melbourne, has two children.

How many sisters have I got in each case?

B Practice

Decide whether the clauses in the following sentences are identifying (they contain essential information) or non-identifying (they contain non-essential information). If the clause is non-identifying, add commas. Can you replace any of these relative pronouns by other relative pronouns?

1 I received six letters yesterday. The letter which included an invitation to their wedding arrived by the first post.
2 The groom who is Erica's cousin is much older than the bride.
3 The bride whose family is quite well-off has just celebrated her 21st birthday.
4 The man who is going to play the organ played at my wedding too.
5 The reception which will be held at the Crown Hotel is for invited guests only.

C Find more examples of relative pronouns in the text and underline them. What other relative pronouns could be used in their place?

D Check your answers with section 2 in the Grammar reference on page 185.

3 Relative pronouns and prepositions

A What changes need to be made to each of these sentences to make them less formal?

1 Mr Walker, with whom I have worked closely for years, is an excellent colleague.
2 The man to whom I complained was extremely rude.

In which of your sentences can you leave out the relative pronoun?

B Check your answers with section 5 in the Grammar reference on page 186.

4 Other relative pronouns

A The relative pronouns *where, why* and *when* have been removed from these sentences from the reading text. Without looking back at the text, fill each gap with the appropriate pronoun. Then check to see if you were right.

1 She recalls the time _____ the telephone rang in the middle of a dinner party. (line 26)
2 Wherever the bombs fall and the bullets fly is _____ you'll find Kate Adie. (line 13)
3 That's the reason _____ she crammed everything she needed into a tiny bag. (line 47)

In which sentences can the relative pronoun be left out?

B Rephrase the clause in italics in this sentence in four different ways.
We visited the house *where Shakespeare was born*.

C Before you do the following exercise, read section 3 in the Grammar reference on page 185.

5 Practice

Fill in the gaps in the following sentences with an appropriate relative pronoun. Indicate where there is more than one possibility and add commas if necessary.

1 I don't like people _____ are big-headed.
2 Have you seen the awful hat _____ Mary's bought for the wedding?

3 She wanted to know the reason _____ I had turned down her invitation.

4 We were unable to get tickets for Madonna's Wembley concert _____ was a sell-out.

5 They have designed a microwave _____ can defrost a frozen chicken in just ten seconds.

6 We went back to look at the house _____ we used to live.

7 'The 10.05 from London Liverpool Street to Norwich _____ is due to arrive at Platform 1 will call at Colchester, Ipswich and Norwich.'

8 Jeremy Irons _____ latest film is shot in Venice has said he'd like to work in the theatre again.

9 It was returned to the person _____ name was inside.

10 Anne's fiancé _____ is based in Manchester is hoping to get transferred to a branch nearer home.

11 We'll have the party on the 23rd _____ is the day _____ he comes out of hospital.

12 The golden eagle _____ eggs are stolen by unscrupulous collectors is now an endangered species.

13 What's the name of the girl _____ got married to Chris Small?

14 Can you think of any reason _____ he might have done it?

15 I prefer to go to Spain in winter _____ there are fewer tourists about.

16 I don't know of any restaurants _____ you can get a decent meal for under £10.

17 What's the name of the singer _____ record is number one just now?

18 Rangers' second goal _____ was scored in the final minutes won them the cup.

6 Relative clauses and prepositions

A Look at the following pairs of sentences.

1 a That's the man to whom I spoke.
   b That's the man I spoke to.
2 a The speaker, about whom I'd heard so much, gave an extremely interesting talk.
   b The speaker, who I'd heard so much about, gave an extremely interesting talk.

What are the differences between the two sentences in each pair? Can you work out any rules from the four sentences?

B Check your answers with section 5 of the Grammar reference on page 186.

7 Expanding texts

A Rewrite these paragraphs about Jana Schneider and Stephen Hendry including the extra information given in *italics*. Add one extra piece of information to each sentence. Add commas where needed and make any other necessary changes. The first piece of information has been added as an example.

Jana Schneider, *who is 39*, has an unusual job for a woman, as she is a war photographer. Jana has travelled all over the world in her job. Her husband, rock musician and composer Tom Wilson, wants her to give up her career, but Jana cannot imagine doing anything else.

She is 39.
Her pictures of the devastation of war have earned her worldwide recognition.
She has been married to Tom Wilson for nine years.

Stephen Hendry is a millionaire though he is still only in his early twenties. Stephen started playing snooker at the age of 12. As the youngest ever world champion at the age of 21, Stephen says his success lies in his killer instinct.

He is a professional snooker player.
His earnings last year totalled over £450,000.
Without his killer instinct he believes he would be just another good player.

B Now write a paragraph about someone you admire. Include at least three relative clauses.

Exam techniques

Sentence transformations

1 Guidelines

Do	Don't
• Read through all the original sentences and the beginnings of the sentences you have to complete.	▶ Don't start writing immediately.
• Look for clues which tell you the type of pattern required.	▶ Don't just write the first thing that comes into your head.
• Start with the patterns that you recognize. Leave the ones you aren't sure about until later.	▶ Don't waste time worrying about the sentences you can't do. Come back to them.
• If you aren't sure, make a sensible guess.	▶ Don't leave any spaces.
• Check for accuracy of grammar and spelling.	

2 Patterns

There are several structures which are often tested with transformations. Learning to recognize what each question is testing is very important. The most common areas are: conditionals; gerunds and infinitives; comparatives; tenses and time phrases, like *it's the first time;* reported speech; passives; prepositions after verbs; phrases for invitations, suggestions, etc.; similar words, like *so* and *such, although* and *despite.*

3 Recognizing patterns

Look at the following sentences. They illustrate typical transformations of the grammar you have covered in units 1–6. Some of the transformations are correct, and some have mistakes. If the sentence is correct, put a tick (√) next to it. If it is wrong, make the necessary corrections.

Example   He doesn't live there any more.
He used ~~to living there~~.
He used **to live there**.

1 You can't drive without a licence.
If you *haven't got a licence, you can't drive*.
2 He prefers staying at home to going out.
He'd rather *to stay at home than to go out*.
3 Have you got an earlier flight than this?
Is this *the earlier flight you've got?*
4 Motorbikes are faster than mopeds.
Mopeds *are not so fast than motorbikes*.
5 He started playing golf six months ago.
He has *been playing golf since six months ago*.
6 I've never eaten snails before.
This is *the first time I am eating snails*.

7 I haven't been to a Chinese restaurant since Christmas.
The last time *I have been to a Chinese restaurant was at Christmas*.

8 We can't buy a new car because we haven't got enough money.
If we *had enough money, we could buy a new car*.

9 'Why don't you apply for the hospital job, Linda?' said Larry.
Larry suggested *Linda should apply for the hospital job*.

4 Practice

Now try out the guidelines and complete the following sentences so that they mean the same as the original sentences. Think carefully about what kind of transformation is expected. Use the clues after each question to help you.

1 A holiday in Miami is cheaper than one in Bermuda.

A holiday in Bermuda _____
Clue What kind of sentence is the original? What's the opposite of *cheaper*?

2 The last time I saw Jimmy was at Stephen's party.

I haven't _____
Clue What tense does *haven't* indicate? Should you use *for* or *since*?

3 'Try going to bed earlier,' the doctor said to Mrs White.

The doctor suggested _____
Clue What structure follows *suggest*?

4 He doesn't go out every night any more.

He used _____
Clue *doesn't* and *any more* are clues.

5 You can't come in unless you are a member.

If you _____
Clue What tense is the verb in the main clause? Which conditional is required here?

6 My grandfather used to take me fishing every Sunday.

My grandfather would _____
Clue Does *would* indicate a conditional sentence?

7 She has been married for a year.

She got _____
Clue *Got* indicates the past tense. What's the action? When did the action happen?

8 I'd rather drive than be driven.

I prefer _____
Clue What structure follows the verb *prefer*? There are two possibilities.

9 He is overweight because he eats so much chocolate.

If he _____
Clue Is he overweight? How can he change the situation? Which conditional is required here?

10 I'll finish this before Monday.

By Monday _____
Clue What tense is often used with *by*?

7

Only skin deep

1

Introduction

1 There is more to a person than their appearance. What else can we talk about when we describe someone?
2 What determines the type of description we give?

Listening

1 Think ahead

Describe the women in the photos and predict what they are like, what jobs they do, and their interests.

2

3

2 Listening

You are going to hear a description of one of these women. As you listen, decide which one is being described and circle the number next to the photograph.

3 Comprehension

A Listen to the conversation again and work out:

who is describing Diana Jacobs.

who the 'describer' is talking to.

what the context of the description is.

Choose a person from list **1**, a person from list **2** and a context from list **3**. What evidence is there in the description that your choices are right?

1 Describer's connection with Diana

potential employer   acquaintance   friend   someone who fancies her

2 Describer's connection with the listener

friend   acquaintance   colleague   member of family

3 Possible contexts

discussion at work   private conversation   formal speech   casual chat

B You are going to hear two more descriptions of the same person. For each description do the same as for **A** above.

C True or false?

Conversation 1

1 The speaker can't go to the airport because she feels ill.

2 She is taller and fatter than Diana.

3 She says Diana will be wearing a dress.

Conversation 2

4 There was live music at Charlie's on Saturday.

5 Mick generally goes out with blondes.

Conversation 3

6 Diana Jacobs went to university.

7 She has done a lot of company law.

8 She works better on her own than in a team.

4 Missing person

Listen to the description of a missing person and complete this report form.

Missing Person

Name of missing person	
Reported missing by	
Address	
Phone number	
Age	
Height	
Build	
Hair	
Distinguishing features	
Clothes	
Last seen by	
Date last seen	14th June
Time last seen	
Place last seen	

Sgt. Paul Banham

Vocabulary

1 Describing people
Vocabulary reference p.197

A How many words do you know for describing what people look like? Write down as many words as you can under the following headings.

age   height   build   hair   complexion   distinguishing features

B Find someone who ...

Look at the photos. Find people who have the following physical characteristics. Use a dictionary to check words you don't know.

Find someone who is:

bald	going grey	plump	slim	tanned
clean-shaven	petite	skinny	stocky	well-built

Find someone who has:

a beard	dyed hair	a parting	a scar	spiky hair
curly hair	freckles	a pony-tail	shoulder-length hair	a spotty complexion

C Modifying adjectives and adverbs

1 Some adverbs like *very* intensify the meaning of adjectives and other adverbs.

2 Look at the following sentences from the listening. Underline the modifiers, then grade them from the most to the least intense.

> *She's very efficient.*   *He's fairly tall for his age.*
> *It's really straight.*   *She usually dresses quite casually.*
> *She's extremely reliable.*   *I think she'd fit in pretty well.*
> *They're often a bit late.*   *He's rather inexperienced.*
> *It was incredibly crowded.*

Which of these words occur only in informal English? Can you think of any other words like *incredibly?*

3 Some adverbs like *fairly* can intensify or reduce the meaning of adjectives and adverbs. Different meanings are conveyed by different stress.
*He's fairly **tall** for his age* means he's taller than you would expect most boys that age to be.
*He's **fairly** tall for his age* means he's tall but not especially so.
Which other modifiers are like *fairly?*

4 Read the Grammar reference on page 186 before you continue.

D Descriptions

Describe one of the people in the photos. Your partner will try to guess who it is. Give a full description including approximate age and height, hairstyle, build, complexion, distinguishing features, and say what you think they are like. Try to include some of the modifiers. When giving your description, leave the most obvious features until last.

E Choose the word which best completes each sentence.

1 She sometimes wears her hair _____ .

  A tied   B loose   C free   D fringe

2 He has a _____ complexion.

  A white   B spotted   C clear   D brown

3 Last year's cycling accident has left him with a large _____ on his left cheek.

  A mark   B cut   C wound   D scar

4 Mark's hair is already _____ , which isn't surprising as his father lost all his hair at an early age.

  A bald   B parting   C retiring   D receding

5 People with red hair often come out in _____ when they sunbathe.

  A stubble   B moles   C freckles   D blemishes

2 Word building

Look at these sentences from the listening and study the notes below.

  'I know it's an *inconvenient* time.'

  'It's *impossible* to drive.'

The negative prefixes *un-, dis-, in-, im-, ir-* and *il-* can be added to some adjectives to make opposites. The following general rules may help you decide which prefix to use, but remember there are exceptions.

  im- before a word beginning with *m* and *p*   *immature, impractical*

  ir- before a word beginning with *r*   *irrational*

  il- before a word beginning with *l*   *illiterate*

There are no rules of use for *un-, in-* and *dis-* but it is useful to know that *un-* is the most common negative prefix.

Look at these adjectives, some of which were in the Introduction on page 75, and try to add the correct prefix to make the opposite.

caring	fair	logical	patient	responsible	sociable
enthusiastic	fit	organized	polite	secure	

3 Phrasal verbs

In one of the listening passages, the police officer says, 'There's a good chance he'll *turn up*.' There are several phrasal verbs formed from *turn*. Complete the following sentences with the verb *turn* in the correct tense and one of the words below. Make any other necessary changes to the sentence.

down   into   out   over   to   up

1 '_____ that radio! I can't hear myself think!' Alan shouted.

2 When water freezes, it _____ ice.

3 In Agatha Christie's novels the murderer always _____ to be the least likely person.

4 We had to _____ their invitation as we had already arranged to go out that day.

5 When the omelette is cooked on one side, _____ .

6 The room was so cold that they had to _____ the heater to maximum.

7 In six months the tiny puppy _____ a huge dog.

Writing

Bringing descriptions to life

> The first thing everyone notices about him is his height – he is tall, almost two metres. The second thing is how skinny he is. He is as thin as a rake. He looks as if he has not eaten for months and yet he is always
> 5 eating. He never bothers much about his appearance, except for his hair. I joke about him looking like an angry hedgehog when he gets out of bed in the morning – his short, brown hair all spiky and sticking out. He spends hours trying to comb it flat but with no success.
> 10 He is patient and kind. He always helps me with my maths, even if it means giving up a night out with his friends. He is also calm. I've only ever seen him get angry once.
> We get on each other's nerves sometimes, but I
> 15 wouldn't change him for the world.

1 Model

Read the description above. Do you think the writer is describing a friend, her father or her brother? Give reasons.

2 Making descriptions interesting

What makes the description come to life is the detail and examples that we give.

A Giving details

What do we learn about the person in the description? Make notes under these headings where information is given.

Physical appearance	Character
1 Hair, eyes, complexion	1 General qualities
2 Height, build	2 Habits
3 Typical clothes	3 Abilities
4 Distinguishing features	4 Moods

B Giving examples

1 Underline the parts of the description which give examples for the notes you made under 'character'.

2 Choose words from the list below to complete the following sentences. Then make similar sentences of your own with the remaining words.

affectionate	ambitious	brainy	nervous
reliable	reserved	sentimental	shy

a My brother always came top of the class at school. He's very _____ .

b She's _____ . She won't stop until she gets to the top.

c She's very _____ . She never asks anyone round to her house and generally keeps herself very much to herself.

3 Think, plan, write

Write about 100 words to describe either your favourite person, your least favourite person, or one of the people in the pictures in this unit. Try using this plan.

Paragraph 1 say who you want to describe and why

Paragraph 2 physical description

Paragraph 3 character description

Paragraph 4 conclusion – sum up your feelings about this person

8 Information

Sleep tight

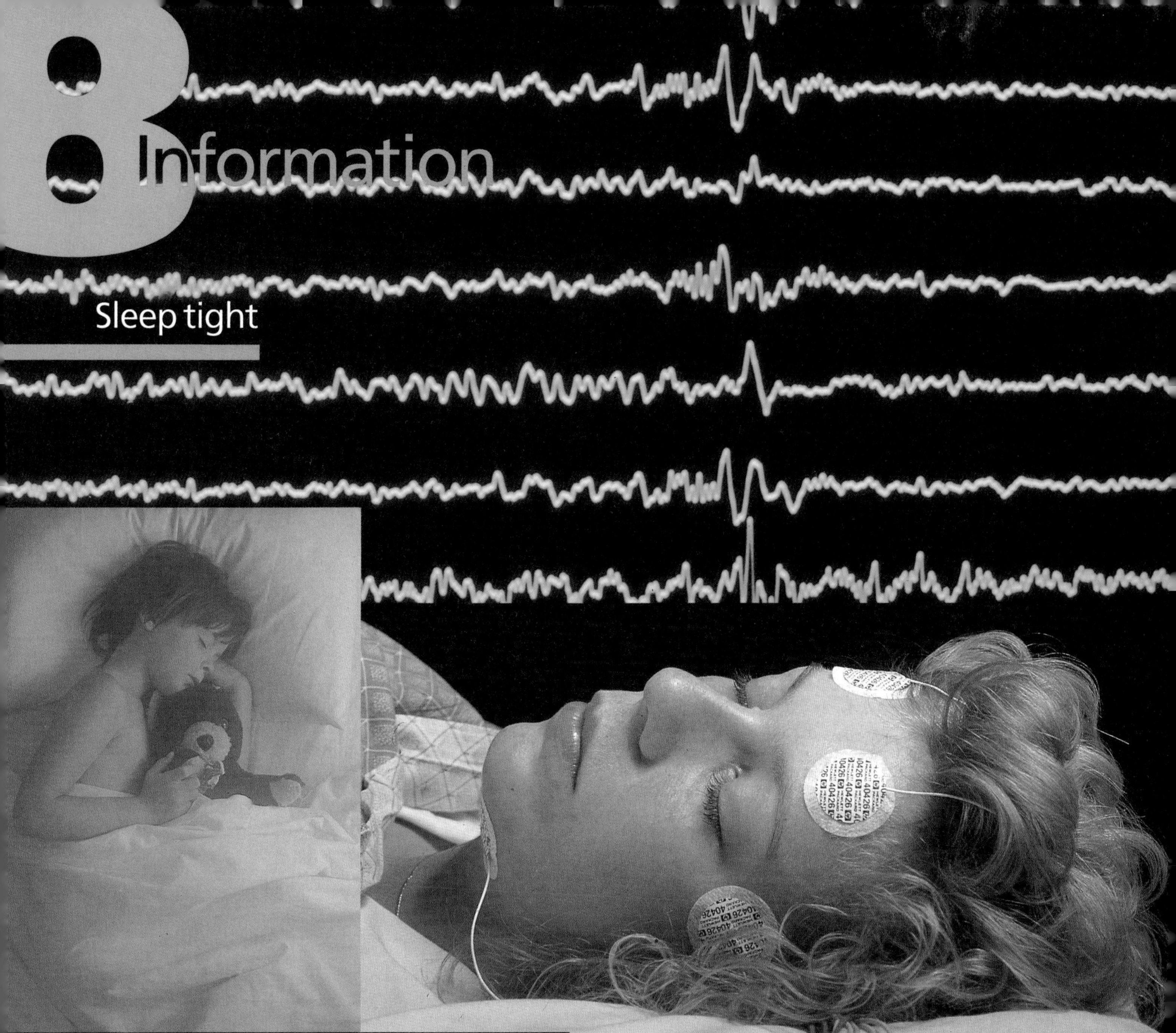

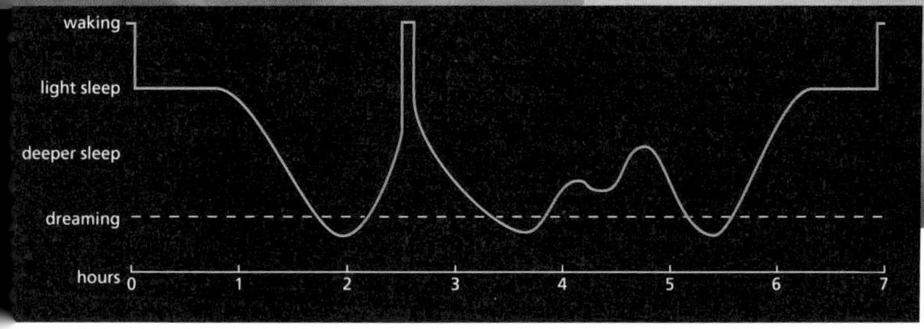

Introduction	**A** What do you think is happening to the woman in the photograph? According to the information given in the graph, do we dream when we are in *light sleep* or when we are in *deeper sleep*?

B What time do children under seven go to bed in your country?

C How much sleep do you usually have? How much sleep do you need? What effect does lack of sleep have on you?

D What advice would you give to someone who had trouble getting to sleep?

Reading

1 Think ahead How many different words do you know for *sleep* in English?

2 Reading Read the text through quickly. Do you think it comes from an encyclopaedia, a scientific journal, a magazine, or a school textbook? Give a reason for your choice.

Kip, nap, doze, forty winks, shut-eye and snooze are all expressions we use to describe that mysterious state, sleep. We all do it, we can't get by without it
5 **and by the time we reach old age most of us have spent 20 years sleeping. Yet nobody knows why we do it.**

Most scientists reckon that by resting our bodies, we allow time for essential maintenance work to be
10 done. Any damage that there is can be put right more quickly if energy isn't being used up doing other things. Injured animals certainly spend more time asleep than usual while their wounds are healing. And quite a few illnesses make us feel
15 drowsy so our body can get on with curing us.

Sleep is controlled by certain chemicals. These build up during the day, eventually reaching levels that make us tired. We can control the effects of these chemicals to some extent. Caffeine helps to keep us
20 awake while alcohol and some medicines make us sleepy.

By using electrodes, scientists are able to study what goes on in people's heads while they sleep. They have discovered that when we first drop off
25 everything slows down. The heart beats more slowly and our breathing becomes shallow. After about 90 minutes our eyes start to twitch and we go into what is called REM sleep. REM stands for Rapid Eye Movement, and it's a sign that we've started to dream. 30

You have dreams every night, even if you don't remember them. There are all sorts of theories about why we dream. One is that it gives the brain a chance to sort out the day's activities, filing everything away in the right place. Another is that 35 the brain gets bored while we're asleep and organizes its own entertainment – a sort of late-night cinema!

A lot of people say they have to have eight hours' sleep every night while others seem to manage on 40 a lot less. One thing's for sure, we all need some sleep and going without it can have some very strange effects. An American disc-jockey, who stayed awake for 200 hours to raise money for charity, thought things were bursting into flames 45 all around him after 120 hours without sleep. He survived the ordeal but was depressed for three months afterwards.

Humans are unusual in the way they sleep. Most animals have a sleep during the day and tests 50 have shown that a siesta can be beneficial for us too. It's even been recommended that airline pilots should have a nap during long flights so that they are more alert for the tricky business of landing.

So next time you nod off after Sunday lunch in 55 front of the telly, don't feel embarrassed about it. Science, after all, is on your side.

3 Points of view What's the longest you have gone without sleep? What was the reason? How did you feel?

4 Comprehension

A Read the questions, then read the text again carefully and choose the best answer for each question. You must be able to explain your choice.

1 Most scientists think we sleep because
   A all our energy has been used up.
   B our brains are tired and need to rest.
   C our bodies need to carry out repair work.
   D our bodies contain too many chemicals.

2 What have scientists discovered about dreaming?
   A Some people never dream.
   B Most people dream for ninety minutes every night.
   C People's eyes move when they are dreaming.
   D People dream for different reasons.

3 What does the writer say about the amount of sleep we need?
   A Most people need eight hours' sleep a night.
   B Not everyone needs the same amount of sleep.
   C People who don't get enough sleep get depressed.
   D People who sleep too little start imagining things.

4 What does the writer say about people's and animals' sleeping habits?
   A People and animals have similar sleeping habits.
   B People would benefit from copying animals' sleeping habits.
   C People need more sleep than animals.
   D Animals need more sleep than people.

B Vocabulary
Choose the best meanings for these words and phrases from the article.

1 yet (line 6)   A and   B but   C so
2 to some extent (line 19)   A occasionally   B partially   C totally
3 he survived the ordeal (line 47)
   A he got through a difficult experience
   B he made a lot of money for charity
   C he didn't suffer any after-effects
4 alert (line 54)
   A calm and relaxed   B cool and prepared   C awake and ready
5 tricky business (line 54)
   A boring day   B exciting prospect   C difficult task

C Reading between the lines
1 What bed-time drinks would you not recommend for someone who had problems getting to sleep?
2 What age group might be embarrassed about 'nodding off in front of the telly'? Why?

D Paragraphs
Read paragraphs 2–7 again. What question could each paragraph answer?
Example   paragraph 2 *Why do scientists think we sleep?*

5 Over to you

Do you remember a particular dream? What makes it memorable? Is it a recurring dream or a nightmare? Working in groups, see if you can find any explanations for your dreams.

6 Sweet dreams?

Now write down the description of your dream, including as many details as you can.

Grammar and practice

1 Passives

A Form and use

1 Read these sentences from the text. Underline the verbs. Which are passive and which are active? Name the tenses.

  a Any damage that there is can be repaired if energy isn't being used up doing other things . . .

  b Sleep is controlled by certain chemicals.

  c We can control the effects of these chemicals to some extent.

2 How is the passive formed?

3 Rewrite sentences a and b putting the passive verbs into the active form and the active verbs into the passive form. How do the changes you have made affect the meaning?

  Only one of the sentences has an agent, i.e. the person or thing responsible for the action. Why has an agent been included here but not in the other sentences?

B Read the Grammar reference on pages 186–7 before doing the following practice exercises.

2 The agent

Why is there no agent in the following sentences? Match the sentence with the most appropriate reason, a–d. There may be more than one reason.

Example   The secretary was given a pay rise.

        c The agent is obvious. It must be her boss.

1 Gaugin's most important paintings were produced during his time in Tahiti.

2 Silence must be observed at all times.

3 The house had been re-decorated since my last visit.

4 I was told to be here by five at the latest.

5 I've been robbed.

6 Smith was given a five-year sentence for his part in the robbery.

a The agent is probably not known.

b The agent is not considered important.

c The agent is obvious.

d The agent has already been mentioned.

3 Practice

A Advertising

Match the products and services in the photos with sentences 1–5 from their advertisements and brochures. There is one extra product. Which words helped you make your choice?

Fill the gaps in the sentences with one of the verbs from the box. Use the correct form and tense of the passive.

1 This product should reach you in perfect condition. If it does not, please return the product and its wrapper, stating when and where it _____ .

2 We insist our shoes _____ by a trained assistant.

3 Every effort _____ to ensure that a warm welcome awaits all our guests.

4 Once opened, this pack should _____ in an airtight container and _____ in a cool place, ideally the refrigerator.

5 Any electrical work that _____ to install this appliance should _____ by a qualified electrician or a competent person.

buy	fit	offer	require
carry out	make	place	store

B Put the following passages into the passive. Do not include the agent unless it is important.

1 The police arrested Smith at Newtown Hospital last night. Doctors were taking him to the operating theatre when the police arrived. One of his accomplices had accidentally shot him in the knee during the get-away. The police are interrogating Smith at Sunhill Police Station. They will charge him with armed robbery. They have charged him twice for similar offences in the last five years.

2 The government will close three more coal mines over the next two years. They have already closed a total of six since they came into office. They are asking miners to consider voluntary redundancy.

C Services

1 Fill the gaps in the hotel brochure below with the passive form of one of the verbs underneath. All verbs should be in the present simple tense.

THE GEORGE HOTEL

A friendly atmosphere _____ (1) at the George Hotel which _____ (2) in a quiet residential area in the historic heart of Norwich, just a few minutes' walk from the city centre. All 30 bedrooms _____ (3) to a high standard and most have en suite facilities. All rooms _____ (4) with colour TV, tea and coffee-making facilities and direct-dial telephones. Some rooms _____ (5) for non-smokers. A full English breakfast _____ (6) in the price and _____ (7) between 7 a.m. and 10 a.m. in the Breakfast Bar. Dinner is available between 7 p.m. and 10 p.m. and can _____ (8) at Reception. A supplement of £3 _____ (9) for a single room.

| book | charge | equip | furnish | guarantee |
| include | reserve | serve | situate | |

2 Now write a similar text about the hotel in the photograph. Use the information in the key and your imagination to write about the hotel.

4 Friday the 13th

Fill each gap with one word only.

Fear of Friday 13th, and of the number 13 generally, is _____ (1) as triskaidekaphobia. A recent survey carried _____ (2) in Britain revealed that 41% of British people feel uncomfortable about Friday 13th while 4% live in dread of it.

The reluctance of superstitious sailors to sail on Friday 13th was once considered to _____ (3) reached such a level that _____ (4) 1791 the government _____ (5) to prove that the superstition was a fallacy. Construction was started on a new ship on Friday 13th; she was named HMS *Friday*; she was launched on a Friday _____ (6) she began her first _____ (7) from London on a Friday. Neither the ship _____ (8) the crew was ever heard of _____ (9).

Richard Hall, from Sheffield, has _____ (10) involved in four crashes on Friday 13th. He has also _____ (11) several bones, fallen into a river, been knocked down by a motorbike and walked through a glass door. Now he _____ (12) gets out of bed on _____ (13) day.

Friday 13th interferes _____ (14) hospital schedules because many patients refuse to have operations on that date but it _____ (15) not seem to be the case that _____ (16) accidents happen on Friday 13th than on any _____ (17) Friday.

Serious numerologists claim that the number 13 is not really as _____ (18) as people say. What it really brings is surprises, _____ (19) can be good as _____ (20) as bad.

8 Information

Remember, remember

Introduction   What is happening in the photos? Are fireworks and fires associated with any special festivals in your country? What is celebrated or remembered? Describe one festival.

Listening

1 Think ahead   What do you know about Bonfire Night in Britain? Look at the statements in 3A (some are true and some are false) and try to work out what events are remembered.

2 Listening   Listen to an interview about the origin of Bonfire Night. Were your predictions right?

3 Comprehension

A True or false?
Listen to the interview again and decide whether the statements are true or false.
1 Professor Ellett is an expert on Guy Fawkes.
2 Guy Fawkes organized the plot to blow up Parliament.
3 Guy Fawkes wanted to rule England.
4 England was a Catholic country in those days.
5 The government was told about the plan.

6 Guy Fawkes was arrested in the Houses of Parliament.
7 All the conspirators were caught.
8 Guy Fawkes was burnt to death.

B Now listen to part of a radio broadcast giving information about Bonfire Night celebrations in the local area. Fill in the spaces in the information sheet below.

	Venue	Date	Time of firework display	Entrance fee Adult	Child
1	The Green Man	4 Nov	_____	_____	_____
2	_____	5 Nov	_____	£3.50* *and includes _____ and a baked potato	_____
3	_____	_____	6 p.m. and 9.30 p.m.	_____ †and includes _____	£1.25†

4 Over to you

Compare the festival you described in the Introduction with what you've heard about Bonfire Night. For example, is any special food or drink associated with your festival?

Grammar and practice

More passives

A Look at the two pairs of sentences below. In which sentence does the speaker present the information as being factual? How do the passive forms *is said* and *is considered* alter the meaning of sentence b in each pair? What other verbs could replace them?

1 a Professor Ellett is one of the leading authorities on 17th century British history.
  b Professor Ellett is considered to be one of the leading authorities on 17th century British history.
2 a Guy Fawkes had the fuse in his hand.
  b Guy Fawkes is said to have had the fuse in his hand.

B Now read the Grammar reference on page 187.

C Practice

You are preparing a news report for a radio station. Not all the information you have received from reporters has been confirmed as factual. You have underlined these bits in your notes. Write up your news report using the present passive form of the

verbs below, followed by the infinitive or perfect infinitive to show what information is unconfirmed.

say   believe   report   think

Example Elizabeth Taylor was not accompanied by her husband. He is in Switzerland.
  He is believed / thought, etc. to be in Switzerland.

1 A Boeing 747 has crashed in Peru. The plane was carrying 250 passengers. Several of the passengers were British. The plane was on a routine flight between Madrid and the capital, Lima. It ran into problems as it was coming in to land.
2 An Essex man has dug up some coins in his garden. He uncovered the coins late yesterday afternoon. The coins are Roman. They date from the first century BC.
3 The police are looking for two men in connection with a robbery which took place at Goodbuy Supermarket at 5 p.m. yesterday. One of the men has a scar on his left cheek. The other speaks with a northern accent. The robbers got away with more than £10,000 in used banknotes.

Vocabulary

1 Celebrations; food and drink

Vocabulary reference p.198

A Choose the word which best completes each of the following sentences.

1 The last family _____ was on the occasion of Sarah's 100th birthday.
   A anniversary   B together   C meeting   D gathering

2 We packed sandwiches, fruit, cold chicken and cheese into a hamper and set off for a _____ lunch in the country.
   A buffet   B picnic   C four-course D snack

3 Victor put two spoonfuls of sugar into his tea and _____ it quickly.
   A beat   B stirred   C added   D whisked

4 The dessert was so delicious that I decided to have a second _____ .
   A repetition   B time   C course   D helping

5 Cooked vegetables are less nutritious than _____ vegetables.
   A raw   B stodgy   C ripe   D bland

6 The religious _____ went through the centre of the town and back to the cathedral.
   A parade   B band   C procession   D march

7 He put the meat in his mouth and _____ it for several minutes.
   A chewed   B swallowed   C sipped   D chopped

8 She put the cake in the oven to _____ for an hour.
   A make   B cook   C bake   D poach

B Describe how to make a special dish or drink that you have when you celebrate a festival in your village, town or country. Use the Vocabulary reference on page 198 to help you.

2 Sleep

Vocabulary reference p.198

Using the clues to help you, find eight *sleep* words in this puzzle.

1 extend your arms and legs when you are tired or when you wake up
2 when you sleep badly, you _____ and turn
3 sleep lightly
4 short sleep
5 bad dream
6 open your mouth wide and breathe in when you are sleepy
7 opposite of *asleep*
8 breathe noisily while you sleep

```
N  L  O  P  S  A  A  R  T
A  I  U  R  T  O  S  S  E
P  A  G  I  R  W  L  L  O
E  I  A  H  E  N  P  S  R
Y  A  U  Q  T  R  B  S  C
A  N  M  F  C  M  O  N  C
W  D  A  V  H  D  A  O  A
N  I  A  W  A  K  E  R  S
R  U  S  L  D  O  Z  E  E
```

3 Confusing verbs

The verbs *raise* and *rise* are often confused. So are *lay* and *lie*. Before you do the following exercise, check that you know how to form the past tense, present participle and past participle of these verbs. Also make sure that you understand the different meanings (*lie* has two different forms and meanings).

Fill the gaps with the appropriate form and tense of *lay, lie, raise* or *rise*.

1 Please _____ your hand if you want to ask a question.
2 _____ in bed on a Sunday morning is one of life's pleasures.
3 When you've finished _____ the table, could you give me a hand with these potatoes?
4 Prices _____ 10% since this time last year.
5 People often start _____ about their age when they reach 40.
6 The subject of inflation _____ by some of the delegates at yesterday's conference.

4 Phrasal verbs with *up*

Look at this sentence from the reading passage on page 88, line 10. 'Any damage that there is can be put right more quickly if energy isn't being *used up* doing other things.'

Use up means to use totally. The word *up* adds a sense of completion to the meaning of the verb. There are some more common verbs of this type in list A. Match them with one of the nouns in list B and make sentences which illustrate the meaning of the verbs.

Example *I was so furious that I tore the letter up and threw it in the bin.*

A   B
1 tidy up   letter
2 tear up   desk
3 drink up   present
4 eat up   milk
5 fill up   mess
6 clean up   dinner
7 wrap up   car

5 Phrasal verbs with *get*

A Some of the most common phrasal verbs in English are *get* + particles. Can you guess the meanings of these phrasal verbs from their context in the reading passage on page 88?
. . . so our body can *get on* with curing us. (line 15)
We can't *get by* without it. (line 4)

B Fill the gaps in the following sentences with *get* + one of the particles below, making any other necessary changes. Use a dictionary to check your answers.

away   by   down   on   out   over

1 She decided to leave home to _____ from her parents.
2 Mary Lou asked me how Neville _____ at school.
3 Eric _____ with his brother when they were young but they're quite good friends now.
4 Even if you haven't time for a proper holiday, try and _____ to the coast for a few days.
5 I hate winter; the cold weather and short days really _____ me _____ .
6 When we were in Greece, we _____ with sign-language and the half dozen words of Greek that we knew.
7 Keith still can't _____ the shock of winning so much money.
8 The prisoner _____ by climbing over the high wall that surrounds the gaol.

Writing

Describing an event

1 Model

The title of this model composition is *Describe a festival or celebration in your town or country.* Read the composition and make brief notes on the answers to the questions in the margin. Which paragraph do you find most interesting? Why?

Which festival?
Where? When? Why?

How is it celebrated?
(general)
What happens?
(details)

Food?
Drink?

How does it end?

Australia Day, which is a national public holiday, is celebrated on January 26th, in the middle of the Australian summer. It commemorates the foundation of Sydney in 1788.

Australia Day is a family day, and many families go out for a picnic. Some people go to the beach, where they go surfing or sunbathe, but the residents of Sydney head for The Rocks, the oldest part of Sydney and the site of the first colonial settlement. The Rocks, which overlooks Sydney Harbour, is packed on this day. Parades with brass bands march through the narrow streets and hundreds of small boats take part in races in the harbour.

Wherever people go, it is customary to have a barbecue and drink beer. The traditional food is 'Pavlova' a sweet cake made of meringue with fruit on the top, and 'damper', a bread made with flour, water and sugar, cooked in the fire.

The festivities in Sydney end with a huge firework display. The yellows, blues and greens light up the night sky and fall like shooting stars into the water below.

2 Making writing interesting

A When we describe a place or an event, the details we give make it interesting and bring it to life. These details can be factual or descriptive or a mixture of the two. Find examples from the model and write them under these headings: Factual details ('in the middle of the Australian summer'); Descriptive details ('*narrow* streets').

B A procession
Look at the description of a parade on page 97. Dots (•) indicate points where details can be added. Some suggestions of the type of details you can include are given underneath. Add one more example to each list then rewrite the text including information from the lists.

The parade passed •1 through the •2 town. •3 People stood •4 on both sides of the road watching it. At the head of the parade was the band, composed of men and boys wearing •5 uniforms, blowing •6 trumpets and banging •7 drums.

1 How?	solemnly, briskly, . . .
2 Which part?	outskirts of the, centre of the, . . .
3 How many?	(large) crowds of, dozens of, . . .
4 How/doing what?	pressed close together, cheering, . . .
5 What like?	spotless, military, scarlet and black, . . .
6 What like?	gleaming, shiny, . . .
7 Size?	large, enormous, . . .

C Read the paragraph below and rewrite it to include details at the places marked •.

• Men carry the • wooden platform on their shoulders, weighed down by the • weight. On the platform there is a • cross surrounded by • candles and • flowers. Men wearing • red robes and • pointed hats walk • in front of the platform, carrying • crosses in their hands.

3 Think, plan, write

Describe in 120–180 words a festival or special celebration that takes place in your village, town or country.

A Decide which festival you are going to describe and jot down some ideas using the questions below to help you.

Paragraph 1
Is it a local or national festival?   Where / when / why is it celebrated?

Paragraphs 2 and 3
How is it celebrated?   Is there a parade or procession?
Do people wear special costumes?   Is there any singing or dancing?
Do you have special food or drink?   Do events happen in any special order?

Paragraph 4
How does it end?   Is there a bonfire or firework display?

B Write the composition from your notes. It may help you to describe the events in the order in which they happen. Remember that it is better to write about fewer things in more detail than everything with no details.

C Check through your composition for correct spelling, grammar and punctuation.

Exam techniques

Guided writing – interpreting visual information

1 The task
Guidelines, p. 24

The guided writing always has three parts – the instructions, the information and the paragraph openings. In this question, the information is mainly visual. Read it all.

2 Information

The new mayor of the village of Tarnforth is trying to decide on the best site for this year's November 5th celebrations and the best time to start the event, which lasts about two hours and is also attended by people from Gosforth and Wickham. He is considering four sites, marked on the map as A, B, C and D and three starting times: 6 p.m., 7 p.m., or 8 p.m.

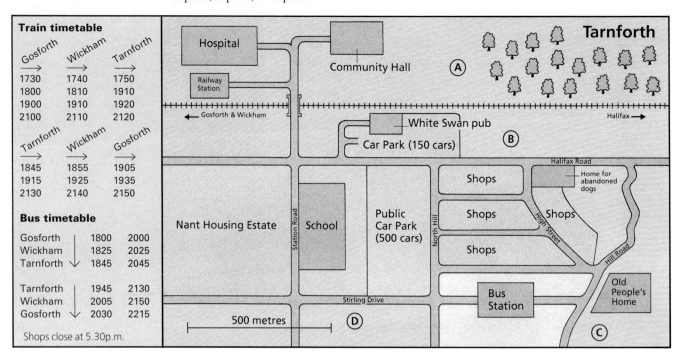

Complete the three paragraphs, writing 50–60 words for each.

1 In my opinion the best site for the bonfire and firework display is . . . because . . .
2 I don't think it is a good idea to site the bonfire at . . . because . . .
3 I think the best time to start the celebrations is . . . because . . .

3 Think, plan, write

A What needs and problems are associated with fireworks, bonfires, public events, crowds, etc.? Make a list of your ideas.

B Study each of the sites A–D, and note down the advantages and disadvantages of each site, referring to your list.

C Choose the sites which you think would be the best and the worst. Use your notes from B to write the first two paragraphs, explaining your choices.

D Now look at the timetables and work out which starting time is best for people travelling to Tarnforth by bus and by train. Remember that they also have to get home again.

R2 Revision

This section gives you extra practice in the grammar and vocabulary covered in Units 5–8. Before you begin, remind yourself of this language by reading the Grammar reference notes on pages 183–187 and the Vocabulary reference on pages 197–198. This is not a test so you should refer to Units 5–8 and the reference sections as you work through these exercises.

1 Vocabulary multiple-choice

Choose the word or phrase that best completes each sentence. Look up any words you don't know when you've finished.

1 The car is old but reliable; so far it hasn't let me _____ .
   A in   B up   C down   D through

2 Susan _____ as a nurse for three years before her marriage.
   A has worked   C worked
   B has been working   D is working

3 Jan didn't check she had enough petrol before she left, _____ was careless of her.
   A what   B it   C that   D which

4 It's not true. He's _____ a lot of nonsense!
   A speaking B saying C talking D telling

5 Dot and Andy set _____ on the first leg of their journey on March 1st.
   A off   B in   C to   D for

6 I slept really badly; I _____ and turned all night long.
   A revolved B twisted C turned D tossed

7 Add the sugar _____ the mixture and beat well.
   A with   B in   C to   D into

8 She finds it difficult to manage on her pension – she just gets _____ .
   A by   B out   C over   D on

9 _____ he took off his dark glasses, I recognized him.
   A Whenever   C As soon as
   B Then   D While

10 You might get there on time if you _____ now.
   A will leave   C would have left
   B leave   D are leaving

11 It is _____ impossible to guess my boss's age. He could be anything between 35 and 55.
   A quite   C very
   B rather   D extremely

12 Prices _____ considerably since this time last year.
   A raised   C have raised
   B rose   D have risen

13 'When I _____ my hands, stop,' the teacher instructed.
   A smack   B clap   C slap   D shrug

14 You won't do it _____ you try harder.
   A in spite of B unless   C if   D in case

15 After three days of torrential rain, the roads turned _____ rivers.
   A to   B into   C out   D over

16 The house, _____ Shakespeare was born in, is open to the public.
   A where   B which   C that   D whom

17 If he _____ more slowly, he would have been able to stop.
   A had been driving   C has driven
   B drove   D didn't drive

18 She has red hair and a _____ complexion.
   A white   B pale   C spotted   D freckles

19 They sat down to a _____ meal.
   A five-coursed   C five courses
   B five-course   D five course's

20 He's above _____ height; about 1 metre 78 cm.
   A medium   B normal   C average   D usual

2 Topic vocabulary

Complete the sentences with one word related to *food* and *drink*.

1 He always has two _____ of bread and a cup of coffee for breakfast.

2 If you're on a diet, remember that chips are much more _____ than boiled potatoes.

3 The butter was so cold that I couldn't _____ it on my bread.

4 Taking the bottle from the table, he _____ himself another glass of whisky.

5 'A packet of tea and a _____ of jam, please.'

6 If you leave the butter out of the fridge too long, it'll _____ .

3 Gap filling

Look back at the Exam techniques section on pages 30–31 to remind yourself how to work through gap filling exercises. Then fill each gap with one word.

Lisa Simmonds was in her kitchen when she heard the terrified screams of her three-year-old son, Barney. 'It wasn't the sound of a little boy _____who_____ (1) had fallen over and hurt his knee,' Lisa recalls. 'There was a terror in his voice I'll _____never_____ (2) be able to forget.' She raced outside where she found her son barely visible: an _____enormous_____ (3) snake was coiled _____around_____ (4) his body.

Lisa and her husband, Dan, live in a tropical part of Queensland, Australia. The Australian rain forests are home to a variety of wildlife, including the Rain Forest Python _____which_____ (5) can grow _____up_____ (6) to nine metres long. _____approximate_____

As _____soon_____ (7) as she saw the snake wrapped around her son's body, Lisa recognized it was a python. These dangerous creatures coil _____themselves_____ (8) tightly around their victims, breaking and crushing their bones, before swallowing _____them_____ (9).

'The snake _____had_____ (10) coiled itself four or five times round Barney's body; his face was red and his eyes bulging,' Lisa remembers. She ran to get a spade _____repate_____ _____from_____ (11) the garden shed and beat the python several times, _____taking_____ (12) care to avoid hitting her son, but the python would not let go. _____In_____ (13) the end she was _____so_____ (14) scared that she started hitting it with her fists. When it _____finally_____ (15) uncoiled itself and fled, Lisa saw that it was five metres long.

Lisa's husband arrived home just _____when_____ (16) she was carrying her injured son inside, and they rushed him to the hospital. He was suffering _____from_____ (17) shock and had a fractured left leg. Luckily, he was out of hospital and back to normal within days. Lisa, _____however_____ (18), still hasn't got _____over_____ (19) the shock and now never lets her son out of her _____eyes_____ (20).
_____sight_____

4 Transformations

Before you begin, look back at the Exam techniques section on pages 80–81, which gives advice on how to do transformations. Then complete each unfinished sentence so that it means the same as the sentence printed before it.

1 That girl's mother used to work with mine.
   That's the girl _____
2 I've never eaten with chopsticks before.
   It's _____
3 She forgot to add salt, so the food was tasteless.
   If _____
4 Having made all the arrangements, they decided to go anyway.
   Since _____
5 They'll have to cancel the picnic.
   The picnic _____
6 I haven't been to the dentist's for over two years.
   It's _____
7 We didn't go because we couldn't afford it.
   If we _____
8 The fire will go out if someone doesn't put some more coal on.
   Unless _____
9 The police are questioning a man in connection with the burglaries.
   A man _____
10 It is essential that you eat the soufflé as soon as it's cooked.
   The soufflé _____

5 Word building

Use the word in capitals at the end of each of these sentences to form a word that fits in the blank space.
1 Sue went red with _____. EMBARRASS
2 Graham hates queuing; he's very _____. PATIENT
3 Don't believe a word Tom says. He's a terrible _____. LIE
4 Deb's a very warm and _____ person. CARE
5 The man spoke with a _____ accent. SOUTH
6 The woman has blonde shoulder-_____ hair. LONG
7 Applicants must be under 25, hard-working and _____. ENERGY
8 Many modern refrigerators never need to be _____. FROST

You are now ready to do Progress test 2.

9 Interaction

Hooked

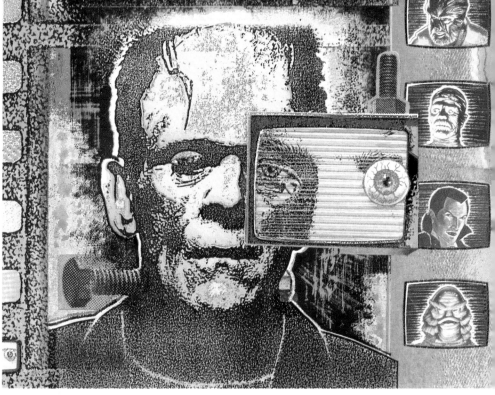

Universal monsters

Dracula has risen from the grave . . . and he's not alone. Frankenstein, the Mummy, and even the Creature from the Black Lagoon are among the foul fiends also set to appear on your screen when you buy **Universal Monsters**. This game will breathe new life into the undead stars of Universal's horror film classics and bring them into your home. Not to be played late at night.

A lost childhood

We live in a seaside town. On sunny days you would expect 13-year-old boys to be down at the sea, brown and healthy, having the time of their lives. Instead, they and their friends retire into darkened rooms with the curtains drawn, playing computer games hour after hour, killing or being killed by weird creatures which pop up on the screen. The boys and their friends have pasty, unhealthy faces, and they have become aggressive and irritable. It breaks my heart to see my boys wasting their young lives on this rubbish.

Toys for boys and games for girls

Barbie Goes Shopping will soon be nestling incongruously on the shelves of computer game shops alongside Pitfighter, Streetfighter and Bad Dudes vs Dragon Ninjas. Nintendo have at last brought out a computer game aimed at girls.

Since Nintendo's Gameboy hit the British market from the States back in 1988, it has been just that – a toy for the boys.

Despite this, there are no plans to bring out a Gamegirl. If the company started to market its product at females, admits a spokeswoman, there is a danger that boys would stop buying it. 'Girls don't mind joining in male pursuits, but it never works the other way round,' she explains.

Introduction

A Read the three extracts. What have the extracts got in common? Where do you think each one is from? Which one matches the illustration?

B Why are games like the one described in the first extract so popular?

C Do you think the parent in the second extract is right to worry about the boys?

D Is it true that girls don't mind playing boys' games but that boys don't like playing girls' games? If your answer is yes, how do you explain this?

Listening

1 Think ahead

addicts

advisers

aerials

average

compensation

equipment

eyes

fingers

intended

screens

sold

A Read this information about computer games. Fill the gaps with words from the list on the left.

1 There are at least 50 million Nintendo _____ around the world.
2 Fifty per cent of Japanese homes have Nintendo games connected to their TV _____ .
3 The hand-held Gameboy was _____ for 18 to 25-year-olds, but is being played by six-year-old children.
4 An American girl who played with her Gameboy for two hours a day for a year has developed numbness and tingling in her _____ . She is suing the Nintendo company for $10,000 _____ .
5 Five hundred Nintendo _____ answer 500,000 queries a week from players with problems.

B Make a list of as many ways as possible that computer games could be harmful.

2 Listening

A Listen to the first part of the recording.

1 What is the speaker introducing?
  a an interview with a psychologist
  b a university lecture
  c a radio phone-in programme
  d a television documentary
  e a radio discussion

2 How many people are you going to hear in the next part?

B Listen to the rest of the programme. Are any of the harmful effects you listed in Think ahead B mentioned by the speakers?

3 Points of view

Do you think Marion Jeffries is over-reacting? Whose view do you most agree with?

4 Comprehension

A Read the statements below, then listen to the second part of the programme again. Decide whether the statements are true or false.

1 Marion Jeffries thinks her son spends too much time playing computer games.
2 She is worried because her son doesn't mix with other children.
3 The child psychologist thinks Marion has good reason to be worried about her son's behaviour.
4 The psychologist expects Adam to lose interest in computer games soon.
5 According to the head teacher, children who play computer games do badly at school.
6 The head teacher advises Marion to take the game away from the boy.
7 According to Oliver's research, computer games affect everyone in the same way.

B Listening between the lines

1 What do you think Adam's personality was like before he became addicted to his computer games?
2 Why do you think the child psychologist suggests that Marion should try ignoring her son?
3 What does Oliver Newton mean by 'outlet for their aggression'? What other outlets for aggression can you think of?

C Read these extracts from the radio programme. Match the words or phrases in *italics* with the definitions.

1 If I shout to get his attention, he *loses his temper*.
2 When he's finished playing, he's completely *uncommunicative*.
3 What should I do about Adam's *obsession*?
4 He's like a two-year-old having a temper *tantrum*.
5 Obsessions like this are *a passing phase*.
6 It might just *do the trick*.
7 . . . if he continues to play *for hours on end*.
8 That'd be *asking for trouble*.
9 He's got a *flair* for computers.

a for a long time without stopping, continuously
b something you can't stop thinking about
c become very angry
d succeed in producing the right result
e a habit or stage in a person's life that does not last
f increase the chance of problems occurring
g a sudden noisy or violent outburst of anger
h unwilling to talk or listen to other people
i a special talent

5 Vocabulary

Fill the gaps in these sentences with a word formed from the word in capital letters.

1 Some parents worry about their children's _____ to computer games. ADDICT
2 They believe that playing games for too long can be _____ to their children's health. HARM
3 In particular, parents are afraid of changes in their children's _____ . PERSON
4 Some parents have frequent _____ with their children about how often and how long they should play these games for. ARGUE
5 There is no _____ proof that computer games are dangerous. SCIENCE
6 Although the basic _____ is relatively cheap, the computer games themselves are expensive. EQUIP
7 Computer game companies employ special _____ to help people who get into difficulties with their games. ADVICE

6 Over to you

Marion Jeffries thinks her son is addicted to computer games. What other common kinds of addiction are there? Rank all the addictions you can think of in order of seriousness, starting with the most serious.

Grammar and practice

1 Suggestions, advice and warnings

A Rank these three statements in order of strength.
1 You really ought to stop worrying.
2 Don't stop your son from playing altogether, or you might make the situation worse.
3 You could try ignoring Adam altogether.

Which statement is:
a a suggestion – an idea or plan put forward by someone?
b a piece of advice – someone's opinion or recommendation?
c a warning – strong advice with a mention of what may happen if this advice is not followed?

B Here are some more extracts from the radio programme. Are they suggestions, advice or warnings?
1 If I were you, Marion, I'd point out to Adam that he could do damage to his eyes.
2 I wouldn't do that.
3 Encourage him to keep up his other hobbies, otherwise he'll lose all his friends.
4 Why don't you tell him he's got a flair for computers?

C Advice and suggestion phrases
1 Sentence 1 above starts with *If I were you*. Do you know any similar ways of giving advice which start with *If I were . . .*
2 Rephrase sentence B4 above, starting with these phrases.
   What about . . . ?
   You could . . .
   How about . . . ?

D What does Marion Jeffries mean when she says, 'I shouldn't have bought it for him. I realize that now.'?

E Check your understanding of suggestions, advice and warnings in the Grammar reference on page 187.

2 Practice

A Respond to these statements with suggestions or advice.
1 'I need to find a way of earning money so that I can afford a holiday next summer.'
2 'I'm finding it really difficult to revise for my school exams.'

3 'My parents are always arguing. I don't know what to do.'

B What would you say to your friends in these situations? Give them warnings.
1 Your friend has got a new car and drives too fast.
2 Your friend always drinks too much alcohol at parties.
3 Your friend, who has plenty of money, has got into the habit of stealing small things from shops for fun.

C Read this brief news report. What should or shouldn't the airport worker have done?

An airport baggage handler was in a plane's luggage compartment waiting for the last bag. He was tired after working an 80-hour week, so he lay down to rest and unfortunately fell asleep. When he woke up the plane had taken off. He cried for help and was freed by the flight crew. When he got back home, he was sent a bill for £298 – the cost of the return flight.

3 Dialogue completion

Complete this conversation between two friends.

John   You look terrible. Are you all right?
Alan   Yes, thanks, I'm just very tired.
John   What _____? (1)
Alan   Quite early, actually. The problem was I couldn't get to sleep.
John   _____? (2)
Alan   It was the next door neighbours again. Every night they stay up late talking in loud voices and playing music.
John   _____? (3)
Alan   I have asked them. They said they'd try and be a bit quieter, but it hasn't really made much difference.
John   What about _____? (4)
Alan   That's not a bad idea, I could do with some proper legal advice.
John   I could _____. (5)
Alan   Thanks, that would be very useful. I've never been to a solicitor before.
John   The problem is, the law works slowly and solicitors aren't cheap.
Alan   I know, and all the time I'm getting more and more exhausted.
John   You know, I think if I were you, _____. (6)
Alan   That's a bit drastic, isn't it? Perhaps I'll just call the City Council.

4 Fluency

A Work in groups of three or four. Each choose a different problem from the list below. Think about how the people with the problems are behaving and how they have changed recently. Decide exactly why you are worried.

- Your sister is addicted to gambling. You know she rarely wins, and loses much more money than she earns each week.
- Nearly all your friends smoke, and they want you to start. You hate smoking, and want your friends to stop.
- You think your best friend might be taking drugs.
- Your friend has just got a credit card and is spending far more money than he can afford.

B Now take it in turns to present your problems to the group. The rest of the group should give their advice. Make sure the advice you give is clear and helpful.

5 Linking ideas

A These extracts from the reading and listening texts each include two main ideas. Find these ideas and underline the words which link them. The first one has been done for you.

1 The boys and their friends have pasty faces <u>and</u> they have become aggressive and irritable.
2 Since Nintendo's Gameboy hit the British market in 1988, it has been a toy for the boys. Despite this, there are no plans to bring out a Gamegirl.
3 Girls don't mind joining in male pursuits, but it never works the other way round.
4 Don't let him give up his other hobbies, otherwise he'll lose all his friends.
5 Although the children who play these games behave more aggressively, they also develop improved powers of observation.

B Discuss these questions about the sentences in A above.

1 How are the two ideas in the extracts related? Match each extract with one of these definitions.
   a one idea is an addition to the other
   b the two ideas are in contrast to each other
   c one idea is conditional on the other
2 Which words are used to link contrasting ideas?
3 Can you think of any more words or phrases which link contrasting ideas?

C Before doing the next exercise, read the Grammar reference on page 188.

6 Practice

Link these pairs of contrasting sentences in as many ways as possible.
1 John's very fat. He does a lot of exercise.
2 We've got three television sets at home. I never watch TV.
3 I drink several cups of coffee every night. Coffee keeps me awake.
4 I went to work as usual yesterday. I had a terrible cold.
5 My brother can't find a job. He is very well qualified.
6 My sister always gets good marks in exams. She never does any revision.

On the right track

EURORAILING

Thanks to long vacations, students are in the enviable position of being able to travel round Europe by rail and see the sights on the cheap. This article points out some of the pros and cons of travelling by train.

5 The sense of freedom offered by rail travel is unrivalled by any other, except perhaps the less safe option of hitch-hiking. Trains are also a great way to meet local people and, compared with other long-distance modes of transport, the Greenest you can get. Rail travel allows you to explore the hidden corners of the
10 continent, especially areas where rural lines are still open and trains are still the most common form of public transport. It's also a relaxing way to travel, whether you're using it as a cheap bed for

| Introduction | If you had as much money and time as you wanted, what kind of holiday would you choose to have? Which methods of transport would you use? |

Reading

1 Think ahead

Imagine you're going on a month's holiday travelling around Europe by train. What problems might you encounter? Make a list. What precautions would you take?

2 Reading

The leaflet above gives advice to students on travelling round Europe by train. As you read it, underline any of the ideas you thought of in the Think ahead section.

3 Points of view

What would be the best way for a visitor without a car to travel round your country visiting places of interest?

4 Comprehension

A Match the eight paragraphs of the leaflet with these possible titles. Write the paragraph numbers in the spaces.

A word of warning ___   Possible problems ___
Financial considerations ___   A final piece of advice ___
Packing the essentials ___   Making the most of long holidays ___
Getting the most out of your holiday ___ Trains! They're the best ___

B Read the questions, then read the leaflet again. Choose the answer which you think fits best.

the night, or as a ring-side seat for a series of stunning views.

15 The first step before you go is to choose one of the Eurorail schemes available. After that, there are a few tips to bear in mind before you leave. Budgeting always causes headaches and it's worth finding out which are the 'expensive' and the 'cheap' countries. It's sensible to take some cash, but you should take most of your money in traveller's cheques. Choose a well-known 20 brand and buy small denominations.

Your most important piece of equipment is your backpack, and it's worth choosing one that's comfortable and light, sits just above your hips, and is 'high' rather than 'wide' when full. A day-pack is useful for sightseeing, and a pair of comfortable walking 25 shoes is vital, along with dark, hard-wearing clothes. As a general rule, put out everything you want to take – then halve it. Some things, however, should not be left behind. An alarm clock (so you don't miss those early trains); a scarf to cover your shoulders or legs for visits to churches or mosques; photocopies of all your 30 important documents – best packed separately or given to a travelling companion; toilet paper, soap and a universal plug; a Swiss army penknife; numerous plastic bags; a water bottle and a small first aid kit.

The fun really starts once you're out there, of course – hunting for 35 a hostel at 10 p.m., being ripped off by a taxi driver who claims there are no buses to your campsite or being turned away from a famous tourist attraction for wearing shorts. There are compensations for these frustrations (which make the best stories afterwards, anyway!), but many problems can be avoided 40 if you're aware of the potential pitfalls before you leave.

The golden rule is not to try to cram too much into the time available. Trying to see the whole of Europe in a month, by spending every night on a train and an afternoon in each capital city will result in an unsatisfactory blur of shallow impressions. It 45 is also a recipe for disaster, as you will be tired, grumpy and unreceptive for most of your trip. Instead, try to vary your route, mixing visits to cities with relaxing spells on the beach or in the countryside.

Each year a few unlucky travellers have their valuables stolen. 50 The best way to prevent this is to carry them with you at all times, preferably in a money belt or a neck pouch. This is especially important on night trains, where most thefts occur. Another sensible precaution is not to sleep rough – you're just asking for trouble. Watch out for conmen at stations: they'll try to persuade 55 you to accept a room, tempting you with glamorous pictures of a hotel which turns out to be awful and whose price will have doubled by the time you reach it. Far better to go and see accommodation yourself before accepting it. And, if you're on a tight budget, it's always worth asking if they've got anything 60 cheaper.

● ●

These ideas are really just common sense, but it's amazing how often they're overlooked. But the most important tip of all is – have fun!

1 In comparison with hitch-hiking the writer says that travelling by train is
   A more dangerous.   C just as dangerous.
   B less dangerous.   D not dangerous.

2 When packing for a rail holiday, the writer advises students to
   A take everything they want.
   B take more than they think they'll need.
   C take half of what they really want to take.
   D leave behind nothing they think they'll need.

3 According to the writer, the best thing about bad experiences on holiday is that
   A you usually forget about them later.
   B you often receive compensation later.
   C you usually find them funny at first.
   D you can tell people about them later.

4 When planning a route, the writer advises students
   A to see as much as possible in the time they have.
   B to visit places but also rest from time to time.
   C to go sightseeing in the afternoons and travel by night.
   D to see everything in a month.

5 What should travellers do to prevent their valuables from being stolen?
   A They should keep them with them all the time.
   B They should not travel on trains at night.
   C They should not fall asleep on trains.
   D They should be especially careful at stations.

5 Over to you   What is the most interesting journey you have ever had? Tell your group about it.

Vocabulary

1 Travel and holidays
Vocabulary reference p.198

A Modes of transport
Complete these sets of travel words.

1 car	to _____	to go by road
2 _____	to travel on a train	to go by_____
3 ship	to _____	_____
4 _____	to fly _____	to go by _____

B Noun-verb collocations
If the vehicle and the verb can be used together, tick the correct space in the table. For example, you can say *catch* or *miss a bus*, but not *catch* or *miss a bicycle*.

Types of vehicle	car	bicycle	boat / ship	bus	motorbike	plane	taxi	train
Verbs catch / miss				✓				
get into / get out of								
get on / get off								
ride								
take								
drive								

C Fill the gaps in the following sentences with one of the following words.
trip   journey   tour   excursion
1 Do you know, my _____ to work took over four hours this morning.
2 For our holidays next year, we're going on a ten-day _____ of the Australian outback.
3 We always go on a day _____ to France in December to buy Christmas presents.
4 The price of this holiday includes a full-day _____ to a place of cultural interest.
5 He's hoping to go on a(n) _____ to the Himalayas next year.

D Choose the correct word to fill the gaps in these sentences.
1 Next year, we're going on a cheap _____ holiday to Portugal. The flight and the hotel are included in the price.
   A packet   B package   C overall   D inclusive
2 Have you ever been on a guided _____ of Westminster Abbey?
   A journey   B sightseeing   C trip   D tour
3 I've just come back from a business _____ to New York.
   A trip   B journey   C excursion   D travel
4 Last year, we drove non-stop from Paris to Madrid. This year we're going to _____ our journey in Bordeaux.
   A stop   B pause   C break   D interrupt
5 The sea was so rough that the _____ took nearly six hours.
   A voyage   B flight   C passage   D cruise

2 Word building

Roots

1 What are the roots of these nouns from the reading passages in this unit? What parts of speech are the roots?

goodness   observation   reaction   amusement   valuables

Example   The root of the noun *goodness* is the adjective *good*.

2 What are the roots of these adjectives from the passages? What parts of speech are they?

darkened   addictive   resentful   unrivalled   unlucky   glamorous

Example   The root of the adjective *darkened* is the adjective or noun *dark*.

3 What are the roots of these adverbs from the passages? What parts of speech are they?

honestly   enviably   especially

4 You may find it useful to learn sets of words based on the same root. Fill the gaps in this table with the missing words. The first one has been done for you.

verb root	noun	adjective	adjective with opposite meaning
satisfy	*satisfaction*	*satisfactory*	*unsatisfactory*
receive			
communicate			
compete			
succeed			
attract			

3 Colloquial language

The words and phrases in *italics* in these extracts from the Eurorailing leaflet are all informal or colloquial English. Match them with their meanings.

1/2 There are a few *tips* to *bear in mind* before you leave.

3 Budgeting always causes *headaches* . . .

4 . . . being *ripped off* by a taxi driver . . .

5 . . . many problems can be avoided if you're aware of the potential *pitfalls* before you leave.

6 . . . you will be tired, *grumpy* and unreceptive for most of your trip.

7 . . . mixing visits to cities with relaxing *spells* on the beach . . .

8 . . . if *you're on a tight budget*, it's always worth asking if they've got anything cheaper.

a bad-tempered

b unexpected difficulties

c you haven't any money to spare

d pieces of advice

e think about / remember

f cheated / misled

g worrying problems

h periods of time

4 Phrasal verbs

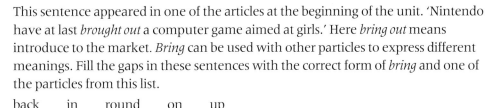

This sentence appeared in one of the articles at the beginning of the unit. 'Nintendo have at last *brought out* a computer game aimed at girls.' Here *bring out* means introduce to the market. *Bring* can be used with other particles to express different meanings. Fill the gaps in these sentences with the correct form of *bring* and one of the particles from this list.

back   in   round   on   up

1 Last year the government _____ a new law making it compulsory for people to wear seat belts in the back of cars.

2 I _____ by my parents to know the difference between right and wrong.

3 Don't feel sorry for him. He _____ all his problems _____ himself.

4 Visiting Spain again _____ so many childhood memories.

5 It took doctors an hour to _____ him _____ after the accident.

Exam techniques

Vocabulary multiple-choice

1 Guidelines

Do	Don't
Before the exam ● Train yourself to notice word combinations when you are reading or listening to English. Similarly, record and learn words in combinations wherever possible (e.g. *to burst into flames, to burst out laughing*). **In the exam** ● Read each sentence carefully to try and understand what the sentence will mean when the gap is filled. ● Study the four choices. If you think you know the right answer, check that both the meaning and the grammar are correct. ● If you aren't sure, try to eliminate three of the four alternatives, starting with the words that don't make sense. ● Then think about the grammar, especially tenses, gerunds and prepositions. ● If you still can't decide, guess.	▶ Don't always think of words as single isolated items. ▶ Don't look at the four choices or guess the answer until you've tried to understand what the sentence means. ▶ Don't just choose the first word which seems to have the right meaning. ▶ Don't leave any unfilled gaps.

2 Guided practice

Many of the common problem areas are practised here. Questions 1–7 each test a different area of grammar and vocabulary, and there are clues to help you with these. As you work through the exercise, follow the guidelines. When you have chosen your answer, think of reasons why the other three alternatives should be eliminated in each case.

1 If I'd known it was going to be so sunny, _____ my sunglasses.
   A I'd wear   B I'll wear   C I'd have worn   D I wear
   Clue What kind of conditional is this?

2 We'd better _____ really early. It's a very long journey.
   A set up   B set off   C set down   D set on
   Clue Which of these four verbs means *leave?*

3 My father _____ five languages fluently.
   A speaks   B talks   C tells   D says
   Clue Which verb goes with *language*?

4 My friend and I agreed to go to France for our holidays. It was a _____ decision.
   A joint   B collective   C agreed   D twin
   Clue This is a set phrase which was used in Unit 4.

5 _____ I'm eating less than usual, I still seem to be gaining weight.
   A Because   B If   C Although   D Unless
   Clue Decide on the meaning of the sentence, then check the grammar.

6 There is no _____ evidence for the existence of UFOs.

    A scientific   B science   C scientist   D scientifically

    Clue What part of speech is *evidence*? What part of speech is needed here?

7 Even though he's 21, he hasn't got a job and is still financially dependent _____ his parents.

    A on   B for   C from   D of

    Clue What preposition follows *depend*?

3 Practice

Now try the rest on your own.

8 In the last year the _____ of inflation has slowed down considerably.

    A growth   B increase   C decrease   D rate

9 I never take much on holiday with me, just _____ clothes and a couple of books.

    A few   B little   C a few   D a little

10 I heard strange noises in the street last night, so I looked out of the window to see what was going _____ .

    A on   B off   C in   D up

11 I need eight hours' sleep a night, _____ my brother gets by on only five or six.

    A except   B however   C whereas   D because

12 I really enjoyed the novel you lent me, but the ending was very _____ .

    A predictable   B predicted   C predicting   D prediction

13 My sister lives in a tall _____ of flats in the town centre.

    A house   B tower   C skyscraper   D block

14 Can you check my work to see if I've _____ any mistakes.

    A done   B made   C brought   D had

15 My sister won't _____ me borrow her bicycle.

    A allow   B let   C permit   D leave

16 I can honestly say I've never seen _____ boring film.

    A so   B so much   C such a   D such

17 I'm like Mum, whereas my brother takes _____ Dad.

    A on   B in   C after   D over

18 There's no need to be nervous. You're quite capable _____ your driving test.

    A of passing   B passing   C to pass   D pass

19 Do you think you could possibly _____ favour?

    A make me a   B do me a   C do my   D make my

20 He went into the manager's _____ and lodged a complaint.

    A study   B office   C desk   D bureau

21 I'm really looking forward _____ home at the weekend.

    A to going   B gone   C going   D to go

22 I went on a day _____ to Belgium last week. It was really cheap.

    A trip   B journey   C voyage   D tour

23 You won't pass your exam _____ doing a lot more practice.

    A except   B although   C without   D unless

24 I was brought up in a small house _____ the suburbs of Manchester.

    A out of   B on   C off   D in

25 If _____ John, tell him I'll phone him later.

    A you see   B you saw   C you'd seen   D you'll see

Writing

Informal letters

1 Model

As you read this letter, underline the features that indicate it is an informal, not a formal, letter.

> 17, The Avenue
> Southampton
> Hants
>
> 25th July
>
> Dear Sam,
>
>   Thanks for your letter. I'm glad you're coming at last. Do you think we'll be able to meet up?
>
>   I can understand you being a bit worried - I'll never forget my first trip abroad. Anyway, you asked for some advice, so here goes!
>
>   First of all, pack some warm clothes. You never know what the weather's going to be like - even in the summer. And it's definitely worth bringing an umbrella.
>
>   As far as money's concerned, the golden rule is not to carry too much around with you, I'd say £50 at the most. Most places take credit cards now, and there're always traveller's cheques.
>
>   Finally, a few things to remember - banks, pubs and restaurants open and close at rather strange times, and public transport can be unreliable. As a general rule, the best way to meet people is to start talking to them. We're not really unfriendly, it's just that we're not very good at making the first move.
>
>   Give me a ring when you arrive and we'll arrange a get-together.
>
> Love,
> Anna

2 Language points

A Some features of informal letters are the same as for formal letters, for example

1 The general layout: the way you write your address and date; where you start and finish writing.
2 The division of what you write into paragraphs.

B We tend to write informal letters when we are writing to someone we know well. We want to sound friendly, so we write more or less as we speak. Here are some examples of informal language taken from the model. Did you underline them?

1	Contracted verb forms	*I'm glad you're coming.*
2	Questions	*Do you think we'll be able to meet up?*
3	Informal words	*a get-together*
4	Colloquial expressions	*here goes!*
5	We usually use the person's first name	*Dear Sam, Love Anna*
6	We often end with *Love*. Other endings include	*All the best, Yours, Best wishes.*

3 Think, plan, write

Write a letter giving advice to a friend who is planning to spend a week in your country. Write 120–180 words.

A Before you write, look back at the Eurorailing leaflet on pages 106–7, and list all the advice expressions you can find.

B Although in real life people do not plan informal letters, you still need to practise planning your composition. Make notes of what you are going to say, using the advice expressions you have listed. Then divide the notes into paragraphs. Look at the letter to Sam to get ideas.

C When you write the letter, make sure that you use the features of informal letters listed above, and no formal language.

10 Restrictions

Within limits

1 Ceremonial guards

2 Doctors

4 Heads of state

3 Professional ballet dancers

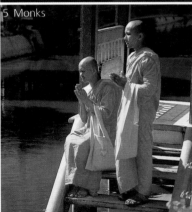

5 Monks

6 Sumo wrestlers

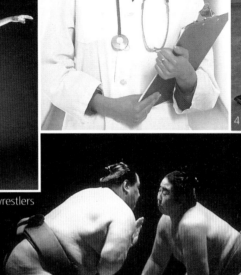

7 Schoolboys

8 Top fashion models

Introduction

A Look at the people in the photographs and discuss your answers to these questions.
1 Who has the hardest life?
2 Who has the easiest life?
3 What makes these people's lives harder or easier than the others?

People's lives are governed by a variety of restrictions, from national laws to rules and regulations associated with their jobs. Think about the special restrictions which govern the lives of some of the people in the photographs and compare ideas.

Examples *Ceremonial guards have to wear special uniforms and take part in official ceremonies.*

Heads of state can't go anywhere without bodyguards.

B Can you think of people whose lives are restricted in other ways?

Listening

1 Think ahead

What rules or restrictions are associated with these four photographs?

2 Listening

You are going to hear four extracts of conversation. As you listen, match them with the photos above.

3 Points of view

1 Do you think the age at which people are allowed to marry should be the same for boys and girls? Give your reasons.
2 At what age do you think boys and girls should be allowed to marry without their parents' permission?

4 Comprehension

A Matching

Read the questions below, then listen to the first three conversations again and choose the correct answer.

1 Which of these situations is a foul in the game described in the first conversation?

2 Which of these students is wearing the correct uniform described in the second conversation?

3 Which of these situations illustrates where the homeless girl spends the night?

B True or false?

Conversation 1

1 Players aren't allowed to carry the ball.

Conversation 2

2 At St Mary's you had to stay at school even if you had no lessons.

3 The girl thought that wearing the correct uniform and shoes was sensible.

4 Alison once wore jeans to school and changed into her uniform in the headteacher's office.

Conversation 3

5 The girl ran away from home when she was 14.

6 The girl was forced to stay in a children's home until she was 16.

7 She went straight to a hostel when she ran away.

Conversation 4

8 In France, girls can get married younger than boys can.

C Vocabulary

In English there are a number of adverbs which have two forms. In some cases the two forms have different meanings. For example, *rough* and *roughly*.

*Diana has been sleeping **rough**.* in the open air, or outside

*Her parents treated her **roughly**.* violently, or cruelly

Here are some more pairs of adverbs. Decide which form should go in which sentence.

1 a He _____ refused to help his mother with the housework.

 b He tripped and fell __ on his face. flat, flatly

2 a In some countries old people travel _____ on the buses.

 b There's no one listening, so we can talk quite _____ . free, freely

3 a Some people work _____ and get very little money.

 b Other people _____ do any work and are paid a fortune. hard, hardly

4 a Where's Gloria? I haven't seen her _____ .

 b Don't worry, she's coming. She always arrives _____ . late, lately

5 a It is _____ known that the President is about to resign.

 b At the dentist, you have to open your mouth _____ . wide, widely

6 a Be careful not to drive _____ the edge of the cliff.

 b Someone I know _____ had a terrible accident last week. near, nearly

5 Fluency

Working in pairs, act out one of these situations. Instructions for Student B are on page 174.

Situation 1 – Student A

You are a famous sumo wrestler training for the world championships. You are tired of weighing 180 kilos, and want to be slim. Tell your trainer you have decided to go on a diet, and explain why.

Situation 2 – Student A

You are a ceremonial guard. You think your uniform is ridiculous and want to wear something more normal. Persuade your commanding officer to let you.

Grammar and practice

1 Modal verbs

A Obligation and necessity

Read these sentences from the conversations in the listening, and underline the verbs which express obligation and necessity.

1 You must come and watch the match on Sunday.
2 If we're going to work together, I need to know what your parents were like.
3 I hate being moved on – I suppose it's something I have to put up with.
4 In Greece boys must be 18 to get married.

Which sentence expresses:
a a necessity?
b a strong suggestion or invitation?
c a legal obligation or law?
d a personal obligation outside the speaker's control?
What grammatical differences are there between the verbs in 1 and 4, and those in 2 and 3?

B Rewrite these sentences, without changing their meaning, and without the verbs in *italics*. The first one has been done for you.

1 You *mustn't* drive if you've drunk too much alcohol.
It's against the law to drive if you've drunk too much alcohol.
2 You *shouldn't* sunbathe for too long. It can damage your health.
3 British people *needn't* vote in general elections if they don't want to.
4 Soldiers *don't have to* wear uniforms when they're off duty.
5 You *mustn't* worry about me. I've travelled on my own before.

C What is the difference in meaning between these sentences?
1 I didn't need to hurry. There was plenty of time.
2 I needn't have hurried. There was plenty of time.
In which sentence did the speaker hurry?

D Fill the gaps in these sentences with *didn't need to* or *needn't have* and the correct part of the verb in *italics*.
1 I went to the airport to meet him. Unfortunately he was ill and had to cancel his trip, so I _____ *drive* all that way.
2 I was about to go shopping, when Dad arrived home with everything we needed, so I _____ *go* after all.

3 The car was really dirty, but then it rained for a couple of hours, so I _____ *wash* it.
4 I carried my umbrella round all day but it didn't rain once. I _____ *take* my umbrella.
5 Last year my father won £1 million. He _____ *work* any more, so he gave up his job.
6 That was a lovely meal, but you _____ *go* to so much trouble.

E Check your understanding of these verbs in the Grammar reference on page 188.

2 Practice

A Read these extracts from a speech made by a college director talking to a new group of students. Choose the best verb to fill the gaps.

1 Most importantly, you _____ enrol and pay your fees, otherwise you won't be allowed to start your course.
 A must   C don't need to
 B don't have to   D should
2 This is a no-smoking college. That means that you _____ smoke inside the building at any time.
 A mustn't   C don't need to
 B shouldn't   D don't have to
3 The college regulations say that you _____ attend a minimum of 80 per cent of your classes.
 A should   C don't need to
 B need   D must
4 In fact, if you want to do well in your exams, you _____ try to attend all your classes.
 A must   C have to
 B should   D don't need to
5 If you have no classes, you _____ stay at the college. You can go home if you like.
 A have to   C mustn't
 B don't have to   D shouldn't
6 If you are planning to come by car, and want to use the car park, you _____ get a permit from the college office.
 A will need to   C should
 B won't need to   D shouldn't

B This leaflet gives tourists information about driving on British motorways. *Must* is used for all legal obligations, *should* for anything which isn't law, and *need* for things that are physically necessary. Read the leaflet, and fill the gaps with the affirmative or negative form of one of the three verbs.

Drive carefully ... ⚠️

Although motorways are safer than other roads, nevertheless accidents do sometimes happen – and they can nearly always be avoided.

Before you leave

▶ If you are feeling tired, you _____1 drive.
▶ Learner drivers _____2 not use motorways.
▶ Petrol stations may be up to 80 miles apart on some motorways. You _____3 make sure you have enough petrol before joining the motorway.

As you go

▶ Drive at a safe speed. You _____4 under any circumstances drive faster than 70 m.p.h.
▶ If you have a mechanical problem and you _____5 stop, pull on to the hard shoulder and switch on your hazard warning lights. You _____6 use the hard shoulder for casual stops.
▶ If driving long distances makes you feel sleepy, you _____7 stop regularly at service stations and walk about.

hard shoulder – area at the side of a motorway where drivers are allowed to stop in an emergency

... arrive safely

3 Permission

A This chart gives information about the ages at which young people in Britain are allowed to do certain things. Study the information and make sentences using *can* and *be allowed to*.

Examples   *When you're 12 you're allowed to buy pets.*
You can't buy pets until you're 12.

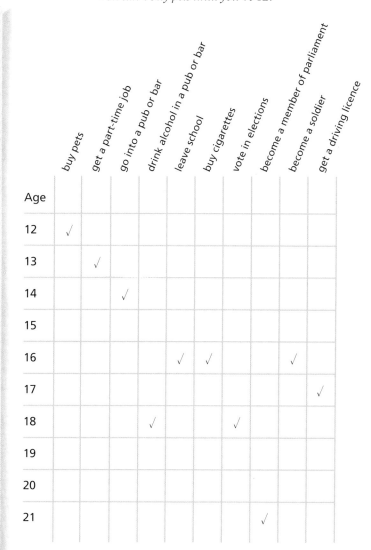

Age	buy pets	get a part-time job	go into a pub or bar	drink alcohol in a pub or bar	leave school	buy cigarettes	vote in elections	become a member of parliament	become a soldier	get a driving licence
12	✓									
13		✓								
14			✓							
15										
16					✓	✓			✓	
17										✓
18				✓			✓			
19										
20										
21								✓		

B Check your understanding of ways of talking about permission in the Grammar reference on page 189.

C Make a similar chart like this for your country. Compare charts with other students.

4 Do as you're told

You have won a local election, and have the power to introduce new local laws. Write a public notice listing your new laws. Write about 80 words.

Writing

An informal talk

1 Formal or informal?

In Paper 2 of the exam you may be asked to write what you'd say in a particular situation. This could be a formal speech, like the kind made at weddings or to mark someone's retirement (formal speeches will be practised in Unit 11). Or it could be something informal, like what you would say if you were explaining things to a friend.

A On what other occasions do people talk formally and informally? Compare ideas with a partner.

B Read these extracts and decide whether they are formal or informal.

1. Ladies and gentlemen, it is my pleasure to welcome you all to what promises to be a memorable occasion. Before I introduce this evening's conductor, I would like to say a few words about the pieces the orchestra is going to play.

2. Okay, lads, that wasn't a bad first half, but what were we saying before the game? Move into space. And you're still hanging on to the ball for too long, aren't you? Move it around a bit, you know, get in behind them, keep them guessing, especially the goalie.

3. So, when you've whisked the egg mixture for a couple of minutes, add a little water or milk and carry on whisking for another minute. By now the oil in the pan should be hot enough . . .

4. When I was first approached by the committee to present these awards, I wondered what I could possibly have done to deserve such an honour. As someone who writes only the occasional letter, I still find it incredible that novelists can spend several years on one book.

C For each extract, answer as many of these questions as possible.
1. Who, or what kind of person, is speaking?
2. Who is this person speaking to?
3. Where and when are they speaking?
4. What is the speaker's purpose? For example, is it to explain or describe something, to instruct or advise someone, etc.?

2 Talking informally

A The following features should be included in this kind of composition. The examples are from the four extracts above.
1. verb contractions, e.g. *when you've whisked the egg*
2. informal or colloquial words, e.g. *goalie, a couple of*
3. phrasal verbs, e.g. *carry on whisking*
4. conversation fillers, e.g. *okay, you know, so*
5. questions to the listeners and question tags, e.g. *What were we saying before the game? You're still hanging on to the ball for too long, aren't you?*

B Because informal talks are written more or less as we speak, they do not have to follow a set structure, as formal speeches do. This does not make informal talks easier to write, as they must still have a structure, but you have to plan it for yourself. Be careful not to use any formal language.

3 Model

A As you read this composition, answer the questions from 1C.

> Right then, crossing the road is something you all do from time to time, isn't it? Maybe you do it on your way to school, or when you go shopping for your mum and dad. And of course, roads are
> 5 dangerous, aren't they? Well, I'm here to teach you how to cross roads safely.
>
> Of course, the best way is to use zebra crossings or footbridges, if there are any. If not, choose a place where you can see a long way in both
> 10 directions. Don't cross between parked cars if you can help it. Okay?
>
> Then stand near the edge of the pavement and listen and look all round for traffic. If there's anything coming, let it go, then listen and look
> 15 again. When there's nothing coming from either direction, walk straight across. Don't run, or you might fall and hurt yourself. And as you're crossing, go on looking and listening, just in case there's something coming. You can never be sure.
> 20 Most of all, you must be sensible near busy roads. Don't forget that roads aren't playgrounds.

B What examples are there of the features which were listed in 2A?

4 Think, plan, write

A You are going to write 120–180 words for this title.
You are with a small child who is very worried about starting school next week. Reassure the child and talk about your experience of starting school.

B Plan what you want to say, and divide your ideas into paragraphs. There is no set plan, but here is one idea.
Paragraph 1   the subject of school as an introduction
Paragraph 2   what happens on the first day
Paragraph 3   some things you liked about starting school
Paragraph 4   something encouraging as a conclusion

C Make a list of special words related to the subject, and any informal words and expressions you would like to use.

D As you write each paragraph, use the features you studied on the previous page, and the phrases you have just listed. You are talking to a small child, so don't use any formal or difficult words.

E When you have finished, read your composition imagining that you are talking to the child. It should sound friendly and informal. Finally, check it for grammar, spelling and punctuation.

The law of the jungle

LAWS ARE MADE TO BE BROKEN.

THE LAW IS AN ASS.

LAWS ARE LIKE NETS: LITTLE FISH SLIP THROUGH THEM, BIG FISH BREAK THROUGH THEM AND ONLY MEDIUM-SIZED FISH GET CAUGHT.

THERE'S ONE LAW FOR THE RICH AND ANOTHER FOR THE POOR.

IT IS WRONG FOR PEOPLE TO TAKE THE LAW INTO THEIR OWN HANDS.

Introduction

A Which of these ideas about laws do you agree with?

B Are there any laws in your country which a lot of people ignore?

Reading

1 Think ahead

You are going to read about a man who took the law into his own hands. Try to guess what happened by interpreting the headlines and the photographs on the next page.

2 Reading

Now read the articles opposite and check your predictions.

3 Points of view

From what you have read about the Dryden case, do you think that the judge in the case was right to sentence him to life imprisonment? Give your reasons.

4 Comprehension

A Read the questions, read the articles again, then choose the best answer for each question.

1 Dryden shot Collinson because Collinson
   A had demolished his bungalow.
   B was going to demolish his bungalow.
   C had brought the police with him.
   D wanted to demolish the bungalow in broad daylight.
2 Why did the police go to Dryden's house with Collinson?
   A They were going to demolish the house.
   B They were going to arrest Dryden.
   C They thought Dryden might become violent.
   D They wanted to keep the public away.
3 Which of these aspects of Dryden's behaviour did the writer of the second article find most worrying?
   A his ability to make rockets   C his interest in weapons
   B his obsession with his bungalow   D his mania for collecting American cars
4 When Dryden first appeared in court, some people demonstrated to show
   A their support for Dryden.   C their disapproval of the killing.
   B their sympathy for Collinson.   D their approval of the killing.

B Reading between the lines
1 Why do you think Dryden was obsessed with not giving in to 'bureaucratic busybodies'?
2 Why do you think Collinson had wanted to be open about the demolition of Dryden's bungalow?

TV killer of council planner gets life

Albert Dryden immediately after shooting dead Harry Collinson, a council planning officer

The man seen by millions of television viewers shooting dead a council planner in a dispute over his bungalow was jailed for life at Newcastle crown court yesterday.

Albert Dryden, a former steel worker, shot Harry Collinson, a Derwentside council officer, in June last year. The planner had gone with other council officers, accompanied by police and press, to impose a demolition order on Mr Dryden's bungalow at Butsfield, near Consett, which had been built in breach of planning regulations.

Mr Dryden had threatened violence against the council officers before and for this reason police were standing by, but none had anticipated he would open fire.

With the television cameras running, Mr Dryden calmly shot Mr Collinson, and then tried to shoot other officers.

Mr Collinson had organised the demolition during the day because, he told colleagues, he wanted to be open about it. It could have been carried out at night as Mr Dryden had not moved into the house.

Obsession that led to gun murder

Duncan Campbell on the man who bought his first weapon from a friend when aged 11

Albert Dryden's bungalow was an obsession in his life that was to become fatal. Long before he gunned down Harry Collinson, he had let it be known that he was prepared for many to die if his home was demolished because of his breach of planning rules.

He had told one local reporter that he had plans to load up his car with explosives and blow up the civic centre. He also said that he had acquired a machine-gun and had been practising.

A bachelor of 51, he had lost his job at British Steel's Consett works 12 years ago.

He spent £13,000 of his redundancy pay on what he saw as his dream home, doing almost all the work on it himself. It was a big and crazy scheme involving the excavation of 2,000 tons of earth.

Mr Dryden knew early on that he would encounter planning problems. He became obsessed with not giving in to what he saw as bureaucratic busybodies.

His hobbies included making rockets out of metal tubes and launching them. He claimed he had got into trouble with the RAF because one of the rockets had nearly struck a Vulcan bomber. Another hobby was old American cars. He had six at the time of the killing and said he had collected 49 over the years.

But it was his obsession with weapons that was the disturbing element of his eccentricities.

He was only 11 when he paid a school friend 10 shillings (50p) for a .455 revolver. He obtained a firearms certificate for a .22 rifle in 1957 but this was revoked three years later after police had found a sawn-off shotgun and the means of making ammunition in his home.

After his arrest over the killing, police found an arsenal of weapons, many of them home-made.

He did not lack local sympathy, and friends demonstrated on his behalf when he made his first magistrates' court appearance.

They claimed he was a very caring man who had looked after his widowed mother Nora up to her death two years ago, and had cared for a handicapped brother.

Defence psychiatrists suggested that Mr Dryden was mentally ill and not responsible for his actions when he opened fire. But a psychiatrist for the prosecution said Mr Dryden's responsiblity was 'not substantially impaired' and he knew what he was doing.

3 What motive might Dryden have had for wanting to blow up the civic centre?

4 What reasons might the local council have had for refusing planning permission for Dryden's bungalow?

C Vocabulary

1 What evidence is there in the two articles that these words could all be used to describe Dryden's character?

considerate	individualistic	odd	stupid
crazy	lazy	paranoid	unintelligent
hard-working	mentally unbalanced	self-centred	violent
independent	normal		

2 Divide the words into two groups.

a Words which a friend might use in Dryden's defence.

b Words which a colleague of Collinson might use.

Are there any words which don't go in either group? Who might use them?

Vocabulary

1 Clothes and uniforms   Vocabulary reference p.198

A Clothes

1 Clothes can be categorized in many ways. List as many items as you can under the following headings.

Winter clothes   Summer clothes   Sportswear   Indoor clothes   Nightwear

Can you think of any other categories of clothes?

2 Think about all your clothes and decide what you would wear on the occasions below. Describe the clothes you have in mind, mentioning material, colour, pattern and style. The Vocabulary reference on page 198 will help you.

a a formal interview tomorrow   c a day on the beach at the weekend

b a friend's birthday party this evening

Example   *For a formal interview tomorrow, I'd wear my lightweight cotton suit. It's pale green, and looks very smart.*

Compare ideas in pairs, and give reasons for your choices.

3 How many different items of clothing will you wear tomorrow? Think about what you'll be doing and list the clothes. Compare lists with other students.

B Uniforms

In the listening exercise on page 114, a student talked about her school uniform. Even if people don't wear a uniform, they often wear special clothes. Describe the clothes the people in the pictures are wearing.

Think of another group of people who wear distinctive clothes. Describe the clothes to a partner, who should try to work out who wears what you are describing.

C Phrasal verbs related to clothes

Fill the gaps in the sentences below with the correct form of one of these verbs.

put on   take off   try on   wear out

1 I've only had these shoes for a couple of months and they _____ already.

2 Why are you _____ your overcoat? Do you think it's going to turn cold?

3 These boots are killing me! I can't wait to get home and _____ them _____ .

4 I wish I could find some jeans I really like. I must have _____ at least ten pairs.

2 Formal and informal language

The articles about Albert Dryden on page 121 include these words and phrases used mainly in formal English. Can you think of more informal equivalents?

Example   dispute (line 3)   *row* or *argument*

1 anticipated (line 21)   5 obtained (line 80)

2 acquired (line 48)   6 revoked (line 82)

3 encounter (line 61)   7 on his behalf (line 91)

4 disturbing (line 76)   8 not substantially impaired (line 105)

3 *Too, enough, very*

A Fill the gaps in these sentences about Albert Dryden with *too, enough* or *very*.

1 Nobody anticipated that he would get angry _____ to open fire.

2 They claimed he was a _____ caring man who had looked after his widowed mother until her death.

3 He had also cared for a brother who was _____ disabled to look after himself.

B Which of the three words, *too*, *enough* and *very*:

a intensifies an adjective or adverb?

b means *more than is needed or wanted*?

c means *sufficient*?

Which of the three words can come

d before an adjective or adverb?

e after an adjective or adverb?

f before an uncountable noun or a plural countable noun?

C Practice

Use the information given to complete the unfinished sentences. If possible, complete the sentences in two different ways, with *too* and *enough*.

1 When I was sixteen, I fell in love with a boy of 18. We wanted to get married, but my parents said no. They wanted me to wait for two or three years.
My parents thought we _____ .

2 We've been looking for a new flat for ages. There's a fantastic one right in the town centre but we can't afford the rent.
Unfortunately, this flat _____ .

3 I was thinking of going to India for my holiday next year, but I don't think I could stand the high temperatures.
I think India _____ .

4 My brother started training to be a teacher, but he gave up after a year because he found he didn't have the patience necessary for the job.
My brother gave up the idea of teaching because _____ .

4 Prohibition

Choose the correct word to fill the gaps in these sentences.

1 He was found guilty of dangerous driving and _____ from driving for three years.
A forbidden B banned C prevented D stopped

2 Smoking is strictly _____ on underground trains in London.
A prohibited B banned C disallowed D prevented

3 It is now _____ for all passengers in cars to wear seat belts.
A enforced B obliged C allowed D compulsory

4 Because he got home two hours late, he was _____ to go out for a week.
A forbidden B prohibited C prevented D banned

5 Relatives were only _____ to visit patients on weekday afternoons between four o'clock and half-past five.
A let B prevented C permitted D prohibited

5 Phrasal verbs

These phrasal verbs have been used in this unit.

carry out   hang up   look after   move in   run away   turn up

Fill the gaps in the sentences below with the correct form of one of the verbs, and make any other necessary changes.

1 It's no use _____ ten minutes before the play starts and hoping to get a good seat.

2 My little brother hated school so much that he _____ three times in the first week.

3 Don't leave your clothes on the floor. _____ them _____ in the wardrobe.

4 The builders haven't finished work on our new house yet. I don't know when we'll be able to _____ .

5 I hope the government doesn't _____ its threat to raise taxes.

6 Nurses who _____ old people have a very difficult job.

Exam techniques

Listening – predicting the topic of a recording

1 Guidelines

Do	Don't
• Listen carefully to the instructions on the cassette.	• Don't try to look through the whole paper.
• Try to build up a picture of the topic of the recording. Read all the questions, alternative answers and statements and look at any illustrations.	▶ Don't try to answer any questions at this stage.
• From the picture you have built up, predict the kind of things you might hear.	▶ Don't worry if there are gaps in your knowledge. The fact that you know something about the subject will help you to understand the recording.

2 Practice

A Here is a typical set of true/false statements that you might meet in the exam. Read them and work out as much as you can about the recording they are based on. There are some questions to help you.

1 The incident the speaker describes took place last weekend.
2 The noise started early in the afternoon.
3 The music was so loud that the speaker couldn't hear her own TV.
4 Two teenage musicians were responsible for all the noise.
5 The speaker had a phone call from the local police.
6 The police could not stop the noise because it was too late.
7 The police told the speaker to contact the Department of the Environment immediately.

a *Do you think the incident referred to in statement 1 was something pleasant or unpleasant? What makes you think this?*
b *How many people were involved in the incident?*
c *What sort of music do you think the speaker could hear?*
d *How do you think the police became involved?*
e *How could the Department of the Environment be involved in this incident?*
f *What possible endings are there to this story? Which ending do you think is most likely?*

B Listen to the recording. Were your predictions correct? Was anything you heard surprising?

C Read the statements 1–7 again, and check that you understand them. As you listen to the recording for the second time, decide whether the statements are true or false.

11 Skills and abilities

Geniuses

Introduction

A How old were you when you could read, write, speak fluently, play a musical instrument, and speak a foreign language?

B Reading

Read this newspaper article and find out how old Nicholas MacMahon was when he was able to do the same things. What other extraordinary things could Nicholas do at an early age?

The four-year-old undergraduate

A CHILD prodigy of four is studying at university because he is too clever for school. Nicholas MacMahon is receiving computer lessons at Brunel University in
5 London. A senior lecturer at the university, Valso Koshy, said the boy was remarkably intelligent.

Nicholas spoke fluently before he was one. At 18 months, he was taking telephone
10 messages. Conversational French followed. These are the trademarks of a highly-gifted child, unusual but not unique. The strange thing about Nicholas is his reading – he taught himself to read before
15 he could speak.

Ms Koshy, an expert on gifted children, says Nicholas is quite exceptional. Yet 'exceptional' understates his bizarre ability to read, almost from birth. 'He was talking
20 when he was one and we realized from the start he could already read,' his father said. 'Soon after he was correcting my spelling, words like caterpillar. Now he identifies insects by their Latin names.'
25 The list of achievements is impressive, but frightening. A four-year-old who can tell a Boeing 747 from a DC10, devours encyclopaedias, reads the *Daily Telegraph* and is well on the way to becoming a violin
30 virtuoso is not normal.

C Points for discussion

1 Which of Nicholas' accomplishments do you find the most amazing? Why?
2 What kind of talents can people be born with? What other kinds of talent are there? Which talents can be improved through practice?

Reading

1 Think ahead

Before you read the text, try to answer all the following questions.

1 When is your birthday?
2 What day of the week were you born on?
3 What day of the week did your tenth birthday fall on?
4 What day of the week was 1st April 1933?

2 Reading

Scan the text to find the answers to the following questions.

1 When was autism first named?
2 How many children are born autistic?
3 Which film is about an autistic savant?

Autism is a mental disease which prevents those who suffer from it from communicating with the outside world. Victims seem to live in a world of their own which, even now, doctors are unable to penetrate. The illness was first given a name in 1943, and yet doctors have made very little progress in their understanding of the disease since then. According to statistics, between two and four children out of every 10,000 are born autistic.

The mysterious power of **the brain**

Often victims are not able to speak, read or write. But what is most extraordinary about the illness is the fact that in other areas many of the children can perform almost super-human feats of the brain. One of the more common skills these so-called autistic savants have is calendrical calculation, that is the ability to say which day of the week a particular date falls on. Jackie, for instance, who is now 42, could do this from the age of six, when she first began to talk. She can tell you what day of the week it was on 1 April 1933 with scarcely a moment's hesitation. But if you ask her how she does it, she'll say she doesn't know.

Leslie Lemke only has to hear a piece of music once and he can play it back on the piano note-perfect. Yet he has never had any formal musical training, is blind and has an IQ of 58. If you ask Richard the route of any bus in the London district, he will give you an answer immediately. Stephen Wiltshire has exceptional artistic talents and, like both Leslie and Richard, combines this talent with a remarkable memory, and can draw buildings with complete architectural accuracy, sometimes only hours after seeing them for the first time. Other savants are able to carry out amazing mathematical computations in their heads, but cannot add up simple numbers.

The mystery of how savants perform such tricks is as elusive to the medical world as it is to Jackie and the others like her. Certain common characteristics have, however, emerged. Strangest of all, perhaps, is the fact that about 85 per cent of all recorded cases are male. But what is also puzzling is why the range of savant skills is so narrow: these include music (usually the piano), calendrical or other mathematical calculation, art, extra-sensory perception, extraordinary sensitivity of touch or smell and (more unusually) mechanical ability.

It has been suggested that autistic people do not suffer; that they are perfectly happy to remain in their own world and that a cure is only necessary in order to reduce the terrible pain of rejection felt by the victims' families. This controversial opinion is, however, only held by a few.

The subject has become the focus of particular media interest since Dustin Hoffman's portrayal of an autistic savant in the film *Rain Man*, for which he won an Oscar. This has increased public awareness of the disease and hopefully will result in more money being given to research and a cure being found sooner rather than later.

3 Points of view

Is it right to make money from films like *Rain Man*, about people's illnesses and suffering?

4 Comprehension

A Read the questions below, then read the passage again. Choose the answers which you think fit best.

1 What is autism?
 A a common illness   C an infectious disease
 B a physical illness   D a disease of the mind

2 What is particularly unusual about autistic people is that many of them have
 A extremely poor memories.   C extraordinary natural talents.
 B larger-than-average brains.   D well-above-average intelligence.

3 Medical research has discovered that
 A autism does not affect the sexes equally.
 B autistic people feel rejected by their families.
 C only a few autistic people suffer intense pain.
 D autistic savants all have a wide variety of skills.

4 Following the success of the film *Rain Man*
 A people have given more money to research on autism.
 B the media have shown a greater interest in autism.
 C the public have become knowledgeable about autism.
 D researchers have found a cure for autism.

B Reading between the lines

1 Do you think Leslie Lemke is a brilliant musician? Why? Why not?
2 Why is it impossible to tell whether autistic people are happy or not?
3 What do you think the family of an autistic child would find most difficult or painful?
4 Why would the media have become especially interested in autism after Dustin Hoffman won his Oscar?

C Vocabulary

Find other words in the passage which have similar meanings to the words given. Where there is more than one word with a similar meaning, this is indicated.

1 disease (line 1)
2 ability (line 15), two possibilities
3 extraordinary (line 11), three possibilities

D Meanings in context

Six words from the article are shown below, each followed by three words which are synonyms in certain contexts. Which words mean the same in the context of the article? There may be more than one possibility.

1 progress (line 6)   advance, movement, headway
2 extraordinary (line 11)   curious, strange, odd
3 scarcely (line 19)   barely, hardly, only just
4 training (line 23)   background, instruction, tuition
5 characteristics (line 35)   facts, features, traits
6 focus (line 48)   centre, target, object

5 Over to you

Should people with mental 'disabilities' live in the community or be separated from other people? Give reasons for your opinion.

Grammar and practice

1 Can, be able to

A The structures *can* and *be able to* are often inter-changeable as in these examples from the reading text.

1 Often victims *are not able to* speak, read or write.
2 Other savants *are able to* carry out amazing mathematical computations in their head but *cannot* add up simple numbers.

In sentences 3 and 4 it is not possible to use the *can* form. Why not?

3 She *hasn't been able to* finish all the letters yet.
4 *To be able to* take part in the Olympic Games, you need to be an amateur.

B Practice

Look at the following sentences. Rewrite them using the alternative form where possible. If both forms are possible, but one is more usual, underline the more usual form. If it is not possible to use the alternative form, say why not.

1 He's able to run 100 metres in just over 12 seconds.
2 I was able to climb a mountain without getting out of breath when I was younger.
3 They had eaten such a big breakfast that they weren't able to finish their lunch.
4 The climbers won't be able to reach the summit if the blizzard continues.
5 Even if you'd come over, I wouldn't have been able to spend much time with you.

C In sentences 1 and 2 below, the *can / be able to* forms are interchangeable but in 3 they are not. Can you think why?

1 Before Dave started smoking, he *could / was able to* hold his breath for three minutes.
2 Despite their attempts, the doctors *couldn't / weren't able to* save the woman's life.
3 After nine hours the firefighters *could / were able to* put out the fire.

D Check your answers with the Grammar reference on pages 189–90.

2 Other ability structures

In sentences 2 and 3 in C, *can* and *be able to* forms can be replaced by the verbs *manage* and *succeed*.

Examples   After nine hours, the firefighters *managed* to put out the fire.
After nine hours, the firefighters *succeeded* in putting out the fire.

Can you think why it is not possible to rephrase sentence 1 using these verbs?

3 Practice

A Fill in the gaps with the verb in capitals along with another appropriate verb, making any other necessary changes. The first one has been done for you.

1 He *managed to win* the election, despite strong opposition. MANAGE
2 Although they searched for several hours, the rescue party _____ the climbers. SUCCEED
3 He did his best but he _____ all his work before the boss got back. BE ABLE TO
4 Jerry was thrilled when he _____ his driving test first time. SUCCEED
5 Although there were several people in the house, the burglar _____ and steal the video without being noticed. MANAGE
6 Ann _____ three lengths of the pool when she was Bobby's age. BE ABLE TO
7 Richard's interview was this afternoon, wasn't it? I wonder if he _____ the job. MANAGE
8 I was so tense that I _____ despite the fact that I was extremely tired. BE ABLE TO
9 The police _____ the man from his fingerprints. BE ABLE TO
10 Despite the fact that he didn't have a corkscrew, he _____ the bottle. SUCCEED

Which sentences can be rewritten using *could / couldn't*?

B Fill in the gaps with one of the following structures in the correct tense, along with any other words that are necessary, such as other verbs and prepositions. Use each structure once only.

succeed

learn how

manage

be good

Evelyn Glennie was born in Scotland in 1965. As a young child, she loved music and _____ her reluctant parents to let her have music lessons. She was delighted to find that she _____ it. Then, when she was ten years old, she became profoundly deaf. She was determined to carry on with her music, however, and _____ feel music through her body. She earned a place at the Royal College of Music, where, despite her deafness, she _____ several major prizes. She is now one of the world's best, and most popular, percussionists.

Now write a similar paragraph using as many of the above structures as you can. It could be about someone famous or simply a friend.

C Quiz

Think of something you can do or used to be able to do. It could be a sport or an activity like tossing a pancake, whistling or walking on your hands. The other students will ask you questions to find out what it is. Answer only *yes* or *no*. Here are some suggested questions.

Can you still do it?

Did you learn how to do it?

Did someone teach you how to do it?

Can anyone do it. Do you need special skills?

Is it easy to do?

Do you need special equipment to do it?

4 One giant leap

Fill each gap with one word only.

'Being in space is an exhilarating experience,' recalls astronaut Buzz Aldrin, member of the three-man _____ (1) which made history over 25 years ago _____ (2) they succeeded in being the first men ever to set _____ (3) on the Moon. 'Just being _____ (4) to float around is amazing. Unfortunately, the space suits were _____ (5) restrictive so we weren't able to move about very easily. They made the job of _____ (6) moon rock and soil to bring _____ (7) to Earth much more difficult. The surface of the Moon is covered in a fine powder and because there isn't _____ (8) wind or weather on the Moon, Neil's famous first footprint should _____ (9) be there until it is disturbed _____ (10) other visitors.

'On our _____ (11) to Earth, we were put in quarantine. It was still not known _____ (12) life existed on the Moon and it was feared that organisms from the Moon _____ (13) infect animals and plants on Earth. Hopefully, in the _____ (14) 25 years man will be setting _____ (15) permanent bases on the Moon or even on Mars. I don't see much _____ (16) in just sending astronauts there.

_____ (17) of short trips, which are not a very efficient allocation of resources, we should be sending people there to stay.

'In time, _____ (18) possibly not in my lifetime, people will be born on Mars. They will be our "Martians", _____ (19) the green creatures that science fiction writers write _____ (20).'

11 Skills and abilities

The good old days?

Introduction

Which film stars from this list have you heard of?

Jason Connery	Sean Connery	Cary Grant	Meryl Streep
Julia Roberts	Clark Gable	Marilyn Monroe	Jack Lemmon
Dustin Hoffman	Glenn Close	Kirk Douglas	Michael Douglas
Katharine Hepburn	Robert de Niro	Arnold Schwarzenegger	Richard Gere

What films are they famous for? What kind of character is each star best known for playing?

Listening

1 Think ahead

In what ways are the film stars of today different from the film stars of the past?

2 Listening

You are going to hear some people talking about film stars. Listen to part one and put a tick (√) next to the film stars in the list who are mentioned. What is the main point of the discussion?

3 Points of view

Which of the actors mentioned do you like? What special qualities do you particularly like about them?

4 Comprehension

A Read the questions, then listen to part one again and choose the best answers.

1 What does John say about Clark Gable, Marilyn Monroe and Katharine Hepburn?
  A They were all good actors.
  B Clark Gable was a better actor than Marilyn Monroe.
  C Katharine Hepburn was the only good actor.
  D None of them was a good actor.

2 What do they say about actor sons of famous fathers?
  A None of the sons are better actors than their fathers.
  B All of the sons are better actors than their fathers.
  C Two of the sons are better actors than their fathers.
  D Only Michael Douglas is a better actor than his father.

3 What do they say about Arnold Schwarzenegger?
  A He takes his acting seriously.   C He is one of the best actors around.
  B He is a very popular actor.   D He is unattractive.

4 What does John say about Meryl Streep?
  A She is better than Katharine Hepburn.   C She is very adaptable.
  B She isn't as good as Katharine Hepburn.   D She is very dedicated.

B Opinions

Listen to part two of the discussion. The first time you listen, tick (√) the correct column to show who likes which actors.

	Jill	John	Ron	Gloria
Cary Grant				
Dustin Hoffman				
Robert de Niro				

As you listen for a second time, fill in the table below. Put a tick (√) if the quality is mentioned.

	Cary Grant	Dustin Hoffman	Robert de Niro
professional			
charismatic			
good at accents			
attractive			
dedicated			
good sense of humour			
versatile			

5 Over to you

1 Do you think acting is a natural talent or an acquired skill? Can it be inherited?
2 Why do children of famous people often follow their parents into the same kind of work? Does this just happen with famous people?

6 Move with the times

The people you have just been listening to were discussing whether film stars of the past were as good as those of the present. Write about 60 words comparing something else in the past and present. Here are some ideas: sports, fashion, politicians, comedians, buildings, popular music.

Grammar and practice

Question tags

A Listen to these examples of question tags from the listening.
1 Gloria   That was the one with Jack Lemmon, wasn't it?

2 Gloria   He's got a really good sense of humour too, hasn't he?

In which sentence is Gloria asking a question? In which sentence does she simply expect agreement? How do you know?

B Listening
1 Listen to the following sentences and decide if the speaker is asking a real question or expecting agreement. Put Q or A next to the sentences.
a You couldn't lend me a fiver, could you?
b It isn't 3 o' clock already, is it?
c He'll never pass his exams, will he?
d You can come tomorrow, can't you?
e Let's have a break, shall we?
f You know Jane, don't you?
2 Listen again. This time repeat the sentences after the speaker.

C Forming question tags
Look at the above examples. What are the rules for forming question tags?

D You are going to hear some incomplete sentences. The question tags are missing. Repeat the sentences after the speaker and add the missing question tags. Use falling intonation on all the tags.

Vocabulary

1 The senses

Vocabulary reference p.199

Complete the following sentences with one appropriate word connected with the senses. All of these words are in the Vocabulary reference on page 199.

1 The man's _____ was so bad that we almost had to shout to make ourselves understood.
2 Angela's _____ wasn't good enough to read the last line of the optician's chart.
3 Don't _____ that plate! It's very hot.
4 When you have a cold, you don't enjoy eating as you can't _____ your food.
5 The woman only caught a _____ of the thief as he ran away.
6 He cooks with garlic so often that his whole house _____ of it.
7 As a child, I was told that _____ at people was rude, and that I should look at them out of the corner of my eye.

2 Money

Vocabulary reference p.199

A All the missing words in the following sentences are connected with money. Choose the best word to fill the space from the four options given.

1 You can often find _____ in the sales.
   A bargains   B refunds   C prices   D rates
2 The service in the restaurant was so bad that they decided not to leave a _____ .
   A donation   B fine   C collection   D tip
3 James decided to _____ all the money he had in his account and close it.
   A withdraw   B purchase   C inherit   D borrow
4 With a small loan and his _____ he had just enough to pay the deposit on the new car.
   A saves   B budget   C savings   D income
5 Although we live in a fairly _____ society, there is still a lot of poverty.
   A wealth   B affluent   C poor   D mean
6 To become a member of the club, you have to pay a membership _____ of £10.
   A entry   B price   C sum   D fee
7 Mary has decided to ask her boss for a(n) _____ .
   A rise   B income   C credit   D wage
8 Keith was furious! The vase that he'd paid £100 for at the auction turned out to be _____ .
   A invaluable   B worthless   C priceless   D costly

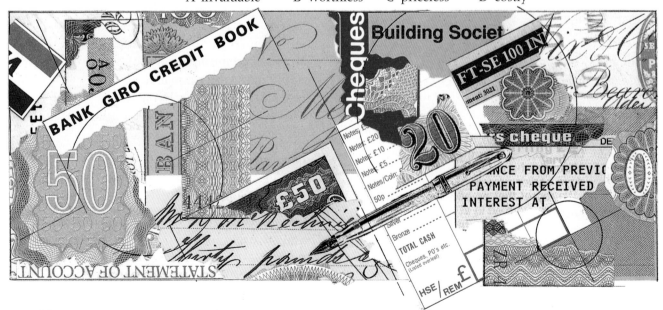

B Money quiz

1 Who gets a pension?
2 Who gives pocket-money?
3 Who gets a grant?
4 Who do people give tips to in your country?
5 Why might you have to pay a fine?
6 Why might you ask for a refund?
7 How can you pay for purchases?
8 What's the difference between a gross salary and a net salary?
9 Who pays a mortgage?
10 Who pays rent?

C Phrasal verbs

The phrasal verbs below can all be used when talking about money. Fill the spaces with an appropriate verb, making any necessary changes.

pay back	pay into	pay off	put down
put towards	run out	save up	take out

1 Every month Richard _____ a third of his salary _____ his deposit account and gives another third to his mother to pay for his keep.
2 Jill and Mike _____ to get married since their engagement last April.
3 If you _____ a deposit of £100, you can pay the rest in easy instalments.
4 Graham _____ a bank loan last week to pay for the extension to his house.
5 Don't lend Sharon any money. She never remembers _____ .
6 They hitch-hiked round the world and came back six months later when their money _____ .
7 My parents said they _____ £50 _____ the cost of the repair if I was prepared to pay the remainder myself.
8 He went bankrupt last year and _____ his debts for several years to come.

3 Word building

A There are several examples of adjectives which end in -al in the reading passage on page 126, for example *musical*. How many others can you find? Can you think of any other adjectives ending in -al?

B Other typical adjectival suffixes are: -ful, -ous, -less, -ed, -ish, -y. Give at least two examples of adjectives which fit in each category.

C Fill the gaps in these sentences with a word related to the word in capital letters.
1 He's quite _____ in many ways. He still plays with a rubber duck in the bath. CHILD
2 Richard is reasonably _____ that he'll get the job. CONFIDENCE
3 The new model has automatic windows and a more _____ engine. POWER
4 It was _____ of him to start smoking again after all this time. FOOL
5 He wouldn't have failed the exam if he hadn't made so many _____ mistakes. CARE
6 One of their daughters married a _____ businessman. WEALTH
7 She decided to have a siesta even though she was _____ to sleeping in the afternoon. CUSTOM
8 It is _____ to swim there because of the currents. DANGER
9 Although they have the same surname, they are not _____ . RELATE
10 It was the most _____ situation I've ever been in. EMBARRASS

Writing

The formal speech

In paper 2 of the exam you may be asked to write either an informal talk or a formal speech. Informal talks were covered in Unit 10. How many situations can you think of when you might be asked to make a formal speech?

1 The features of formal speeches

Formal speeches generally follow the pattern of introduction, followed by main message, then conclusion. Each of these sections includes some of the features listed below. What is included depends on the occasion, the purpose of the speech, and the audience.

1 The introduction could include opening remarks, welcome, thanks, information about yourself, reason for the speech.

2 The main message depends entirely on the subject of the speech. Personal feelings as well as factual information are often included here.

3 The conclusion can include the reason for the speech repeated, thanks, hand over to someone else.

2 Model

Read the following speech and note which of the features from 1 appear. The title of the composition is, *You have been asked to make a speech to introduce a famous former pupil who has been invited back to your school to open a new swimming pool.*

Ladies and gentlemen, let me introduce myself. My name is Emily Foster and I am captain of the school swimming team. As you all know, we are here this afternoon for the official opening of the new swimming pool. To do this we have a former pupil,
5 who I am sure needs no introduction from me, David Stigwood.

David Stigwood, as you know, is an accomplished film director and has made films both for television and the cinema. His best-known film is probably 'Night and Day', for which he was awarded an Oscar.
10 Mr Stigwood was a pupil here from 1960-67. During this time, he helped set up the film club, which, he will be pleased to know, still runs today.

Now all that remains for me to do is to thank Mr. Stigwood, on behalf of everyone here, for agreeing to come along this
15 afternoon to open the new pool. We know how busy he is and would just like to say how much we appreciate it. Ladies and gentlemen, please welcome David Stigwood.

3 Formal phrases

List the formal phrases Emily uses. What is each phrase used for? For example, *Ladies and gentlemen* is used to get the audience's attention and start the speech.

4 Think, plan, write

A popular teacher at your school is taking early retirement. Write the farewell speech that you will make to mark the occasion. (120–180 words)

A Look at the features of formal speeches. Decide which features you will need to include in your introductory and concluding remarks. Make a list.

B Think about what you are going to say in the main part of your speech, and make notes. It might help to base your speech on a person you know. These questions may give you some ideas.
How long has the teacher been at the school?
What subject does he or she teach?
Has the teacher ever taught you? For how many years?
What good qualities does the teacher have? Give examples.
How do you feel about the fact that the teacher is leaving? Why?
What are the teacher's future plans?

C Decide which of these ideas to include. Put them in the order in which you will mention them.

D Divide your notes into three or four paragraphs, and decide which of the formal phrases you will need to join your ideas together. Here are some other phrases:
Fellow pupils and members of staff   Today is a sad occasion
We are sorry   We hope   We wish you/him all the best in . . .

E Write the speech out in full, in correct, formal English.

Exam techniques

Letter expansion

1 Guidelines

Do	Don't
● Read the letter from beginning to end before starting to write.	▶ Don't do the sentences out of order. Start with the first and work through to the last.
● Check for punctuation to see if there are any question marks or exclamation marks.	▶ Don't assume that all the sentences will be statements.
● Underline all the verbs, then look for clues which indicate what tense to put the verbs in.	▶ Don't assume that you will be using the same tense throughout.
● Decide what kind of words are missing, e.g. articles, possessive adjectives, pronouns, relative pronouns and conjunctions.	▶ Don't add words except where there is a slash.
● If you don't know, make a sensible guess.	● Don't use contractions if it is a formal letter.

2 Practice

Try out the guidelines on the following letter. Use the clues and questions to help you decide what tense to put the verbs in.

Dear Mr Stigwood,

I be / headmaster / Bradham Grammar / you study / 1960–67.

a) _____

We just finish build / new swimming pool.

b) _____

I write / ask you if you perform / official opening.

c) _____

This be / Friday October 10th / three o'clock / afternoon.

d) _____

I not know if you be / Britain / date / whether you have time.

e) _____

I realize you be / extremely busy man / I be most grateful if you be able / attend.

f) _____

I look forward to hearing from you.

Yours sincerely,

Hugh Dobson.

a)	*be*	Is this his position now?
	study	What do the dates tell you?
b)	*finish*	What tense do we use with *just*?
	build	Does the infinitive or gerund follow *finish*?
c)	*write*	Is this action past or present?
	ask	What is the reason for the action?
	perform	What kind of sentence is this? It isn't a conditional.
d)	*be*	We use this tense to refer to events in the calendar.
e)	*know*	This verb can be used in only one of the present tenses. Which one? Remember to make it negative.
	be; have	See *perform*
f)	*realize*	Usually like *know*.
	be	The present, the future or the past?
	be able; attend	Which conditional is this?

12 Speculation

Follow that

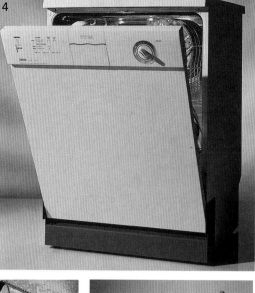

Introduction

gadget (colloq)
small mechanical
device or tool: *a new
gadget for opening
tin cans.*

appliance piece of
equipment for a
particular purpose
in the house, esp.
one that works by
electricity or gas.

A Read the dictionary definitions of *gadget* and *appliance*.
1 Look at the photos and decide which objects could be described as appliances,
   which as gadgets, and which as either appliances or gadgets.
2 What do you think the gadgets and appliances are used for?

B Read these three descriptions and try to match them with three of the objects
above. Would you buy any of them? Why? Why not?

▶ Make fuel from waste
paper – reuse your old
newspapers and paper
waste to produce fuel
briquettes. They are easy to
make, non-toxic, cost nothing
and burn steadily for up to
two hours. ■

▶ Forecast the weather
electronically with this sleek
and accurate digital
barometer which gives the
temperature, humidity, an
illustrated weather forecast,
barometic pressure trend
chart, plus alarm clock.
Requires 4 x AAA
batteries. ■

▶ This long reach flexible
torch is invaluable for seeing
clearly behind large
household appliances,
heavy furniture and in small
awkward areas for
maintenance and DIY.
Pocket clip gives hands-free
advantage. Requires
2 x 1.5v batteries. ■

C Points for discussion
1 What gadgets or appliances do you have, at home or at work, which you couldn't
   do without? What are they for?
2 Have you ever bought a gadget that didn't live up to your expectations, or one that
   was particularly useless? What was it, and why was it disappointing?

Listening

1 Think ahead

What special equipment do you need to pick up satellite television where you live? What difficulties might you have if you tried to install the system yourself?

2 Listening

You are going to hear part of a panel game called 'Follow That'. Did you think of the problem which is described?

3 Comprehension

A Read the questions below, then listen to 'Follow That' again. Choose the best answer or ending.

1 The rules of the game say that
   A you lose points for a wrong answer.
   B you have to answer as a team.
   C you can get five points for a correct answer.
   D you can't answer the other team's question.

2 Who is the central character in Anita's story?
   A Anita's husband   C a relative
   B a friend   D a neighbour

3 What happened the first time Eric went up the ladder?
   A He fixed the satellite dish.   C He dropped the satellite dish.
   B He fell off the ladder.   D He broke the ladder.

4 What was the TV reception like after Eric's second trip up the ladder?
   A They couldn't get a picture.   C They couldn't get a very good picture.
   B They couldn't get any sound.   D They couldn't get a picture or sound.

5 The final outcome of the story was that the satellite dish
   A burnt a table.   C caused an explosion.
   B fell off the wall.   D set a building on fire.

B Listening between the lines

1 Do you think they have different people on the team in this game every week? Give reasons for your answer.

2 Why did the presenter say to Nigel 'You might have to go for the next one on your own.'?

C Vocabulary

Match the words and phrases from the recording with their meanings.

1 The ladder was *wobbly*.
2 But it seems a bit obvious. There's probably *a catch*.
3 Your team is *in the lead*.
4 Eric isn't really bothered about doing things *properly*.
5 At a *crucial* point in the match . . .
6 Am I *on the right track*?
7 If you're going for *full marks* . . .
8 It must have been something *flammable*.

a maximum points
b hidden problem or difficulty
c easily set on fire
d not firm or steady, likely to move about
e correctly, in the right way
f getting the right idea
g winning
h very important

4 Over to you

A You are going to discuss the following question.
Which of these technological inventions has had the greatest effect on people's lives – the telephone, the computer or the television?
If you already have an opinion, jot down two or three ideas of how the invention has affected people's lives. Mention positive and negative effects.

B If you haven't got an opinion, use the following questions to help you decide.
1 How many people have one?
2 Where is it used?
3 What did people do before it was invented?
4 What has it enabled people to do that they couldn't do before?
5 How else has it changed people's lives?

C Get into groups with others who share your point of view. Together note down as many arguments supporting your opinion as you can.

D Split up into small discussion groups with someone in each group arguing for each invention. Try to convince the others of your point of view.

E Write about 80–100 words to sum up your point of view. The writing section in Unit 3, page 36, gives useful language for expressing opinions.

Grammar and practice

1 Certainties and possibilities

A Read these sentences from 'Follow That'.

1 The dish might have reflected the sun onto something in the other house.
2 Well, it can't have been anything solid, like a table, because the dish had only been up for an hour and a half.
3 It must have been something flammable and near the window.
4 It was net curtains at the window.

How certain is the speaker of each extract about what caused the fire? What structures or words helped you answer?

B Look at the sentences below which are also from 'Follow That'. In all of them the speakers show their attitude to what they are saying. Which:
a is fairly certain the idea is right?
b isn't sure about the idea?
c is fairly certain the idea is not right?

1 Could be anything, couldn't it? It could be a dishwasher.
2 There again, it might be a portable phone.
3 Well, if it wasn't a phone, it must be satellite television.
4 No, it can't be a dishwasher. They're quite old, aren't they?

C Read the extracts again and underline the words or structures which the speakers use to indicate their attitudes. Think of other words or structures you know which have similar meanings, for example, *maybe*.

2 Past, present or future?

A Read the following dialogues and decide whether speaker B is talking about a past, present or future event or situation. Which structure follows the modal verb in each case?

1 A I saw Joe in a new car the other day.
  B He must have sold his old one, then.
2 A I haven't seen Jenny for ages!
  B She might be studying. She's got exams soon.
3 A Isn't Mick coming?
  B He might come later.
4 A I'm starving!
  B So am I. It must be almost lunchtime.

B Now read the Grammar reference on pages 190–1.

3 Practice

Use an appropriate modal verb to rephrase the parts of the sentences in *italics*. The first one has been done for you.

Fiona I've seen Rachel out with another boy so *I'm pretty sure she isn't going out with Robert any more.* (1)

  . . . she can't be going out with Robert any more.

Pat I can't find John anywhere. Have you seen him?
Liz *Maybe he's in the canteen.* (2)
Pat No. I've looked there.
Liz Well, *perhaps he's gone home early.* (3) He sometimes does on Thursdays.

Linda It was an excellent meal. Steve's a good cook, isn't he? We had pork casserole for the main course and a lemony pudding for afters.
Bev *I'm quite sure it wasn't pork that you had.* (4) Steve's a vegetarian.

Douglas Maggie still isn't speaking to me. I sent her some flowers like you suggested.
Michael *Perhaps they haven't arrived yet.* (5)
Douglas No. *I'm sure she's got them.* (6) The shop promised they'd be delivered first thing.
Michael Well, if that's the case, *I guess she's still very angry.* (7)

Jack What's the time?
Bill Three o'clock.
Jack *That's impossible.* (8) I left the house at one!
Bill *Maybe your watch is slow.* (9)
Jack So it is. I forgot to take it off when I had a bath last night. *Water's probably got into it.* (10)

4 Picture discussion

Work with a partner. You are going to take turns to ask each other questions about the two photographs.

Photograph 1

Photograph 2

Student A

You are an oral examiner. Think of some questions to ask your partner. Start by asking questions on what is happening in the photograph and then ask some more general opinion questions about the subject. There are brief notes on the photograph and some general question ideas on page 174.

Student B

You are an FCE candidate. Spend a few minutes thinking about what is happening in photograph 1, then answer your partner's questions. Try to include some of the structures you have studied in this unit, for example *might be, can't have (done)*.

Now exchange roles and repeat the sequence of activities with photograph 2. There are brief notes on this photograph and some general question ideas on page 174.

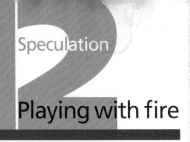

Living on the edge

Volcanic eruptions have been a fact of life since the earth first formed as a solid planet, and they have taken a huge toll of human life over the centuries. One of the earliest recorded
5 disasters was the Vesuvius eruption in AD 79 which buried the Italian city of Pompeii under ash, killing an estimated 16,000 people. The most violent eruption of modern times was in Krakatoa, Indonesia, in 1883 when more than
10 36,000 people were killed and debris was scattered across the Indian Ocean as far away as Madagascar, off the east coast of Africa.

There are about 500 active volcanoes in the world today, though it is always unsafe to
15 assume that any volcano is on the retired list. The types of eruption vary greatly. The simplest kind, found in Hawaii and Iceland, is a more or less continuous fountain of fire, sometimes reaching incredible heights. Next in order of
20 complexity are eruptions that follow the Stromboli* pattern, where the lava is less fluid

*__Stromboli__: a continuously active volcano off the northeast coast of Sicily

and the rate of eruption is not so high – from one every few seconds to one every couple of hours.
25 But even well-behaved volcanoes can turn nasty if water gets into them. It boils to produce steam and this increases explosive power. When a section of rain-sodden ground fell into Mount Etna in 1979, blocking the flow of
30 lava, pressure built up so much that when it was released the huge explosion killed nine tourists who were peering inside.

Even more dangerous is the *nuée ardente* – a burning cloud – which would kill anyone
35 caught in it almost instantly. It occurs in volcanoes where the lava is viscous and rich in gas. Pressure builds up gradually and imperceptibly, though towards the end a distinct swelling of the mountain may be
40 detected, as if it is getting ready to give birth. When the eruption finally happens, the gas is released like the fizz in a well-shaken bottle of champagne throwing out a mass of dust, ash and solid chunks of lava at speeds of up to 100
45 kmh and temperatures between 100 and 900 °C. The hot gases destroy the delicate tissues of the lungs, which can no longer absorb oxygen from the air. Death is by suffocation.

Studies by volcanologists show that there
50 is no real evidence of an accelerating pace in the number and frequency of eruptions, but

Introduction

1 What natural phenomena are shown in the pictures on these two pages?
2 What effect can these phenomena have on the landscape and on people's lives?

Reading

1 Think ahead

How many countries can you name where there are volcanoes? List them.

2 Reading

As you read the text for the first time, tick off any of the places which are on your list.

3 Points of view

1 Have you ever seen a volcano or a volcanic eruption? What was it like? How did you feel?
2 If you haven't seen one, would you like to? Why? Why not?

4 Comprehension

A Read the questions below then read the passage again. Choose the answer which you think fits best.

1 How do 'Stromboli' eruptions differ from 'Hawaiian' eruptions?
   A They are more spectacular.   C They are more dangerous.
   B They are less frequent.   D They are less complex.
2 If you were caught in a *nuée ardente* you would be killed by
   A flowing lava.   C flying pieces of lava.
   B poisonous gases.   D hot gases.

that increasing world populations mean that when a volcano does erupt, it may well affect more people. In fact, this is already happening. The eruption of Pinatubo, in the Philippines, in 1991 has affected the entire world population. More than a year after the eruption, a belt of ash and chemicals still circles the Equator at an altitude of about 20 miles, disrupting the ozone layer and the planet's climate.

Volcanologists also warn that we have yet to see the full capacity for devastation of a volcanic eruption in the modern world. If a major eruption were to occur in Japan, New Zealand or California, as is possible in the near future, we might be counting the dead in millions rather than tens of thousands, and looking at the destruction of a nation's economy and a serious destabilization of world power rather than the loss of a few billion pounds.

There are 15 capital cities in the world in a position to be wiped out or seriously damaged by volcanic eruptions. So why do people continue to live alongside them? Many are poor and have little choice, while others disregard the risk – which is, after all, rather less than smoking or driving a car. But it is the land around volcanoes which attracts people; the soils from volcanic ashes are light, easily worked, drain well and are full of plant nutrients. A light fall of ash, though it may destroy one year's crop, pays back in future years by the fertility it adds to the soil. Coffee in Colombia, vines in Italy, and rice in Japan are just a few of the crops that flourish on volcanic soils.

In Italy, New Zealand, the United States and Iceland the subterranean heat is used to generate electricity. And in many places, the ability of the lava flows to concentrate minerals makes them attractive to mining companies.

People will clearly not abandon the mountains that have played so large a part in the history of the Earth and its civilization, though some of them may one day wish they had. Although growing scientific understanding is helping to predict when a volcano may be about to erupt, we will never be certain.

3 Studies by volcanologists show that volcanic eruptions
  A are likely to happen more often in the future.
  B can have a serious effect on the environment.
  C will occur in Japan, New Zealand and California.
  D will destroy or damage many major cities.

4 Some people continue to live alongside volcanoes because
  A they don't realize how risky it is. C they can make their own electricity.
  B they enjoy taking risks.   D they can farm the land profitably.

B Reading between the lines
1 Why do you think it is always unsafe to assume that any volcano is 'on the retired list'? (line 15)
2 What do you think a 'well-behaved volcano' is? (line 25)

C Vocabulary
Rewrite the formal words and phrases in *italics* in informal English.
1 they have *taken a huge toll of human life* (line 3)
2 *an estimated* 16,000 people (line 7)
3 *the rate of eruption is not so high* (line 22)
4 *the entire world population* (line 56)
5 *in a position to* be wiped out (line 72)

5 Over to you
Environmental disasters are not all natural. What man-made environmental disasters are there? Choose one and discuss its causes and its effect on the environment. What can and should be done to prevent it happening?

Vocabulary

1 Science and the environment

Vocabulary reference p.199

Choose the best word to fill the spaces from the four alternatives given.

1 If we go on using up non-renewable _____ like coal and gas at the present rate, we will soon have none left.
   A products   B resources   C sources   D materials

2 Environmentalist groups like Greenpeace are concerned about the dumping of nuclear _____ at sea.
   A rubbish   B rest   C residue   D waste

3 Exhaust _____ from cars are one of the main causes of acid rain.
   A smoke   B waste   C fumes   D escapes

4 Scientists made the discovery after years of extensive _____ .
   A investigation   B searching   C research   D experiments

5 The main advantage of the _____ model is that it is very light and easy to carry around.
   A portable   B mobile   C movable   D moving

2 Word building

Look at the following sentence from the article on page 142. 'But even *well-behaved* volcanoes can turn nasty if water gets into them.' (line 25). *Well* can combine with past participles to form adjectives. Put a hyphen (-) between the two words.

attended
built
educated
informed
known
organized
paid
prepared
travelled

A Fill in the spaces in the sentences below with *well* and the appropriate past participle from the group on the left. There are more past participles than you need. Write sentences of your own with the past participles you haven't used.

1 The Olympic Games were very _____ . Everything went according to plan.
2 The charity concert was _____ . All 500 seats had been sold.
3 The film is based on a book by the _____ author, Graham Greene.
4 He reads several newspapers and watches all the current affairs programmes so he's very _____ .
5 She packed an umbrella and a couple of thick sweaters so as to be _____ for the British winter.

B How many of the past participles can combine with *badly* to give the opposite meaning? Do you know any other words that can combine with *well?*

3 Phrasal verbs

In 'Follow That', at the beginning of this unit, Anita said about her neighbour 'He was the first to get colour TV when that *came out.*' Here *come out* means to become available to the public. *Come* can be used with other particles to express other meanings. Try to work out the meanings of the following phrasal verbs from their contexts and explain them.

1 I *came across* some old family photographs while I was looking through some boxes in the cellar.
2 'Why don't you *come round* for a drink on Thursday?' Angela suggested.
3 When Jane heard the news, she fainted. When she *came round*, she didn't know where she was at first.
4 'I'm sorry but I won't be able to see you this evening after all,' Ian apologized. 'Something's *come up.*'
5 'I've *come up with* a brilliant plan. It can't fail.'

Grammar and practice

1 Wishes

A Form and use

Look at this sentence from the article on volcanoes.
  People will clearly not abandon the mountains,
  though some of them may one day *wish they had*.

The sentence could have been written as follows:
  Some of them may one day *wish they had left the
  mountains*.

Under what circumstances would people wish this and
why?

B We use *wish* to talk about situations we would like
to change but can't, either because they are in the past,
or because they are outside our control. Look at these
sentences. Match sentences 1, 2, and 3, with their
endings, 4, 5, and 6, and their uses, a, b, and c.

  1 I wish he would write more often,
  2 I wish he had written more often,
  3 I wish he wrote more often,

  4 but he didn't.
  5 but he doesn't.
  6 but he won't.

  a talking about a present situation
  b talking about a past situation
  c complaining about a present situation

C Check your answers with the Grammar reference
on page 191.

2 Practice

A Rewrite these sentences so that they have similar
meanings to the original sentence. Use *wish* in each
one.
1 I can't afford to go away this year.
2 You never clean the bath when you've finished.
3 Pete didn't remember to send Sally a Valentine card.
4 He's always dropping his socks on the floor!
5 It was a bad idea of yours to invite Darrell.
6 That cake looks lovely. Unfortunately, I'm on a diet.
7 They never listen when I talk to them!
8 It wasn't a good idea for us to come here.

B What do you think the people in the following
situations are thinking or saying? Think of as many
sentences as you can for each of them.
Example   1   *I wish I had been honest.*

Exam techniques

Guided writing

1 Introduction

You are going to read two students' notes and completed paragraphs. Before you begin, look back at the Guidelines in Unit 2 (page 24) to remind yourself of a recommended procedure. Then read through these instructions and information which the students were given.

2 The exam task

Read the following information about the proposed building of an airport on the Caribbean island of St Dominique. Using the information given, continue each of the four paragraphs below in about 60 words each. Give reasons for your answers and use your own words as much as possible.

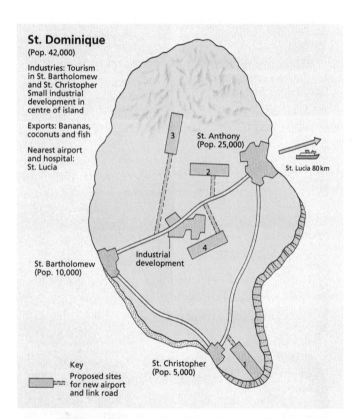

St. Dominique
(Pop. 42,000)

Industries: Tourism in St. Bartholomew and St. Christopher Small industrial development in centre of island

Exports: Bananas, coconuts and fish

Nearest airport and hospital: St. Lucia

St. Anthony (Pop. 25,000)

St. Lucia 80 km

Industrial development

St. Bartholomew (Pop. 10,000)

St. Christopher (Pop. 5,000)

Key
Proposed sites for new airport and link road

St Dominique is one of several retreats popular with the jet set of Europe and the United States. Its beautiful beaches and tropical climate have made it a popular playground with the rich and famous who want to keep out of the public eye. But plans to build an airport on the island may soon change all that. At present it is only accessible by boat. An airport would open it up to package holiday-makers from all over the world. There is concern among some islanders that the jet-setters will pull out. Several residences are already up for sale.

> I wish to protest about the forthcoming plans to build a new airport on the island. No matter where it is situated, we will all be deafened by the noise of aeroplanes landing and taking off!

> It is stupid to assume that the proposed new airport will necessarily mean more jobs for local people. How many local people are trained to work in construction? How many are trained to work as airport personnel? There will be fewer jobs once the ferry service goes out of business.

> Yes, yes, yes to the new airport. More tourists will mean more money, for everyone!

> The fact that the airport company has said that it is willing to pay 75% of the construction and running costs of an accident and emergency hospital is a good enough reason for us to say YES. We need our own hospital!

1 The benefits of an airport would be . . .
2 The disadvantages of an airport would be . . .
3 I think that if they decide to build an airport the best site would be . . . because . . .
4 I don't think it would be a good idea to build the airport at site . . . because . . .

3 Analysis

A Read this student's notes and the completed first paragraph. Decide whether the notes are appropriate and whether the paragraph is a good answer. The questions below will help you to decide. Put a tick (√) or a cross (✗) next to each of the questions. If you put a cross, say what is wrong and show how it can be improved.

The notes

1 Are the notes in note form?
2 Are the notes relevant?
3 Is the information organized?

The paragraph

1 Is the information relevant?
2 Is supporting information given?
3 Is the answer written mainly in the student's own words?
4 Is the answer the correct length?

1 Now: tourists fly → St Lucia then boat 2 hours → St Dominique. Airport = more accessible, more tourists = more money
2 Now: no hospital. Patients → St. Lucia. Air Company pay 75%

1 The benefits of an airport would be . . .

that it would make it much easier for tourists to get to the island. Easier access should mean an increase in tourist numbers, which should, in turn, mean increased income. Another benefit is that it would make the building of a new hospital more likely since the airport company would pay 75% of the building and running costs.

B Follow the same procedure for this student's notes and second paragraph.

Notes: It would be very noisy because no matter where it is situated, everyone will be deafened by the noise of aeroplanes landing and taking off. Famous people - probably film stars and rock stars - go there on holiday who want to keep out of the public eye.

2 The disadvantages of an airport would be . . .

it would be very noisy because no matter where it is situated, everyone will be deafened by the noise of aeroplanes landing and taking off. A lot of rich and famous people go to the island and they will probably want to leave because they want to keep out of the public eye. They wouldn't want to go to the island if there were a lot of package holiday-makers there from all over Europe and the States and some of them have already put their houses up for sale. I think this is because they are worried about the airport. Even if more tourists came in, there wouldn't be any more if some of them left.

4 Practice

You are going to complete paragraphs 3 and 4.

A Before you begin, re-read the information on the previous page.

B Make brief notes for and against each of the four sites.

C Make your choice of answer (remember that there is no right or wrong answer) and choose two or three good reasons to support it. Begin your paragraphs with the words given.

D When you have finished, check what you have written by working through the questions in 3A above.

Writing

Checking your composition

1 Answering the question

A Read this student's answer to the following First Certificate composition title. *In what ways is pollution affecting the environment? What can be done about this?* As you read it, decide if it answers the question or not. If you think it doesn't, say how.

> The issue environmental that are worrying me most is the pollution of the sea. I think that the pictures we saw recently on the TV news while Easter holidays, are still excist in our minds;
> 5 the huge ecological desaster of sea's vital and natural resources caused by leak of petrol-oil from a big tankers. Considering that every day a big part of sea are destroyed from similar accidents which occured all over the world we
> 10 could have estimate that in a half of century there will be no part of the sea without pollution. As a result fishes which are one of the healthier foods will be unsuitable for people. Furthermore many kinds of sea's vital and natural resources
> 15 will dissapear, people won't be able to swim and entertain themselves at sea and so on… Some possible solutions of this disasters are:
> 1) Harder control to ships, wich carry dangerous cargos.
> 20 2) All factories must clean their waste which are near the sea.
> 3) Investigation must be done by scientists in order of finding ways to clean the already polluted parts.

B If you don't answer the question, you will not get many marks – no matter how good your English is. Can you think of a title which the composition does answer?

2 Editing

You can train yourself to check for likely mistakes. Here is a list of some of the things you should check when you are looking through your compositions.

1 Layout
   Is the layout correct? Have you used paragraphs appropriately?

2 Punctuation
   Have you used the correct punctuation?

3 Grammar
   Do the verbs agree with their subjects? e.g. People *are* clever.
   Have you used articles (*the*, *a*, and *an*) correctly? Do demonstrative adjectives agree with their nouns? e.g. *these* problems
   Is the word order correct?

4 Verb tenses
   Have you used the correct tense? Is the choice of tense consistent?

5 Register
   Have you used the correct register, e.g. no contractions or colloquialisms in formal writing?

6 Linkers and markers
   Have you joined information together with appropriate words, e.g. *because*, and made use of relative clauses? Have you introduced ideas with appropriate markers? e.g. *one advantage is*

7 Vocabulary
   Have you used the right word?

8 Spelling
   Is your spelling correct?

3 Practice

Find one mistake in the composition for each category in 2, and correct them.

R3 Revision

This section gives you extra practice in the grammar and vocabulary covered in Units 9–12. Before you begin, remind yourself of this language by reading the Grammar reference notes on pages 187–191 and the Vocabulary reference on pages 198–199. This is not a test so you should refer to Units 9–12 and the reference sections as you work through these exercises.

1 Vocabulary multiple-choice

Before you begin, look back at the Exam techniques section on pages 110–111, which gives you advice on answering vocabulary multiple-choice questions. Then choose the word or phrase which best completes each sentence. Look up any words you don't know when you've finished.

1 The restaurants on the island are expensive, so it's worth _____ a packed lunch.
   A take   B to take   C taking   D taken
2 If I were you, _____ phone and tell her you're going to be late.
   A I'd   B I'll   C I'd have   D I
3 I'm really looking forward _____ to university.
   A to go   B going   C to going   D go
4 The evening with my old school friends brought _____ a lot of happy memories.
   A up   B in   C round   D back
5 You look terribly tired. You really _____ to get more sleep.
   A should   B ought   C must   D could
6 You'd better stop spending money, _____ you'll end up in debt.
   A if   B in case   C otherwise   D unless
7 When I was twelve my parents _____ me stay out until midnight.
   A allowed   B left   C told   D let
8 I'm afraid you're not _____ to take your driving test. You'll have to wait until you're 17.
   A old enough   C very old
   B too old   D enough old
9 What's London like these days? I haven't been there _____ .
   A late   B lately   C later   D latest

10 You _____ put the car in the garage. I'm going out in it later.
   A mustn't   B can't   C haven't   D needn't
11 I can't come out this evening, I've got to look _____ my baby brother.
   A after   B up to   C into   D over
12 My brother didn't telephone while I was out, _____ ?
   A has he   C didn't he
   B did he   D hasn't he
13 When my teacher gave me my homework back, she said I was on the right _____ .
   A course   B way   C direction   D track
14 I've never been very good _____ with money.
   A at dealing   C deal
   B to deal   D for dealing
15 I really enjoy being with my Dad. He's got a really good _____ of humour.
   A way   B feeling   C mood   D sense
16 I'm going to the USA for my holidays. I've been _____ for nearly a year now.
   A investing   C spending
   B earning   D saving up
17 She _____ be a doctor. She doesn't look old enough.
   A mustn't   B shouldn't   C can't   D needn't
18 I'm really tired this morning. I wish I _____ to bed so late last night.
   A hadn't gone   C haven't been
   B didn't go   D don't go
19 Tobacco companies are always coming _____ new ways of persuading people to smoke.
   A out with   C in with
   B up with   D up against
20 That's the first accident you've ever had, _____ ?
   A wasn't it   C isn't it
   B haven't you   D is it

2 Gap filling

Look back at the Exam techniques section on pages 30–31 to remind yourself how to work through gap filling exercises. Then fill each gap with one word.

Britain's most inventive police force has recently introduced a new secret weapon – a fleet of cardboard cut-out patrol cars.

The imitation cars, _____(1) will be cunningly positioned in lay-bys or on bridges, are designed _____(2) frighten speeding motorists into slowing _____(3).

At a cost of £375, _____(4) to £28,000 for the real thing, each car consists _____(5) a thin rainproof sandwich of vinyl-covered card, complete _____(6) all the authentic markings of a real patrol car – including the fluorescent orange stripe along each side.

The Northumberland police force are well-prepared to cope _____(7) a barrage of sarcastic comments from the public. They plan to remind people _____(8) the highly successful fake police officers which have been used now for a _____(9) of years in the area. These _____(10) reduced crime and _____(11) money.

'Initially, this project may provoke a humorous response,' said Chief Superintendent Bob Bensley. 'But we are very optimistic that the cars _____(12) turn out to be a serious and low-cost resource in our campaign _____(13) cut speed and reduce casualties.

Motorists' organizations have welcomed the police initiative, though _____(14) spokesman for the RAC said, 'At the _____(15) of the day, you can't beat a real police car with a real policeman _____(16) the wheel.'

Of course the police realize _____(17) and in fact the imitation cars will not be _____(18) harmless as they might seem. 'There will always be real police officers near each fake,' said Mr Bensley. 'They'll be equipped _____(19) hand-held detection devices, so that if drivers speed up again, they _____(20) be caught.'

RAC = Royal Automobile Club

3 Transformations

Before you begin, look back at the Exam techniques section on pages 80–81, which gives advice on how to do transformations. Then complete each unfinished sentence so that it means the same as the sentence printed before it.

1 I think you should tell the police about the accident you saw yesterday morning.
   If I _____

2 Maybe John's working this weekend.
   John _____

3 I'm really sorry Andrew isn't coming to my party at the weekend.
   I wish _____

4 Riding a bicycle along a pavement is against the law.
   You _____

5 There's no need for you to worry about money. I've got plenty.
   You _____

6 In Spain, it's compulsory to stay at school until you're 16.
   You aren't _____

7 Unfortunately, Nick was too short to be a good basketball player.
   Unfortunately, Nick wasn't _____

8 I can't tell lies very well.
   I'm not very good _____

9 I've never managed to learn to speak a language fluently.
   I've never succeeded _____

10 I'm sure Alison made the announcement. I recognized her voice.
   It must _____

4 Word building

Use the word in capitals at the end of each of these sentences to form a word that fits in the blank space.

1 When Bill and Jean retire, they're planning to spend all their _____ on a Mediterranean holiday. SAVE

2 Third time lucky! After two _____ attempts, Mark's finally passed his driving test. SUCCESS

3 They're an incredibly _____ family. You should see how much food they throw away. WASTE

4 You shouldn't leave _____ things on car seats in full view of people walking past. VALUE

5 I've never had the same opinions as my father. In fact when I was younger we were always having _____ . AGREE

You are now ready to do Progress test 3.

13 Points of view

A burning issue

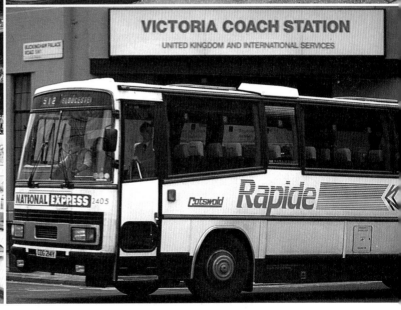

Introduction

A In Britain you are not supposed to smoke in any of the places in the photos. In which places is smoking allowed in your country? In which places is it prohibited? Do you think people should be allowed to smoke wherever they want to?

B What is passive smoking? Do you think it's a health hazard?

C What are the disadvantages of smoking?

Listening

1 Think ahead

1 Which sporting events in your country are sponsored by tobacco companies? Why do tobacco companies use sport for advertising?
2 Should they be forbidden to do this? Why?
3 Make a list of as many arguments as you can against cigarette advertising in general.

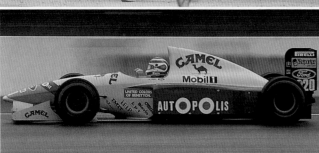

2 Listening

You are going to hear an extract from a radio programme on cigarette advertising. As you listen for the first time, see how many of the ideas on your list are mentioned. Tick them as you hear them.

3 Points of view

Which of the opinions that you heard do you agree with?

4 Comprehension

A Read the statements below, then listen to the broadcast again and decide if they are true or false. Correct the statements which are false.

1 The UK government doesn't support a ban on tobacco advertising.
2 Tobacco companies spend £100 million a year on advertising their products.
3 In the UK, more than 300 people die every day from lung cancer.
4 Christopher Mitchell thinks government health warnings on cigarette packets are ineffective.
5 Shopkeepers in the UK are permitted to sell cigarettes to children under 16.
6 Mark Smith thinks that advertising has no effect on the number of people who smoke.
7 Wendy Johnson thinks people should be able to choose whether or not they smoke.
8 Gordon Jackson is suffering from the effects of smoking.

B Listening between the lines

1 Christopher Mitchell says that he would like to see the government come down harder on shopkeepers who sell cigarettes to children under 16. What do you think happens to shopkeepers who break the law at the moment?

2 Andrew Green says 'You don't see athletes or footballers smoking, do you?' What point is he making?

3 Do you think 'Smokebusters' is a good name for Richard Wells' anti-smoking group? What information would you expect to receive from 'Smokebusters' if you joined?

C Vocabulary

Read these extracts from the programme. Match the words or phrases in *italics* with one of the meanings.

1 Today's biggest cause of *preventable* death and disease is cigarette smoking.

2 Young people are particularly *vulnerable*.

3 It makes young people think smoking is fashionable and the *hip* thing to do.

4 Your clothes all *stink* of it.

5 The government should *take the lead* in persuading people not to smoke.

6 He says he is *sick to death* of people telling him what to do.

7 I think that's *taking it a bit far*.

a go beyond the limits of what is considered reasonable

b can be stopped from happening

c modern, fashionable (informal)

d have an extremely unpleasant smell

e set a good example for others to follow

f unprotected or weak, and therefore easily influenced

g very angry or very bored with something

5 Over to you

A You are going to debate the following question.

Do you agree that the government should take the lead in persuading people not to smoke, or do you think that people should be allowed to choose for themselves whether they smoke or not?
Decide which point of view you support, and get into a group with other people who have a similar opinion to you.

B With the group, make a list of ideas you could use to support your opinion. Here are two ideas to start you off. Which of them supports your view?

• Advertising doesn't make people start smoking. It only influences which brand they smoke.

• Governments have a moral responsibility to protect people, and young people in particular need guidance.

C Now debate the question as a whole class. Each person in each group should talk about one point on the group's list, and be prepared to defend the point.

D Has the debate changed your mind? Write 80–100 words expressing your opinion and backing it up with what you think are the most important arguments. The Writing section in Unit 3 (page 36) gives useful language for expressing opinions.

Grammar and practice

1 Reported speech

A Look at these extracts from the programme.

1 I really don't think the government is doing enough. Some of my friends started smoking at the age of 8!

2 Christopher Mitchell said that he didn't think the government was doing enough and that some of his friends had started smoking at the age of 8.

What usually happens to verb tenses in reported speech? What other changes might we need to make when we report what someone has said?

B Read section 3 in the Grammar reference on page 192 before you do the practice exercise.

C Practice

Report these statements made by the other people on the programme.

1 'I get really angry when I go to sports grounds and see advertising hoardings promoting tobacco.' (Andrew Green)

2 'The government should support the ban but it doesn't because it gets a lot of money from the sale of cigarettes.' (Katie Braithwaite)

3 'I support a ban on tobacco advertising though I'm not convinced it will change people's attitudes towards smoking.' (Wendy Johnson)

4 'It's my body and I can do what I like with it.' (Gordon Jackson)

2 Reported questions

A Look at these sentences.

1 a 'Do you think the government should be supporting the call to ban tobacco advertising?'

  b The presenter asked the listeners if they thought the government should be supporting the call to ban tobacco advertising.

2 a 'Why doesn't the government put a stop to the sale of tobacco altogether?'

  b David Snow asked why the government didn't put a stop to the sale of tobacco altogether.

What other changes (apart from changes in verb tenses) need to be made when we report questions? When do we use *if* in reported questions? What other word could be used instead of *if* in the first sentence?

B Check your answers in section 4 in the Grammar reference on page 192.

C Practice

Report the following questions.

1 'Have you got a light?' the girl asked him.

2 'Do you smoke?' Val asked Rob.

3 'How long has Chris been smoking?' Nick asked me.

4 'Why did you start smoking, Sharon?' Rachel asked.

5 'Would you like to give up?' Julie asked Tim.

3 Changing references

A Time references

Look at this sentence.

  'I'll see you *tomorrow*,' Lizzie told Graham.

We usually report it like this:

  Lizzie told Graham she would see him *the next day*.

However, we can sometimes report it like this:

  Lizzie told Graham she would see him *tomorrow*.

When do we need to change the time reference and when can we keep the same time reference? How would we usually report the following time references?

next week	tomorrow	next month	yesterday
last week	today	three days ago	

B Other references

Read these pairs of sentences and answer the question.

1 a 'Do you think this meat is all right?' Terry asked his wife.

  b Terry asked his wife if she thought the meat was all right.

2 a 'Shall we eat here?' Carol asked Denise.

  b Carol asked Denise if they should eat there.

What other references may have to change when we report speech?

C Read sections C and D in the Grammar reference on page 192 before you do the practice exercise.

D Practice

Put the following sentences into reported speech, making all the necessary changes.

1 'Does this work have to be finished today, Mr. Hunt?' Marsha asked.

2 'Were there any phone calls for me yesterday?' asked Mr Gilbert.

3 'This car was used in a robbery two weeks ago,' the police officer informed Ian.

4 'I wrote to her last week and I phoned this morning,' Dorothy said.

5 'I've arranged to meet them after lunch tomorrow,' Matthew said.

E No change in tense

Look at these sentences.

1 'I'm still fit and healthy.' (Gordon Jackson)
2 Gordon Jackson says that he is still fit and healthy.
3 Gordon Jackson said that he is still fit and healthy.

Sentences 2 and 3 both report Gordon Jackson's comment. Can you think why *be* is in the present tense and not in the past tense in each case? Check your answer in section 3B in the Grammar reference on page 192.

4 Reported functions

A Look at the following sentences.

1 She suggested { talking it over. / (that) they (should) talk it over.
2 She told Bob she was leaving the next day.
3 She told Bob to leave her alone.
4 She asked Bob why he had done it.
5 She asked Bob to leave his keys.
6 She warned Bob not to try and get in touch.
7 Alan advised Bob to try and forget her.

Why is the structure after *tell* different in sentences 2 and 3? Why is the structure after *ask* different in sentences 4 and 5? What structure is used after the verbs *advise*, *warn* and *suggest*?

B Write all the above sentences in direct speech.

C Practice

Complete the following sentences so that they mean the same as the original.

1 'Let's go somewhere new on holiday next year.'
   Mary suggested we _____ .
2 'Don't swim here! There are some dangerous currents.'
   The man warned _____ .
3 'Do you think you could speak a bit louder?' the woman asked the guide.
   The woman asked _____ .
4 'Don't ever do that again!' Sam's mother warned.
   Sam's mother warned _____ .
5 'I wouldn't buy Dave a book if I were you. Why don't you get him a CD instead?'
   Laura advised me _____ .
6 'Stop talking, Claire, and take that chewing gum out of your mouth!' the teacher said.
   The teacher _____ .

5 Fluency

Work with a partner. Act out two of the situations below, taking it in turns to play the role of the police officer and the member of the public. The member of the public should explain what happened, while the police officer should ask questions and make notes. After you have both had a turn as a police officer, write up a report of the questions you asked and the explanations you received.

1 You have lost the keys to your car and are trying to get into it. A police officer sees you. You have no identification on you.
2 You have found a wallet containing £200 in £10 notes. You decide to keep the money but when you try to buy something with it in a shop, you are told that the notes are forgeries. The police are called.
3 A very pleasant man you met at the airport asked you to post a parcel for him when you got to Miami. You agreed. On arrival at Miami Airport, you are searched by customs officers. The parcel is found to contain two kilos of cocaine. The police are called.

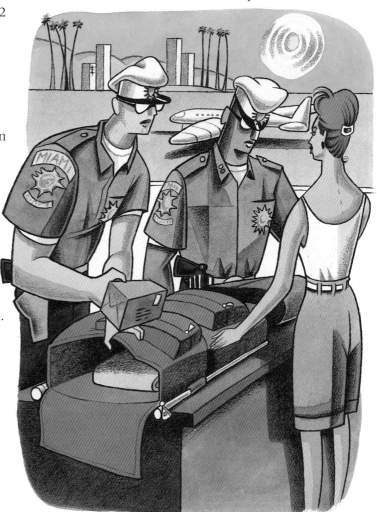

An eye for an eye

Introduction

What message is this poster trying to get across?

Reading

1 Think ahead

What is capital punishment? Do you know which countries have capital punishment? Why do you think they have it? Which countries do not have capital punishment? Why don't they?

2 Reading

As you read the article, check to see if your answers to Think ahead are mentioned, and whether you were right.

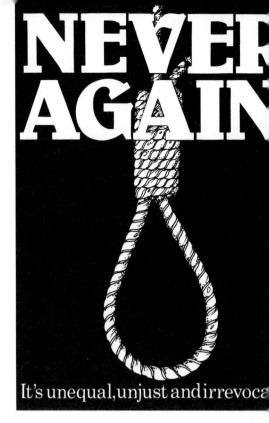

NEVER AGAIN

It's unequal, unjust and irrevoca

THE HANGMAN'S ROPE

The electric chair, the hangman's rope, the guillotine. The debate on capital punishment divides people in Britain very neatly into two groups; those for and those against, because this issue is all black and white; there is no grey area.

Did you know?

In the USA, where over 85% of the population over the age of 21 approve of the death penalty, juveniles and 'mentally deficient' people can be executed. In the many states which still have the death penalty, some use the electric chair, which can take up to 20 minutes to kill, while others use gas or lethal injections.

In Britain, capital punishment lasted until 1965, when it was abolished by Parliament. There have been 14 attempts since then to reintroduce it – all unsuccessful.

FOR

The pro-hanging lobby uses four main arguments to support its call for the reintroduction of capital punishment. First there is the deterrence theory, which states that potential murderers would think twice before committing the act if they knew that they might also die if they were caught. The armed bank robber might, likewise, decide to leave his sawn-off shotgun at home and go back to being an ordinary robber.

Next is the idea of public security. If the death penalty were reinstated, it would mean that a convicted murderer would not be set free after serving 20 years or less of a life sentence and be able to go on to murder again. The general public would, therefore, be safer.

The other two arguments are more suspect. The idea of retribution demands that criminals should get what they deserve: if a murderer intentionally sets out to commit a crime, he should accept the consequences. Retribution, which is just another word for revenge, is supported by the religious doctrine of an eye for an eye and a tooth for a tooth.

The fourth main pro-hanging argument is the most cold-blooded. It is that it makes economic sense to hang convicted murderers rather than have them in prison wasting taxpayers' money.

AGAINST

The arguments against the death penalty are largely humanitarian. But there are also statistical reasons for opposing it: the deterrence figures do not add up. In Britain, 1903 was the record year for executions and yet in 1904 the number of homicides actually rose. 1946 also saw an unusually high number of executions followed in 1947 by another rise in the murder rate. If the deterrence theory was correct, the rate should have fallen.

The second main argument against reintroducing capital punishment is that innocent people are sometimes wrongly convicted and, while people can be released from prison, they cannot be brought back from the dead if they have been hanged.

The other reasons to oppose the death penalty, which are largely a matter of individual conscience and belief, are firstly that murder is murder and this includes state executions. The state has no more right to take a life than the individual. Indeed, the state should set an example to the individual by not taking lives. It is believed to be a measure of its civilization that a state acts more humanely than its citizens. The second is that Christianity preaches forgiveness, not revenge.

3 Points of view   Which of the arguments do you agree with?

4 Comprehension   **A** Read the questions below, then read the article again and choose the best answers.

1 What is the situation regarding capital punishment in the USA?
   A Most Americans are against capital punishment.
   B Only people over 21 can be executed.
   C Not all states have the death penalty.
   D Some prisoners can choose their form of execution.

2 How do people in Britain feel about capital punishment?
   A People either approve or disapprove.
   B People are unsure how they feel.
   C Half are for and half are against.
   D Black people feel differently from white people.

3 Those who are in favour of capital punishment argue that if it were brought back
   A fewer crimes would be committed.
   B people would be less likely to commit murder.
   C there would be fewer bank robberies.
   D criminals would stop using weapons.

4 What do the statistics show?
   A There were more executions in Britain in 1946 than in any other year.
   B In 1903 there were more executions in Britain than in any other country.
   C The death penalty does not appear to deter potential murderers.
   D The death penalty has proved to be an effective deterrent.

B Reading between the lines
1 Which form of capital punishment does the author appear to find the most barbaric? Justify your answer.
2 'There have been 14 attempts since then to reintroduce it – all unsuccessful.' (line 18) What does this tell us about British politicians' views on hanging?
3 What do you think an 'ordinary' robber is?

C Vocabulary
Choose the best meaning for the words in *italics* from the text.

1 a *convicted* murderer (line 33)
   A determined
   B declared guilty by a jury
   C one who has committed murder before

2 The other two arguments are more *suspect*. (line 37)
   A questionable   B understandable   C justifiable

3 The fourth pro-hanging argument is the most *cold-blooded*. (line 45)
   A convincing   B controversial   C unfeeling

4 The arguments against the death penalty are *largely* humanitarian. (line 50)
   A mainly   B especially   C also

5 Over to you   1 Do you think the role of prison should be to punish or to reform criminals?
2 What changes would you make to the system of dealing with criminals in your country?

Writing

The opinion composition

1 Opinion or discussion?

In Paper 2 you are sometimes asked to write a composition expressing your opinion of a statement. This question is different from the *advantages and disadvantages* question in which you have to examine an argument from both sides. In the *opinion* question, you have to decide if you agree or disagree with a statement and back up your opinion with supporting arguments.

2 Models

Read the following model answers to this question.

Some people think that zoos are out-of-date and cruel institutions that should be closed down. Do you agree?

How many arguments do the writers put forward in support of their opinions?

a
I do not agree that zoos are out-of-date and cruel
institutions or that they should be closed down.
  In the first place, <u>zoos are obviously</u>
<u>educational</u>. While children today can learn a lot
5 about wild animals from nature books and
natural history programmes on television, this
is not the same as actually seeing an animal.
You cannot get a feeling of the massive beauty
of an elephant from pictures in a book or images
10 on a television screen.
  What is more, zoos are important centres of
conservation and breeding. Without zoos, many
species would have become extinct. However,
as a result of zoo breeding programmes, many
species can now be returned to their native lands.
15 Although some people argue that it is cruel
to keep animals in zoos, this is not the case.
Generally, zoos have modern buildings and
animals are well cared for in enclosures which
are clean and spacious.
20 In my view, zoos perform a useful and
necessary role in today's society and should
not be closed down.

b
I agree that zoos are out-of-date and
cruel institutions and that they should be
closed down.
  When the first zoos were opened, their
5 main purpose was educational. They gave
people a unique opportunity to see wildlife.
Nowadays, with television and modern
photographic techniques, this educational role
is no longer important. People can learn
10 about wild animals from natural history
programmes on television and magazines.
They do not need to visit zoos.
  However, the main reason I am against
zoos is that I believe it is cruel to keep
15 wild animals in captivity. Many animals are
kept in cages or enclosures which are too
small for them and suffer obvious distress. This
can result in boredom and aggressive behaviour.
  In addition, many animals' lifestyles are
20 turned upside-down. Animals which normally
hunt for their food are fed, and most have
to live in a climate very different from that
of their natural habitat.
  To conclude, zoos have no place in
25 modern-day society.

3 Analysis

A For each composition, underline the writer's main points. The first one has been done for you. What is the function of the rest of the paragraph?

B In composition **a** the writer makes a statement which doesn't support his or her own opinion and then says why it is wrong. Identify this statement. Why are arguments sometimes presented in this way?

C Make a list of the words and phrases which:
a   emphasize that we are reading the writer's opinion.
b   have the following functions: to introduce and sequence arguments; to introduce additional or contrasting information; to summarize.
What other words and phrases can you add to each list?

D Check your ideas in the Writing section on pages 22 and 36.

4 Think, plan, write

You are going to write 120–180 words in answer to the following question.
Parents should never use corporal punishment on their children. Do you agree?

A If you already have an opinion, note down arguments that support it. If you don't, these questions may help you to form an opinion.
1   What methods of corporal punishment are there? Do you feel the same about all of them?
2   Were you ever hit by your parents? Why did they hit you? Was it an effective punishment?
3   What other forms of punishment can parents use? Are these preferable?
4   Do you think that corporal punishment can have any long-term effects on a child?
Exchange ideas with other students and make a note of any interesting new ideas.

B Make a final decision on whether you wholly support the opinion or not, or whether you support it with reservations. Choose two or three of your strongest arguments and think of details to back them up. Write your notes in the correct order for the composition and group them into paragraphs.

C Expand your notes into a full composition.
1   State your opinion clearly in your opening sentences but do not overuse personal opinion words.
2   Introduce each argument with appropriate expressions and follow up your arguments with supporting points. This section can be one paragraph or more.
3   Write your conclusion. It is a good idea to repeat the opinion you expressed in your introductory paragraph but using different words.
Read through your composition to make sure your opinions and arguments are clear, then check grammar, spelling and punctuation.

Exam techniques

Discussing short texts

1 Guidelines

Do	Don't
• Read quickly through the texts the examiner has asked you to read.	▶ Don't read the texts too slowly; you will not have time for a detailed reading.
• As you are reading, look for clues about what kind of text it is.	▶ Don't worry if you can't identify it immediately.
• Answer the examiner's questions as fully as possible. The examiner wants to know how well you express yourself in English not whether you can get all the answers right.	▶ Don't give short answers. If you are not sure of the answer, express your opinion with words and expressions like *I'm not sure, but . . . I think*, etc.

2 Talking about a text

In the oral interview you will be asked to read and discuss a short text which is usually related to the topic of a photograph you have just been talking about. Before you practise this, work through these general questions with a partner.

A What is the text about?

Look for vocabulary clues. What do you think a text containing the words frying pan, beat, eggs, and oil might be about?

B Would you read or hear the text?

1 List all the different types of written text you can think of, e.g. book (travel, cookery, etc.).
2 List the different types of speech you can hear, e.g. part of a conversation.
3 Which of the types you listed in 1 and 2 will be in formal English and which will be in informal English?

C Where is it from?

Look for tense clues. What tenses are common in:

a news reports?
b instruction manuals and cookery books?
c sports commentaries?
d weather forecasts?

D Who is the speaker or writer?

Where does the text come from? If it comes from a cookery book, the writer is probably a cook or chef. Look for pronoun clues, e.g. 'I', which can help identify who is speaking, though you will need to look for other clues, too. What clues might tell us whether 'I' was a man or a woman, a boy or a girl?

E Who would hear or read it?

Who might read:

a a travel brochure?
b a complaint about a holiday?
c an apology for not being able to attend a wedding?

Who might hear:
d a complaint about the service in a restaurant?
e instructions on how to start a car?
f a rail announcement?

3 Practice

Do the following activities with a partner, taking it in turns to be the oral examiner.

A Describe the photos below.

B Now go on to ask some other related questions. Here are some ideas to start you off.

Photo 1   Have you ever had a pet? Which animals do you think make the best and worst pets? Why?

Photo 2   Why do you think animals are kept in conditions like these? How do you feel about it?

C Discuss the texts using questions A–E in 2 and the Guidelines to help you. Justify your opinions wherever possible.

D Match each photo with the text it goes best with. What differences and similarities are there between the photos and the texts?

a It provides an attractive setting for animals as close as possible to their natural habitat. The windows ensure good vision for the public, and the 6-metre-high security mesh over the top of the enclosure allows the cats to climb as in the wild without endangering themselves or the public.

b It's not fair. Andrew's got one. Why can't we have one? Please. I'll look after it. I promise. You won't have to do a thing! I can take it out when I get home. Go on! It won't be expensive – not if we get a small one – they don't eat a lot. Oh, please, can we?

c The UK has around 30 million egg-laying hens. Eighty-five per cent of these hens are housed in battery cages which are made of thin wire mesh with a sloping mesh floor – there is no comfort for the hens. Each cage measures 50 cm x 50 cm and houses up to five birds. Current European Community legislation allows each bird a minimum living space of 450cm^2, less than the size of an A4 sheet of paper. Scientific research shows that this is grossly insufficient space for the hens to behave naturally.

Vocabulary

1 Crime

Vocabulary reference p.199

A Breaking the law

Match these crimes with the pictures below and write a sentence about each, describing what is happening.

1 theft   2 robbery   3 assault   4 vandalism

B Name the criminal

1 A person who steals from a shop as they walk round it.   SH _ _ _ _ _ _ _ _
2 A person who attacks someone in order to steal their money.   M _ _ G _ _
3 A person who steals from houses.   _ _ R _ _ _ R
4 A person who kills someone on purpose.   _ _ _ D _ _ _ _

2 Phrasal verbs

Look at the following sentence from the reading text on page 156. 'The armed robber might *go back* to being an ordinary robber.' (line 30) Here *go back* means to return. *Go* can be used with other particles to express different meanings. Fill the gaps in the sentences below with the correct form of *go* and the appropriate particle.

off   out   over   through   with

1 The room was freezing because the fire _____ .
2 Food _____ very quickly in the summer if it isn't kept in a fridge.
3 The gun accidently _____ as Phil was cleaning it.
4 Mike's spotted tie _____ his striped shirt. They look awful together.
5 The teacher _____ the exam, pointing out all the students' mistakes.
6 In British prisons the lights _____ at 10 p.m.
7 The police officer _____ the suspect's pockets.

3 Word building

A In Unit 3 we looked at four of the most common noun suffixes in English: *-tion, -ence, -ness, -ity*. Another common noun suffix is *-ment*. Find examples of nouns with these endings in the reading text and give their related verbs where possible.

B Complete the following sentences with nouns related to the verbs in capitals.

1 Her resignation was an unfortunate _____ . OCCUR
2 A package holiday includes the flight and the _____ . ACCOMMODATE
3 There was a lot of _____ over what to do next. DISAGREE
4 Patrick's swift _____ saved the man's life. ACT
5 'I really don't mind where we go,' said Jane. 'I have no _____ at all.' PREFER
6 There was a slight _____ behind the bushes. MOVE

14 Cause and effect

That'll teach you

Introduction

A Look at these four photographs, which show different ways of learning.

1 Which of these four situations have you experienced?
2 In which situations did you learn the most and the least?
3 Which situation did you find the most interesting or enjoyable?
4 What made that situation interesting or enjoyable?
5 Have you experienced any other ways of learning? What was good and bad about them?

Discuss your ideas with a partner.

B Education

1 Read these statements about education and decide whether you agree with them.

Education is about learning and remembering information.
The main purpose of education is to prepare people for jobs.
Educated people are more intelligent than uneducated people.
Students learn best by doing practical tasks.
Tests and exams are the best way to find out how good students are.

Compare ideas in pairs or small groups.

2 What do you think the purpose of education is? Has your own education achieved this aim?

Reading

1 Think ahead

Before you read the article on the opposite page, think about how you prepare for examinations. Note down any techniques you find helpful.

2 Reading

Read the article opposite which gives advice about preparing for exams. Does the writer mention any of the techniques you thought of?

3 Points of view

Do you agree that studying with the TV or radio on affects your ability to absorb what you're trying to learn?

4 Comprehension

A Which sentence best summarizes the point Dr Sigman is making?
1 He provides advice about how to prepare yourself mentally for examinations.
2 He helps students prepare mentally and physically for examinations.
3 He says that physical exercise is more likely to bring about examination success than studying and revising.

B True or false?
According to the passage, which of these statements are true and which are false?
1 Students' physical build affects how well they do in exams.
2 There is scientific evidence for the idea that there are two basic types of student.
3 Late-night exercise might make it difficult for students to sleep.
4 People find it most difficult to concentrate in the afternoon.
5 A pilot would find it difficult to land a plane if he hadn't had enough sleep.
6 The author recommends a daytime sleep.

C Fact or opinion?
Which of these statements from the passage express facts and which express opinions?
1 Many people believe that there are two kinds of student.
2 The implication is that students are either intellectual or physical.
3 Recent studies have found that students who take regular exercise generally do better at school than those who don't.
4 Exercise peps you up.
5 You may think you are more creative after 11 p.m.

D Reading between the lines
1 Why do you think some people associate physical fitness with lack of intelligence?
2 Why is outdoor exercise preferable?
3 Why does the writer suggest that students play *pleasant* not *incredible* music?

5 My last exam

Think back to the last exam you took. Write two paragraphs about how you felt before and after the exam. Each paragraph should be about 50 words long. Compare your feelings with other students'.

Exam fitness

Dr Aric Sigman

Research has shown that success in exams depends on *physical* as well as *intellectual* fitness, and while there is no
5 substitute for studying, keeping yourself in good physical shape will help you to make the most of what you've learned. The following advice will enable you
10 to perform at your best at exam time.

Exercise

Many people believe that there are two kinds of student: the fit, sun-tanned type with bulging muscles and a low IQ, and
15 the weak, pasty academics, who wear thick glasses and pass all their exams. The implication is that students are either intellectual or physical, which is not in fact the case. Recent studies have found
20 that students who take regular exercise generally do better at school than those who don't. For example, twenty minutes of aerobic exercise will immediately bring about:

25 ■ an improved performance in IQ tests
■ a reduction in stress
■ improved levels of alertness and concentration
30 ■ faster, clearer, more creative thinking
■ an improvement in your memory.

So, try to do some aerobic exercise at least three times a week. But remember,
35 as exercise peps you up, it's better not to do it near bedtime. It could cause insomnia. And on the exam day, exercise before your exam starts, preferably outdoors.

Body clocks and sleep

40 Our bodies and minds are programmed to run to a particular schedule and our mental and physical abilities change dramatically during a day. For example, concentration, memory and the ability
45 to work with our hands, all reach a peak in the afternoon, and fall to a low in the middle of the night. Our body clocks are set and kept in sync by daylight which also keeps us alert. Confusing your body
50 clock will make you less alert and less effective. Lack of sleep will not stop a surgeon from operating successfully or a pilot from landing a jet, but it will affect a student's ability to read a book and
55 remember things well.

Some points to remember:

■ If you have to get someone to wake you up every morning, you are not getting enough sleep.
60 ■ You should sleep at regular times so as not to confuse your body clock.
■ You must get enough daylight. Study in a well-lit room, preferably near a window.
65 ■ The best times to study are between 9.00 and 12.00 noon, and then late afternoon between 4.00 and 6.00.

■ The worst times are after lunch, because your body clock goes into a
70 dip between 1.00 p.m. and 3.00 p.m., and also late at night. You may think you are more creative after 11.00 p.m., but remember that most exams take place during the day.
75 Studying late at night will disrupt your body clock.
■ A short nap during the afternoon will help you study and could result in an improved performance – just
80 make sure you don't fall asleep during your exam.

Final points

■ Don't study more than four or five hours a day on top of your school or other work.
85 ■ Whatever you tell yourself or other people, studying with the TV or radio on adversely affects your ability to absorb what you're trying to learn. The same goes for any
90 background music which competes for your attention. Choose music you find *pleasant*, not *incredible*.
■ Study with a friend – it helps you to feel you aren't suffering alone.

Grammar and practice

1 Cause and effect

A Read these sentences from the Exam fitness passage and underline the verbs or verb phrases which show the effects of actions. The first one has been done for you.

1 Twenty minutes of aerobic exercise <u>will immediately bring about</u> an improved performance in IQ tests.
2 Aerobic exercise is any activity which makes your heart beat faster.
3 Confusing your body clock will make you less alert.
4 As exercise peps you up, it could cause insomnia.
5 A short nap during the afternoon could result in an improved performance.

B Now work out and note down the causes and effects referred to in each of the above sentences. The first one has been done as an example.

	Cause (action)	Effect (result)
1	20 minutes of aerobic exercise	improved performance in IQ tests

C Make
1 The verb *make* is used in two of the sentences above. What words or grammatical structures follow *make* in each case?
2 Before continuing, check your understanding of *make* in the Grammar reference notes on page 193.

D Using *make*, think of three or four answers to these questions.
1 What makes you laugh?
2 What do you do that makes other people laugh?
3 What makes you feel guilty?
4 What makes you angry?
5 What do you do that makes other people angry or annoyed?

2 Purpose

A This sentence from the text gives advice.
You should sleep at regular times so as not to confuse your body clock.
Which phrase expresses the purpose of the advice, and implies what will happen if the advice is not followed?

B Underline the purpose words or phrases in these sentences.
1 People do exercise to keep themselves fit.
2 I'm going to study really hard this week so I can have Friday off.
3 In order to improve his spoken French, he spent the month before his oral exam in Paris.
4 My friend went to the library so that he could study in peace.

C Check your understanding of purpose expressions in the Grammar reference notes on page 193.

3 Practice

Answer these questions about everyday activities in different ways, using purpose phrases.

Example   Why do people wear clothes?
in order to keep warm
so that they attract attention
to look fashionable

1 Why do people write poetry?
2 Why do young men drive so fast?
3 Why do people go on diets?
4 Why do people go to nightclubs?
5 Why do people take exams?

4 Fluency

Think about what you would do if you were faced with these dilemmas. You may have to justify any actions you decide on.

1 You look out of a window on the 10th floor of an office block, and you see someone on the ledge outside. It's a man who says he's going to jump. What do you do to stop him?
2 Having rescued the man outside the window, you get into the lift to go to the ground floor. The lift starts to descend, but suddenly you hear a strange noise. The cable has broken and the lift is out of control. What do you do?
3 Fortunately, you get out of the wrecked lift with only cuts and bruises, but you decide to go to hospital, just for a check-up. You get into your car and head for the hospital. Soon you're travelling at 110 kmh. You get to the hospital and try to slow down, but the car brakes don't work. What do you do?

Compare ideas in groups. Discuss the probable results of each suggestion and then try to agree on the best course of action for each situation.

14 Cause and effect

Face the music

Introduction

In groups, think of answers to these questions. Spend one minute on each question. In that time note down as many answers as you can.

1 What different kinds of music are there? For example, classical, jazz, etc.
2 On what occasions and in what situations do people listen to or hear music?
3 Other than simple enjoyment, what reasons do people have for listening to music?
4 Are there different times or reasons for listening to particular kinds of music? Think about your own musical tastes.

Listening

1 Think ahead

In recent years people have attempted to make a link between heavy metal music and aggressive behaviour. Do you believe there is any connection between music and certain kinds of behaviour?

2 Listening

You are going to hear an interview with a doctor who has investigated the effects of music. Note down any information you find surprising or particularly interesting.

3 Points of view

1 Discuss any information you found surprising or interesting. Do you believe it?
2 How are you affected by these kinds of music mentioned in the recording?
   Bach   Indian music   harp music   rock music   early classical music

4 Comprehension

A Choose the answer which you think fits best.
1 Researchers have found that people are
   A affected only by music they like.
   B affected only by music they dislike.
   C affected by music they like and music they dislike.
   D unaffected by music whether they like it or not.

2　Dr Ryman became interested in the effects of music
　　A　because of some experiments he did on hospital patients.
　　B　after visits he made to his own doctor and dentist.
　　C　when he was in hospital following an accident.
　　D　after reading the results of research on the subject.
3　At the Los Angeles hospital, doctors
　　A　have found that music can have a similar effect to tranquillizers.
　　B　have replaced conventional drugs with music.
　　C　play music to patients during serious operations.
　　D　use music to prevent back pain in their patients.
4　According to the psychiatrist, Dr Diamond, most rock music
　　A　does not make people feel better.　　C　makes people fall in love.
　　B　is high-energy music.　　　　　　　D　makes people feel better.
5　According to Dr Ryman's colleague, rock music addicts
　　A　are also drug addicts.　　　　　　C　are harmless.
　　B　are intolerant.　　　　　　　　　D　need louder and louder music.

B Listening between the lines
1　Why do so many people listen to personal stereos, especially in public places?
2　What do you understand by this sentence from the interview?
　　'Our patients have had their lives reduced to a hospital bed and a locker.'
3　Why do some doctors prefer to play music to patients than to give them drugs?
4　Why do you think so much research has been done into the link between music and health?

5　Sound effects

Write 50–75 words about a song or piece of music that has a particular effect on you. Describe the music and how it makes you feel.

Grammar and practice

Have / get something done

A Look at these two sentences from the interview.

1　I'd gone to get my blood pressure checked.
2　I had to have a tooth filled.

Who do you think checked the blood pressure and who filled the tooth? Who wanted the blood pressure checked and the tooth filled? Why didn't Dr Ryman do the checking and the filling himself?

B Is there a difference in meaning between these two sentences?
1　I had my tooth filled.
2　My tooth was filled by the dentist.
When might a passive be used instead of *get* or *have*?

C Before you do the next exercise, check your understanding of the verbs *have / get something done* in the Grammar reference on page 193.

D Rewrite these sentences using *have* or *get*. The first one has been done as an example.
1　The mechanic changed the oil in my car.
　　I had the oil in my car changed.
2　The hairdresser cut my hair in a completely different style.
3　A decorator has repainted the front of our house.
4　A friend of mine, who's an electrician, is going to repair my video next week.
5　My jacket is being cleaned at a specialist cleaner's.
6　The town hall has just been rebuilt for the council.

E What do you have done for you, rather than doing for yourself? Make a list and compare with other students.

Vocabulary

1 Education
Vocabulary reference p.199

A Quiz

1 What are the jumbled subjects a–g? Match them with the symbols.

a grayphoge

b shyriot

c thasm

d reofing unalagge

e seccine

f comicnose

g shiplacy tinudeaco

2 What are the three branches of science commonly taught in schools?

3 Many sciences or subjects of study end in *-ology*. How many *-ologies* do you know?

B Fill the gaps in this conversation with the correct form of one of these *exam* verbs.

fail   pass   re-sit   revise   take

Tony   I'm _____(1) an important music exam tomorrow.
Jane   Good luck, I hope you _____(2).
Tony   So do I. I've _____(3) every night for six weeks!
Jane   You've always done well in exams – I'm sure you won't _____(4).
Tony   I hope you're right. I couldn't face _____(5) the exam in December.

C What is, or was, your favourite school subject? And your least favourite subject? Write 50 words about each of these two subjects, explaining why you liked or disliked them.

2 Health
Vocabulary reference p.200

A Find ten medical words in this wordsearch. Here are their meanings.

```
P A T R E A T O S
U B A N D A G E U
S L L I P A P E R
H M I D W I F E G
P L A S T E R A E
B C O F O I N G O
L U H C A T C H N
U R T N E I T A P
D E E S R U N F U
```

People   1 person specially trained to help women to give birth
           2 person who looks after ill people – especially in hospital
           3 person who is ill and needs looking after
           4 doctor who performs operations
First aid 5 long strip of cloth for covering an injury
           6 tablet
           7 patch of material which is stuck on to the skin to protect a small cut or scratch
Verbs   8 Don't come too near me – I don't want you to _____ my cold.
           9 My brother was born deaf but, using the latest techniques, the doctors have managed to _____ him.
          10 In some countries doctors will not _____ people who have no medical insurance.

B Word building

Fill the gaps with words related to the words in capitals.

1 Children often pick up _____ diseases at school. INFECT
2 Our family doctor could find nothing wrong with me, so I had to go and see a _____ . SPECIAL
3 Even though forty cars were involved in the accident, there were no serious _____ . INJURE
4 Before going abroad I had to have seven _____ . INJECT
5 Afterwards my arm was _____ for several days. PAIN

C Confusing words

Choose the correct word to fill the gaps in these sentences.

1 The tablets I took had absolutely no _____ on my headache.
  A power   B effect   C influence   D affect
2 The doctor examined me and then wrote out a _____ for me to take to the chemist.
  A paper   B recipe   C prescription   D ticket
3 I don't mind when you go on holiday. It doesn't really _____ me.
  A effect   B affect   C matter   D suit
4 I've had two teeth taken out – it was OK at the time, but now my mouth really

  _____ .

  A pains   B harms   C hurts   D injures
5 After I'd run for the bus my heart was _____ very hard.
  A beating   B hitting   C striking   D blowing

3 Phrasal verbs

A In the recording, Dr Ryman says 'I don't personally *go along with* everything Dr Diamond says.' *Go along with* is a three-part phrasal verb. Fill the gaps in these sentences with the correct form of a three-part phrasal verb made from the table below. Remember that the three parts of these verbs always stay together.

1 I've _____ an unforeseen problem, which means I'll have to work all weekend.
2 The doctor said I was overweight and advised me _____ my sugar intake.
3 We couldn't buy newspapers on the island so I _____ the news by listening to the radio.
4 I agree with most of what the government does, but I _____ their plan to raise income tax.
5 My friend was running so fast that I couldn't _____ him.
6 My class was almost empty last week – nearly all the other students _____ flu.
7 It's about time someone _____ a new idea for preventing colds.

Verbs	Particle 1	Particle 2
catch	along	against
come	down	on
cut	up	with
go		
keep		

B Can you think of any other three-part phrasal verbs that can be made from the table? Use a dictionary to help you compile a list, and then write sentences using these new verbs.

Writing

The First Certificate composition paper

1 Composition types

Read through these composition titles, which are typical of those you might have in the exam. Match the titles with the appropriate composition types A–E listed below.

A Letter (formal or informal)

B Description (of a place, an object, a person or an event)

C Narrative

D Argument essay (pros and cons or personal opinions)

E Speech (formal or informal)

1 *A group of foreign students will shortly be arriving for a short educational stay in your town. You have been asked to welcome the group officially on behalf of the whole town. What do you say?*

2 *Imagine that you have won a large sum of money and that you have decided to spend some of it on a new house. Describe your dream house and your ideal site.*

3 *Do you think children over the age of 16 should continue to live with their parents?*

4 *A good friend, who is spending a year abroad, has written you an interesting, newsy letter. He / She asks you to write back, giving him / her all your latest news.*

5 *Write a story ending with the words 'That was one of the best days of my life.'*

2 Choosing and planning which compositions to do

A Work through the titles above, noting briefly the things you could write for each composition; jot down single words and ideas. Finally, decide which two compositions you would choose to do.

B Write brief plans for your chosen compositions. Think about how many paragraphs to write and about the contents of each paragraph. Make sure your plan includes all the points in the questions.

3 Writing

A Write one of the essays you have planned, in 120–180 words. Allow about 35–40 minutes.

B Work through this list of check questions.

1 Have you answered the question?

2 Is your composition about the right length? By now, you should know, without counting, how much space 180 words takes up.

3 Is the layout right? This is particularly appropriate for letters.

4 Is the register appropriate? Is it formal or informal?

5 Is your writing accurate? Check grammar, spelling and punctuation.

4 Alternatives

1 Title 1 above is a formal speech. Think of situations in which you might talk *informally* to a group of foreign students.

2 Title 2 asks you to describe an ideal place. What other ideals might you be asked to describe?

3 How is Title 3 different from a *pros and cons* composition?

4 Title 4 asks for an informal letter. In what circumstances might you write a *formal* letter to someone living abroad?

5 Title 5 asks you to write about something that happened to you. Can you think of other *personal experience stories* you might be asked to write about?

R4 Revision

This section gives you extra practice in the grammar and vocabulary covered in Units 13 and 14. Before you begin, remind yourself of this language by reading the Grammar reference notes on pages 192–193 and the Vocabulary reference on pages 199–200. This is not a test so you should refer to Units 13 and 14 and the reference sections as you work through these exercises.

1 Vocabulary multiple-choice

Before you begin, look back at the Exam techniques section on pages 110–111, which gives you advice on answering vocabulary multiple-choice questions. Then choose the word or phrase which best completes each sentence. Look up any words you don't know when you've finished.

1 The gun went _____ as he was cleaning it but luckily he wasn't hurt.
   A out   B by   C off   D over
2 Rosa suggested _____ a suit and tie when he went for the interview.
   A him to wear   C he wore
   B he must wear   D that he wears
3 If you _____ a crime, you must expect to suffer the consequences.
   A perform   B make   C do   D commit
4 Overwork is _____ to cause increased stress.
   A possible   B probably   C obviously   D likely
5 She warned me _____ .
   A to not do it   C I should do it
   B not to do it   D about to do it
6 The doctor has advised him to cut down _____ his drinking.
   A on   B in   C with   D to
7 Hunger and lack of sleep _____ bad-tempered.
   A cause   C result in
   B make me   D make that I am
8 Gordon said that smoking hadn't done him any _____ .
   A harm   B damage   C badness   D hurt
9 I asked _____ the door behind her.
   A her closing the door   C if she closed
   B that she should close   D her to close

10 Jeff wants to look his best at the wedding so he's _____ .
   A to get made a suit   C having made a suit
   B make a suit   D having a suit made
11 Take a _____ nap if you're tired.
   A small   B short   C long   D fast
12 Have you got a light? My cigarette's gone _____ .
   A by   B away   C off   D out
13 Kathryn queued all night so _____ get a good seat.
   A as to   B that she   C she can   D to
14 Last night thieves _____ goods to the value of £10,000 from Goodbuy Supermarket in Elm Lane.
   A robbed   C burgled
   B stole   D shoplifted
15 _____ the gold medal he'll have to do better than that.
   A Winning   C To win
   B In order win   D So that he wins
16 Neil's not very fit. He doesn't _____ any exercise.
   A take   B practise   C make   D have
17 Most pets are well- _____ by their owners.
   A cared after   C cared for
   B looked for   D looked into
18 The main argument _____ a ban on cigarette advertising is that it would be undemocratic.
   A against   B opposing   C opposite   D facing
19 One of the advantages of having a pet is that it _____ you company.
   A gives   B keeps   C does   D makes
20 More than half of the population are suffering _____ malnutrition.
   A with   B for   C by   D from

2 Topic vocabulary

Complete the following sentences with one word related to *health*.
1 The dentist gave me an _____ so that I wouldn't feel anything.
2 My foot is so _____ that I can't walk on it.
3 Despite scientific advances, they still haven't found a _____ for the common cold.
4 The doctor wrote out a _____ and told me to take the tablets for one week.

5 When I broke my arm they had to put it in _____ .

6 Most hospital _____ have over a dozen beds in them.

7 The _____ has performed this operation many times before.

8 'Do you feel any _____ when I press here?' the doctor asked.

3 Gap filling

Before you begin, look back at the Exam techniques section on pages 80–81 to remind yourself how to work through gap filling exercises. Then fill each gap with one word.

If you ask most pet owners what the main benefit of keeping a pet is, the answer will probably be companionship. They are _____(1) not aware that _____(2) pets can be responsible for improving their health. But scientists have now proved _____(3) some owners have always believed, _____(4) is that animals can be good _____(5) you.

A recent study at Cambridge University has shown an improvement in _____(6) the physical and mental _____(7) of new dog owners. This is not just _____(8) of the increase _____(9) the amount of walking they do, either. Owners have also been found to be less _____(10) to suffer from ailments _____(11) as headaches, backache, colds and flu. Owners of cats have shown _____(12) improvements. There is, however, no information so _____(13) on fish or budgie owners.

But whatever pet you have, it _____(14) probably be beneficial to any children in the household. Studies have shown _____(15) pets can improve children's social skills, teaching them, for _____(16), to understand the importance of communication without words. Looking _____(17) a pet is a gentle introduction to responsibility.

For all of us, the action of stroking a pet _____(18) be very therapeutic. This _____(19), in fact, led to _____(20) use of 'Pets as Therapy', where dogs visit long-stay patients in homes and hospitals.

4 Transformations

Before you begin, look back at the Exam techniques section on pages 80–81, which gives advice on how to do transformations. Then complete each sentence so that it means the same as the sentence printed before it.

1 'Bring a sweater with you in case it gets cold at night.'
   She told me _____

2 The builder's going to mend my roof tomorrow.
   I _____

3 You should have an early night, so that you don't feel tired.
   So as _____

4 'Where's that book I lent you?' Dave asked.
   Dave asked _____

5 Chocolate causes some people to come out in spots.
   Chocolate makes _____

6 'Have you got any free time next week?' Mandy asked.
   Mandy asked _____

7 Madeleine wears high heels to look taller.
   In order _____

8 'Why don't you get your hair cut, Gavin?' said Adam.
   Adam suggested _____

9 'I'll have to take out this tooth,' the dentist said.
   The dentist said that I _____

10 'I'll be arriving tomorrow morning,' Jamie said.
   Jamie said that _____

5 Word building

Use the word in capitals at the end of each of these sentences to form a word that fits in the blank space.

1 Drug _____ is a growing problem particularly among young people. ADDICT

2 Most banks have installed video cameras as part of their _____ systems. SECURE

3 Elsa is being kept in an isolation ward because she is highly _____ . INFECT

4 My brother and I were sent to _____ school when we were seven. BOARD

5 Phil was sentenced to seven years' _____ for his part in the armed robbery. PRISON

6 The number of _____ which remain unsolved is still high. BURGLE

You are now ready to do Progress test 4.

Pair work

Fluency (page 5)
Student A
Read these notes about the three applicants' good and bad points. Choose who you would most like to join the expedition. It is up to you to decide whether these people are male or female.

WM Peters
+ Has a reputation for honesty. Strong and fearless. Independent minded. Never gossips about other people behind their backs. A good photographer.
- Can be rather cold towards others. Has no interests outside trekking. Likes to be in charge.

L Palmer
+ Tends to take everything in his/her stride, and does not panic easily. Has a good sense of humour.
- Is very untidy and has no sense of direction. Snores.

F Trueman
+ Young and healthy. Has done weight-training, so would be able to carry heavy loads for long distances. An excellent cook.
- Has little experience of trekking. Is rather shy.

Picture discussion (page 47)
Student A – left-hand photo
This newborn baby boy is being raised to the sky by an old man to receive his name and join his community as a Blackfoot Indian in America.
General question ideas on the theme of families
1 The baby in this photograph is being given a name. How did you get your name? Does your name mean anything? How important are names?
2 How do you think the life of the child in this picture will be different from your life as a child?
3 Are old values being lost in modern life? Which of these values do you think are worth trying to keep?

Picture discussion (page 141)
Student A – photograph 1
This man is taking part in a competition to see who can attract the most worms out of the ground.
General question ideas on the theme of competitions
1 What kind of competitions are popular with adults and children in your country?

2 Why do people go in for competitions? Do you need special qualities to be a good competitor?
3 If you won a lot of money in a competition, what would you do with it? Would it change you?

An audition (page 16)
Student A
You are an actor. Student B is going to phone to arrange an audition for a part in 'Cruiseliner'. You are interested in the part, but you are busy every day next week. Before talking to your partner, note down the things you're doing next week, then try to arrange an alternative time.

Role play (page 115)
Situation 1 – Student B
You are a sumo wrestling trainer. You think Student A just needs to put on 30 kilos to be sure of winning the world championships. Both of you would then be rich and famous. Persuade Student A to eat more.
Situation 2 – Student B
You are the commanding officer of the ceremonial guards. You are fiercely proud of the traditions and uniform, and think they should never change.

Picture discussion (page 47)
Student B – right-hand photo
This picture shows a Japanese couple getting married at the Hilton Hotel in Tokyo. A fog-machine, like those used at rock concerts, is being used to add atmosphere.
General question ideas on the theme of marriage
1 What do you think is a good age to get married?
2 Why do so many marriages end in divorce?
3 What makes a good marriage?
4 What would you look for in a marriage partner?

Picture discussion (page 141)
Student B – photograph 2
These police officers are taking part in the Christmas Tree Patrol which operates for the two weeks before Christmas in some English forests. Their job is to deter or catch Christmas tree thieves.
General question ideas on the theme of the environment
1 Should people have real Christmas trees?
2 Do you think the police force should be involved in the protection of the environment? Are there more important things they could be doing?
3 Do you think the government in your country does enough to protect the environment?

Taking the First Certificate Exam

1 Introduction

This section gives general advice about preparing for the exam and also suggests how you can make the best use of your time during the exam itself.

Everyone's different, however, so what might work for one student might not be so effective for another. You should decide what is best for you.

2 Before the exam – the last few days

1 Don't try to revise the whole of the English language. Spend time on the parts of the exam you worry most about or the parts you know you will find difficult.
2 Look back over your work and make a list of your most frequent mistakes. Work out a revision timetable that covers these problem areas.
3 Stick to your timetable – this will help you to revise systematically and sensibly.
4 Use the Grammar reference and the Vocabulary reference.
5 Don't spend much time on the parts of the exam you are already good at.

3 The day of the exam

1 Before you go into the exam, make sure you know
   - which paper you are doing.
   - how long it lasts.
   - what you have to do.
2 Before you start each paper, decide or make sure you know
   - how many exercises you have to do.
   - what order you are going to do the exercises in.
   - how much time to spend on each exercise.
   - how much time to allow for checking.

The Exam factfile on pages iv – vi will give you this information.

4 During the exam

1 Listen carefully to what the examiner or invigilator says.
2 Read the exam papers to make sure you know exactly what you have to do.
3 Check the following points for every exercise you do
   - Spelling
   - Grammar
     verbs: regular or irregular? tense? form?
            singular or plural?
            word order
   - Layout, paragraphing and punctuation
   Keep checking until time runs out.
4 Don't leave any gaps or any questions unanswered.
5 Don't panic – try not to be too nervous.

5 Papers 1 – 5

All the information you need to know about the exam is in the Exam Factfile at the front of the book. When preparing for a paper, read the Factfile, the Guidelines in the Exam techniques sections throughout the book, and the advice which follows.

Paper 1 Reading Comprehension

A Before the exam
The best way to prepare for this paper is to read as much English as you can. Revise vocabulary from the lists on pages 196–199. If you have recorded new vocabulary, use your own lists too. When you read, practise guessing the meaning of words, rather than always relying on a dictionary.

B During the exam
1 In Section A, check your answers very carefully, thinking about grammar as well as meaning. Don't assume that any question is as easy as it looks.
2 In Section B, read the questions and answers very carefully.
3 Answer every question.
4 Mark your answers on the answer sheet in pencil.

Paper 2 Composition

A Before the exam
1 Look through old exam papers and practise choosing titles quickly.
2 Systematically revise the following:
   • useful topic vocabulary.
   • ways of linking sentences or parts of sentences, e.g. conjunctions and relative clauses.
   • areas of grammar you know you are weak in.
   • phrases used to express personal opinions.
   • the features of formal and informal writing.
   • the rules of paragraphing and punctuation.
   • the layout of formal and informal letters.
3 Practise writing legibly and make sure that you know what 120–180 words of your handwriting looks like.

B During the exam
1 Read carefully through all the titles and choose the two you think you will be able to do best. Decide quickly to leave yourself the maximum writing time.
2 Spend a few minutes making a simple plan for each composition. Decide on the following:
   • the appropriate style, formal or informal.
   • the appropriate verb tenses.
   • the appropriate layout.
   • the number of paragraphs.
   • the contents of each paragraph.
3 When writing, keep your plan in mind. Also keep an eye on the time. Don't spend more than half the time on the first title.
4 Make sure you answer the question and don't write more than 180 words.
5 Finally, check your writing by reading it 'aloud to yourself'. In this way you may 'hear' mistakes. Check the following:
   • grammar   • spelling   • paragraphs   • punctuation

Paper 3 Use of English

A Before the exam
1 Make sure you know how many marks there are for each part of the paper (see the Factfile at the beginning of the book). Work out how much time to spend on each part, and how much to leave for checking. Make sure you know this well, so you don't have to work it out during the exam itself.
2 Decide which order you are going to do the exercises in. Start with something

mechanical, like the Transformations, and leave the Gap fill and the Guided writing until last, when you are warmed up.

B During the exam

1 Stick to the timings you have worked out for each exercise.
2 Do the exercises in the order that suits you.
3 Make sure you leave enough time for the more difficult exercises if you have left these until last.
4 If there's a question you can't answer, don't waste time worrying about it. Go on to something else.
5 Check your work carefully.

Paper 4 Listening Comprehension

A Before the exam

1 Listen to as much spoken English as you can, on TV, radio, etc.
2 Make the most of opportunities to talk to English speakers.
3 Get used to trying to understand without a dictionary.

B In the exam

1 All the instructions are given on the cassette. Listen to them.
2 Try to predict as much as you can from the questions.
3 Don't panic if you don't understand everything the first time.
4 Answer all the questions.
5 Transfer your answers to the answer sheet in pencil.

Paper 5 The Interview

A Before the exam

1 Make the most of every opportunity to speak English. Arrange to meet other students and speak English with them. Always begin your conversations in English when you meet.
2 When you say something short in your own language, work out how you would say it in English. Talk to yourself!
3 When you see a picture, describe it to yourself in English. Look at magazine pictures and list as much vocabulary from the pictures as you can. Find ways to paraphrase words that you don't know.
4 Look back at questions in the Introductions and Over to you sections in this book, and practise answering them. Try to talk for a minute at a time.
5 Practise using more complicated English, like conditionals, in your conversation. You will get more marks if you can use these well.

B During the exam

1 When you go into the examination room the examiner will ask for your name and candidate number, and will ask you a couple of general personal questions to help you relax.
2 In the picture discussion don't try to describe the pictures in too much detail. Try to talk about the themes they illustrate.
3 The examiner needs to hear you talk, so don't just sit waiting for questions. Talk about anything related to the pictures.
4 Show off how good your English is. The examiner likes to hear complicated structures used correctly.
5 Keep talking, and stay calm.

Good luck!

Grammar reference

Terminology

Determiner: definite article

Capital letter: used
1 to begin sentences
2 for all proper nouns (names, days of the week, etc.)
3 nationality adjectives
4 for the first letter of direct speech

Subordinate clause

Sentence

Main clause

Modifier / intensifier: used to strengthen or weaken the meaning of adjectives and adverbs. Some others: *so, very*.

Ungradable adjective: can only be used with 'extreme' modifiers like *absolutely*. Some others: *huge, freezing, furious, terrified*.

Jimmy McGregor was the first man to swim from New Zealand to Australia. When he arrived in Australia, he was met by a TV interviewer. 'Strewth, mate,' said the Australian unbelievingly. 'How did you get to be such a good swimmer? That's an impossible distance you've just swum!'

Question mark: used at the end of a question sentence

Determiner: indefinite article

Apostrophe: used
1 in contractions to show that a letter or letters is/are missing
2 to indicate the possessive, e.g. John's book

Connective: relative pronoun

Connective: conjunction. Some others: *but, so, if*.

Gradable adjective: can be used with modifiers

Speech marks: used to indicate the actual words that someone says. Begin a new paragraph when the speaker changes. Note: other punctuation marks come inside the speech marks.

'As you may know,' replied Jimmy, 'there are lots of lakes in Scotland and, from the age of two, my father used to take me to Loch Lomond, which is one of the biggest. He would row me into the middle, help me over the side, and leave me to swim the twenty kilometres back to the shore.'

'That must have been rather hard for a two-year-old ,' said the Australian admiringly.

'Yes,' agreed Jimmy. 'However, the hardest part was fighting my way out of the sack !'

Quantifier. Some others: *all, both, less, some, several*.

Determiner: possessive adjective. Also demonstrative adjectives *this, that, these, those*

Modifier. Some others: *pretty, quite*.

Comma: used
1 before reporting verbs in direct speech
2 to separate items on a list
3 to divide a subordinate clause from a main clause when the subordinate clause comes first
4 after connecting adverbs
5 around non-identifying relative clauses
6 in front of most conjunctions.

Exclamation mark: used for emphasis instead of a full stop.

Full stop: used at the end of a sentence.

Connective: adverb. Some others: *firstly, in conclusion*.

Unit 1

Describing habitual actions

1 Habitual actions in the present

A The present simple
This is the usual way of expressing present habitual actions.
  *Whenever I go to town, I **spend** too much money.*
The present simple is also used for permanent situations.
  *My uncle **lives** in Bristol, but he **works** in London.*

B Tend to
The verb *tend to* + infinitive can be used to refer to usual or generally occurring actions.
  *She **tends to get up** late at weekends.*

C Other ways of expressing habitual actions in the present
1 Present continuous + *always*
   This is used mainly to refer to another person's actions which the speaker finds annoying.
     *You're **always complaining** about my cooking.*
2 *Will* + infinitive
   This is sometimes used instead of the present simple to refer to behaviour which is characteristic of a particular person.
     *I'**ll sit** for hours watching TV.*
3 *Keep* + *-ing*
   This is often used to refer to habitual actions which are accidental or annoying.
     *I **keep bumping** my head on that tree.*

2 Habitual actions in the past

A The past simple
When a past simple verb refers to habitual or repeated actions it can be accompanied by a frequency expression.
  *When I worked in London, I **usually got** home at six o'clock.*

B Used to + infinitive
This refers to past actions which no longer happen.
  *Before I had a car, I **used to cycle** to work .*
It can also be used to refer to actions that did not happen before, but happen now.
  *I **didn't use to have** foreign holidays. Now I go abroad every year.*
  *We never **used to watch** TV at breakfast time.*
Remember the question form of *used to*.
  *Where **did you use to go** for your holidays?*
Sentences with *used to* do not need frequency adverbs, although they are sometimes included for emphasis.
  *I **always used to be** late for school.*

C Would + infinitive
This refers to habitual past actions.
  *Every summer our parents **would take** us to the seaside.*
Avoid using *would* in questions and negative sentences, as its meaning can be completely different.

D The difference between *used to* and *would*
Used to can refer to permanent situations as well as habitual actions.

*I **used to be able to** see Big Ben from my bedroom window.*
Would can only refer to actions, not situations. You can say *He'**d catch** the 7.30 train*, but not *He'd work in London.*

Used to

Used to has three forms with different meanings.

A Used to + infinitive
This refers to habitual past actions (see note **2B** above).
  *My father **used to smoke** 40 cigarettes a day.*

B To be used to + -ing
This means *to be accustomed to.*
  *I must go to bed early. I'**m used to having** ten hours sleep a night.*

C To get used to + -ing
This means *to become accustomed to,* often to something unusual or strange.
  *If you come to England, you'll have **to get used to driving** on the left-hand side of the road.*

Note Other common verbs which follow the same pattern are *look forward to* and *object to*.

Unit 2

The future

There are many ways of talking about future time in English. This is a summary of the most common forms and their uses.

1 Present continuous

The present continuous is used to refer to future actions or events which have already been arranged.
  *Are you **doing** anything interesting at the weekend?*
  *We'**re spending** the summer with our friends in Greece.*

2 *Will*

A Will + infinitive (future simple)
The *will* future is used to talk about:
1 future facts.
     *The sun **will rise** at 6.30 tomorrow morning.*
2 predictions or expectations.
     *Helen and John **won't be** here on time. They're always late.*
3 strong intentions.
     *When Loretta retires, I'**ll definitely apply** for her job .*
4 instant decisions about the immediate future.
     *The phone's ringing. I'**ll answer** it.*

B Will + be + -ing (future continuous)
This form is used to talk about:
1 events or actions that will be in progress at a specific time in the future.
     *This time tomorrow, I'**ll be travelling** through France.*

2 predicted or expected trends.
> *In the 21st century, people **will be living** to the age of 130.*

C Will + have + past participle (future perfect simple)
Will + have + been + -ing (future perfect continuous)
These two forms are used to talk about:
1 actions or events that will already be completed by a certain time in the future.
> *By the year 2000, I'**ll have left** school and started work.*
2 the continuous nature of actions and events in the future.
> *On Saturday we'**ll have been living** here for three years.*

Note
1 *Shall* is sometimes used instead of *will* after *I* and *we*.
> *In a few days we **shall** have forgotten about the accident.*
2 *Shall* must be used to start questions which are suggestions and offers.
> ***Shall** we phone to see what time the film starts?*
> ***Shall** I carry that heavy case for you?*

3 *Going to* + infinitive

This is used to talk about:
a intentions or plans.
> *After Christmas, **I'm going to get** a job and save up.*
> *What **are you going to do** when you leave school?*
b predictions based on present evidence or knowledge.
> *My nose is tickling. I think I'**m going to sneeze**.*
> *My sister's **going to have** a baby.*

4 Present simple

This tense is used to talk about scheduled, timetabled or fixed events.
> *The match **starts** at 7.30 tomorrow evening.*

5 Other ways of referring to the future

A To be about to + infinitive
This is used to talk about actions or events which we expect to happen in the immediate future
> *I must hurry – the train is **about to leave**.*

B To be on the point of + -ing
This expression also refers to the immediate future.
> *The train is **on the point of leaving**. Close the doors!*

Articles

1 The definite article *the*

Three of the main uses of the definite article are to refer to:
a something that has been mentioned before.
> *Bill: I've got a dog.   Ben: What's **the** dog's name?*
b something there is only one of in a particular context.
> ***The** Queen spent three days in Wales.*
> *Soon after we'd taken off **the** pilot welcomed us on board.*
c something the speaker and listener both know about.
> ***The** film was really good – thanks for recommending it.*

It is also used in these ways:
d with superlative constructions.
> *She's **the** fastest runner in Europe.*
e with adjectives used as nouns referring to groups of people.
> *There's one law for **the** rich and another for **the** poor.*
f with the names of oceans, seas, rivers, mountain ranges.
> ***the** Atlantic, **the** Thames, **the** Alps*
g with the names of some countries and groups of islands.
> ***the** United States, **the** United Kingdom, **the** West Indies*

2 The indefinite article *a / an*

These are the main uses of the indefinite article:
a to refer to something for the first time.
> *I've got **a** dog.*
b to refer to a person or thing (but not a special person or thing).
> *Can I have **a** drink please? Tea, coffee, beer, I don't mind.*
c to refer to a person's job.
> *Alan is **a** telephone engineer.*
d with numbers.
> ***a** hundred, **a** million*

3 Zero article (Ø)

These are the main contexts in which no article is used:
a with plural countable nouns.
> *Ø International footballers are paid too much money.*
b with uncountable nouns.
> *He used to drink Ø beer, but now he drinks only Ø water.*
> *They fell in Ø love while they were in Spain.*
c with the names of towns, cities, states and most countries.
> *Ø New York, Ø Texas, Ø Greece*
d with nouns for certain places or situations.
> *Suzy went into Ø hospital yesterday.*
> *on Ø deck, at Ø home, on Ø holiday, to Ø church, at Ø school*

Unit 3

Gerunds and infinitives

1 Gerunds

Gerunds are verbs that behave like nouns. They are formed by adding *-ing* to the verb base. They can be used in four ways.

A As the subject of a clause or sentence
> ***Eating out** can be expensive.*

B As the object of a clause or sentence
> *My brother enjoys **fishing** but he hates not **catching** anything.*

C After certain verbs
1 After verbs expressing likes and dislikes (but see **2C**2).
> *I don't enjoy **seeing** you like this.*

2 After other verbs such as:

admit, appreciate, avoid, can't help, consider, delay, deny, finish, forgive, give up, imagine, involve, keep, mind, miss, postpone, put off, prevent, report, resist, risk, suggest.

> *Have you considered **buying** a new one?*

D After prepositions

1 After all prepositions except *to*, which is usually followed by the infinitive (see 3 below for some common exceptions).

> *On **opening** the letter, she realized it wasn't for her.*

2 After adjective + preposition combinations such as:

nervous / worried   about
bad / good / clever / skilled   at
sorry / responsible   for
interested   in
capable / afraid / frightened / terrified   of
bored   with

> *I'm interested in **applying** for the job.*

3 After verb + preposition combinations such as:

apologise for, arrest someone for, be / get used to, congratulate someone on, insist on, look forward to, object to, succeed in, warn someone about.

> *My little brother insisted on **coming** with me.*

2 Gerund or infinitive?

Some verbs, adjectives and prepositions must always be followed by the gerund; others must always be followed by the infinitive. Some verbs can be followed by either infinitive or gerund.

A Verbs always followed by the infinitive

The following verbs are always followed by the infinitive:

afford, agree, arrange, ask, appear, attempt, choose, decide, expect, help, hope, intend, learn, manage, need, offer, pretend, promise, refuse, seem.

> *I can't afford **to go** on holiday this year.*

B Adjectives followed by the infinitive

The following adjectives are always followed by the infinitive:

amazed, certain, difficult, disappointed, easy, free, glad, happy, likely, pleased, possible, simple, sure, surprised.

> *The recipe is simple **to follow**.*

C Verbs followed by the gerund or the infinitive

1 With no change of meaning

The verbs *start, begin, continue* can be followed by either the gerund or the infinitive, without changing the meaning of the sentence.

> *Jeff continued **to smoke** despite the doctor's advice.*
> *Jeff continued **smoking** despite the doctor's advice.*

2 With a slight change of meaning

The meaning of the verbs *like, prefer, hate, love* changes slightly, depending on whether the gerund or infinitive follows them.

The gerund is more usual for general statements when the emphasis is on the enjoyment (or not) of the action.

> *Mary prefers **eating out** to **eating** at home.*

The infinitive is more usual for more specific statements where extra information is given.

> *Jane prefers **to eat out** because there's no washing-up to do.*

Note   With the verb *like* + infinitive there is often the added meaning of a preferred alternative.

*I like **to drive** there* may imply *I prefer that means of transport to going by train or coach.*

3 With a change of meaning

The verbs *try, stop, regret, remember, forget, mean, go on* can be followed by the gerund or the infinitive, but with a change in meaning:

Try

+ gerund   to experiment in order to achieve an objective

> *Try **going** to bed earlier and see if that helps.*

+ infinitive   to attempt a difficult action.

> *Jill's been trying **to get** a job since she left school, but with no success.*

Stop

+ gerund   to finish an activity.

> *Stop **talking** and get on with your work!*

+ infinitive   to interrupt one activity in order to do another.

> *Roger stopped **to have** a cup of tea.*

Regret

+ gerund   to be sorry about an action in the past.

> *Many people regret **marrying** young.*

+ infinitive   to be sorry about what you are going to say.

> *Dr. Taylor regrets **to say** that he is unable to see patients without an appointment.*

Forget / remember

+ gerund   to (not) recall an action.

> *I distinctly remember **asking** them to come after lunch.*
> *I won't forget **seeing** Christie win the gold medal as long as I live.*

+ infinitive   to (not) do an action you must do.

> *Ann remembered **to lock** all the doors when she went on holiday, but she forgot **to close** the bathroom window.*

Go on

+ gerund   to continue an action.

> *I'll go on **loving** you until I die.*

+ infinitive   to finish one activity and start another.

> *After seven years of study, Andy went on **to become** a doctor.*

Mean

+ gerund   to involve.

> *Dieting usually means **giving up** sweet things.*

+ infinitive   to be one's intention.

> *I meant **to send** you a postcard but I forgot to take my address book.*

Note   The infinitive is only possible with *mean* in perfect and past tenses.

Verbs of perception

The verbs *see* (*watch, notice,* etc.), *feel, hear, smell* have a different meaning when they are followed by the infinitive (without *to*) or a participle.

+ participle   to experience part of an event

> *I noticed a man **acting** in a strange way.*

+ infinitive without *to*   to experience the whole event

> *I heard my sister **come** in at 1 a.m.*

Unit 4

Comparative and superlative adjectives

1 Forms

A Regular adjectives with one syllable

Adjective	Comparative	Superlative
tall	taller	the tallest
large	larger	the largest
big	bigger	the biggest

Notes

1 Adjectives ending in two consonants or two vowels and a consonant add *-er / -est*.
long, short, bright, smooth, cool, clean, great
2 Adjectives ending in *-e* add *-r / -st*.
nice, late, safe, strange, rude, wide
3 Many adjectives ending in a single vowel + single consonant double the consonant and add *-er / -est*.
fat, thin, flat, sad, wet

B Regular adjectives with two or more syllables

Adjective	Comparative	Superlative
heavy	heavier	the heaviest
modern	more modern	the most modern
important	more important	the most important
common	commoner	the commonest
	more common	the most common

Notes

1 Adjectives ending in *-y* change *y* to *i* and add *-er / -est*.
happy, dirty, funny, tidy, busy, early, empty, dry
2 Most longer adjectives use *more* and *the most*.
comfortable, independent, insignificant, uninteresting
3 Some two-syllable adjectives can form their comparatives and superlatives in two ways: by adding *-er / -est* or with *more* and *most*.
clever, pleasant, gentle, narrow, shallow, simple, tired

C Irregular adjectives

Adjective	Comparative	Superlative
good	better	the best
bad	worse	the worst
old	older	the oldest
	elder	the eldest
far	farther	the farthest
	further	the furthest

2 Comparative and superlative adjectives in context

A More / -er + than

I'm **taller than** my brother.
My brother's **more serious than** me.
I'm **more intelligent than** he is.

Notes

1 If the pronoun after *than* is not followed by a verb, use the object pronoun form – *me, him, us, them,* etc.

2 If the pronoun after *than* is followed by a verb, use the subject pronoun form – *I, he, we, they,* etc.

B The most / -est

I'm **the tallest** student in the class.
My sister's **the most intelligent** student in her school.

C Less + than / the least

That film was **less interesting than** the last one I saw.
It was **the least interesting** film I've seen all year.

3 Qualifying comparative adjectives

a Use these words and phrases to refer to big differences:
far, a lot, much.
Cars are **a lot faster** and **much more comfortable** than bicycles.
b Use these words and phrases to refer to small differences:
a bit, a little, slightly.
The weather's **a bit hotter** than it was yesterday.

Comparative and superlative adverbs

1 Regular adverbs

The majority of adverbs are like this:

Adverb	Comparative	Superlative
slowly	more slowly	the most slowly

2 Irregular adverbs

Adverb	Comparative	Superlative
well	better	the best
badly	worse	the worst
little	less	the least
much	more	the most
late	later	the last

3 Adverbs which are the same as adjectives

Adverb	Comparative	Superlative
fast	faster	the fastest
hard	harder	the hardest

Other adverbs of this kind are:
far, long, loud, straight.

The + comparative + the

This construction draws attention to the link between two actions or situations (when one thing happens, another thing follows). A comparative expression in the first clause is always balanced by a comparative expression in the second clause, but several grammatical patterns are possible here:
a adjective . . . adjective.
The harder a job is, **the more rewarding** I find it.
b adverb . . . adverb.
The sooner we start, **the quicker** we'll finish.

c adjective . . . adverb or adverb . . . adjective.
>   **The easier** a job is, **the more quickly** I do it.
d *more* (+ noun) . . . *more* (+ noun).
>   **The more money** Jack earned, **the more clothes** he bought.
e *less* (+ noun) . . . *less* (+ noun).
>   **The less** Bob earned, **the less food** he could afford.
f *more* (+ noun) . . . *less* (+ noun), and vice versa.
>   **The more** you work, **the less free time** you have.

Other combinations of these patterns are possible. Here are some more examples.
>   **The harder** Joe worked, **the more** he earned.
>   **The more** he ate, **the fatter** he got.

Notice these points about *the . . . the* sentences:
1 Neither of the two clauses makes sense without the other.
2 In writing, a comma is used to separate the two clauses.
3 Both clauses need a verb.
4 In some expressions with *better*, no verbs are needed.
>   Jim   When shall I come round to see you?
>   Tim   **The sooner, the better**.

So and *such*

So and *such* are intensifiers which are used to add emphasis.

1 *So*

a *So* + adjectives (without nouns) and adverbs
>   I find Spanish people **so generous**.
>   Don't drive **so dangerously**. You'll have an accident.
b *So* is also used with *much, many, little, few*.
>   I'm not very hungry. Don't give me **so much** food.
>   I'm surprised there were **so few** people at the theatre.

2 Such

a *Such a* + adjective + singular countable noun
>   Carmen is **such a kind person**.
b *Such* + adjective + plural countable noun
>   Jo and Paul are **such hardworking students**.
c *Such* + adjective + uncountable noun
>   When we were in Spain, we had **such warm weather**.
d *Such* + *a lot (of)*
>   During our week in Thessaloniki we met **such a lot of** nice people and had **such a lot of** fun.

3 *So / such* + *that* clause

That clauses after *so* and *such* express results or consequences.
>   Maria works **so hard that** she's always top of her class.
>   John's got **such a high IQ that** he got into university when he was only 14.

Unit 5

Past Time

1 Past simple

We use the past simple tense when we want to refer to an action or event which is finished and:
1 took place at a specific time and place in the past.
>   Judy **went** to Spain in 1975.
2 took place over a specific period in the past.
>   She **lived** in Spain between 1975 and 1981.
3 was habitual during a specific period in the past.
>   When Judy lived in Spain, she **ate** dinner at about 10 p.m.

Note A past time reference must either be given or understood from the context.

2 Past continuous

We use the past continuous to indicate:
a a continuous event in the past (which may or may not be finished).
>   Dick **was working** for his uncle when I knew him.
b a temporary event in the past which was in progress before another event took place.
>   I'll always remember what I **was doing** when I heard about John Lennon's death.
c an event which started before another event in the past and continued.
>   When Neil and Cathy eventually turned up, all the other guests **were** already **eating** their dessert.
d simultaneous, continuous actions in the past.
>   While I **was trying** to phone her, she **was trying** to phone me!
e repeated actions occurring over a period of time in the past.
>   Before I got my own flat, I **was** always **arguing** with my parents.

3 Past perfect

We use the past perfect to indicate a past event or situation which occurred before another past event or situation.
>   I'**d been** awake for quite a while before the alarm rang.
>   Although I arrived on time, Mike **had** already **left**.

Note A time conjunction sometimes replaces the past perfect to show which of the two past events occurred first. In this case both events can be in the simple past tense.
>   Alex **phoned** me **before** he **left**.

4 Past perfect continuous

We use the continuous form when we want to emphasize the continuity and duration of this event.
>   Brian **had been trying** to get a job for over a year before he was offered his present one.

5 Present perfect

We use the present perfect tense when we want to talk about:

a an event which started in the past, continues in the present and may continue into the future.

*My parents **have been** married for over thirty years.*

b a recent event in the past which has relevance to the present.

*Your taxi **has arrived.***

c an event which happened in the past without saying when it happened (because we do not consider this is important).

Have *you* **seen** *Jill?*

*I've **read** Hamlet but I've **never seen** it performed.*

d an event which happened in the past but in unfinished time (with expressions like *today, this month, this year,* etc.).

*I didn't see Tim last week but I've **been out** with him twice already this week.*

6 Present perfect continuous

We use the continuous form:

a to emphasize the continuity and duration of the event.

*The Smiths **have been living** in the same house ever since they got married.*

The following verbs can be in the present perfect or the present perfect continuous tense with no real change of meaning. The continuous form is, however, often preferred: *live, wait, drive, smoke, work, stay, study, rain.*

*I've **driven** since I was eighteen.*

*I've **been driving** since I was eighteen.*

b to indicate that a continuous activity in the recent past is responsible for a present situation. This activity may or may not be finished.

*I'm not crying; I've **been peeling** onions.*

Participle clauses

A participle clause contains a present participle, e.g. *seeing,* a past participle, e.g. *seen,* or a perfect participle, e.g. *having seen.* It can be used:

a to give more information about a person or thing. It can replace a relative clause.

*The woman **wearing** the funny pink hat is my aunt.*

(replaces *who is wearing*)

*The plane, last **used** in the Gulf War, is now a museum exhibit.*

(replaces *which was last used*)

b to show that the event in the subordinate clause happens at the same time as the event in the main clause. It can replace an *as / when* clause.

***Walking** down the High Street on Saturday, I saw Paul.*

(replaces *As / When I was walking*)

c to indicate that the event in the subordinate clause immediately precedes the event in the main clause. It can replace an *as soon as* clause.

***Realizing** his mistake, Sir Edward apologized.*

(replaces *As soon as he realized*)

d to show that the event in the main clause occurs as a result of the event in the subordinate clause. It can replace a *because* clause.

***Not understanding** Albert's question, I was unable to give him an answer.*

(replaces *Because I didn't understand*)

e to emphasize that the event in the subordinate clause happened before the event in the main clause.

***Having spent** my money on a car, I couldn't afford a holiday.*

Very often the event in the main clause is the result of the event in the subordinate clause.

Note The subject of the participle must also be the subject of the other verb.

Having a bath, the phone rang is not possible.

Unit 6

Conditional sentences

There are four main types of conditional sentence. Each type has a distinctive pattern of verb tenses, and its own meaning.

1 Zero / present conditional (type 0)

A Form

If + present . . . present or imperative

B Meanings

This type of sentence is used to refer to conditions which are always true.

*If **Mike reads** on the train, **he feels** sick.*

(Every time Mike reads on the train, the same thing happens: he feels sick.)

This type of sentence is also used to refer to scientific facts.

*If **you put** paper on a fire, **it burns** quickly.*

It is also used to give instructions.

*If the phone **rings**, **answer** it.*

In zero or present conditional sentences *when* or *whenever* can be used instead of *if*.

2 First conditional (type 1)

A Form

If + present simple . . . *will* future

B Meaning

This type of sentence is used to predict likely or probable results in the future, if a condition is met.

*If **we don't leave** now, **we'll miss** the train.*

*If **we leave** now, **we won't need** to hurry.*

First conditional sentences are often used to express promises, warnings and threats.

*If **you pass** your exams, **I'll give** you a job.*

*If **you don't turn** that music down, **you'll go** deaf.*

C Some modal verbs can be used instead of *will*.

*If we leave now, we **may** catch the train.*

*If you come to London again, you **must** call and see us.*

D Unless or if not

Unless can sometimes be used instead of *if not*.
> **Unless** *we leave now, we'll miss the train.*
> (**If we don't** *leave now, we'll miss the train.*)

3 Second conditional (type 2)

A Form

If + past simple . . . *would / could / might*

B Meaning

This type of sentence is used to speculate about imaginary or improbable situations (the implication is that the conditions will *not* be met).
> **You'd feel** *healthier* **if you did** *more exercise.*
> **If you went** *to Africa,* **you'd have** *to have several injections.*
> (It's not likely you'll go to Africa, but it is possible.)

Second conditional sentences can refer to unreal situations.
> **If people didn't drive** *so fast,* **there wouldn't be** *so many fatal accidents.*
> (Actually people do drive fast and there are a lot of fatal accidents.)

Second conditional sentences are often used to express advice.
> **If I were** *you,* **I wouldn't drive** *so fast.*

C Might / could

Might and *could* can be used instead of *would* in the main clause of second conditional sentences to show uncertainty.
> **If you did** *more exercise,* **you might feel** *healthier.*

4 Third conditional (type 3)

A Form

If + past perfect . . . *would / might / could have* + past participle.

B Meaning

This type of sentence looks back at the past and speculates about possibilities which didn't happen.
> **If I'd had** *your address,* **I'd have sent** *you a postcard.*
> (I didn't have your address, so I didn't send you a postcard.)
> **You might not have crashed** *into the bus* **if you'd been driving** *more slowly.*

Note When the *if* clause comes before the main clause, it is followed by a comma. When the *if* clause comes after the main clause, there is no comma between the clauses.

Unit 7

Relative clauses

1 Form and use

a   A relative clause gives extra information.

b   It is introduced by a relative pronoun: *who (whom), which, that, whose* or there may be no relative pronoun, Ø.

c   The choice of relative pronoun depends on whether:
   • it is the *subject* or *object* or *possessive* of a relative clause.
   • it refers to a *person* or *thing*.
   • the relative clause is *identifying* or *non-identifying*.

d   Relative clauses are common in spoken and written English. However, *non-identifying* relative clauses are more common in written English than in spoken English.

2 Identifying and non-identifying clauses

a   The information given in an identifying relative clause is *essential* to the meaning of the sentence.
> *The man* **who lives at number 36** *has been arrested.*
> *The fingerprints* **that were found on the gun** *were his.*

An identifying relative clause makes clear *which* person or thing we are talking about.

b   The information given in a non-identifying relative clause is *not* essential to the meaning of the sentence.
> *Mr. White ,* **who lives at number 36,** *has been arrested.*

c   Punctuation is important in *non-identifying* relative clauses. A comma is put before the relative pronoun and at the end of the clause, unless this is also the end of the sentence. In *identifying* relative clauses there are no commas.

3 Relative pronouns

A In identifying relative clauses

		Person	Thing
1	Subject	*who (that)*	*that (which)*
2	Object	*Ø (that, who, whom)*	*Ø (that, which)*
3	Possessive	*whose*	*whose (of which)*

The pronouns in brackets are less commonly used.

1   As subject
> *People* **who (that)** *go to university are not necessarily more intelligent than people who don't.*
> *The universities* **that (which)** *opened in the sixties were all campus universities.*

Who and *which* are more usual in writing. *That* is more usual in speech when referring to things.

2   As object
> *That's the woman* **(Ø, that, who, whom)** *I saw.*
> *It was her car* **(Ø, that, which)** *Philip crashed into.*

The relative pronoun is frequently omitted, particularly in speech. *Whom* is formal and is used mainly in writing.

3   As possessive
> *That's the man* **whose** *house was burgled last week.*
> *We arranged to meet at a place* **whose** *location (the location* **of which)** *was to be kept secret.*

Note We usually use *that* (not *which*) after the following words: *all, any(thing), every(thing), few, little, many, much, no(thing), none, some(thing)* and after superlatives. When the pronoun refers to the object, *that* can be omitted.
> *It was something* **that** *could have happened to anyone.*
> *It was the most difficult exam* **(that)** *I'd ever taken*

B In non-identifying relative clauses

		Person	Thing
1	Subject	*who*	*which*
2	Object	*who(m)*	*which*
3	Possessive	*whose*	*whose (of which)*

1   As subject
> *Jim Kerr,* **who** *is lead singer with the rock band 'Simple Minds', is the Rector of Edinburgh University.*
> *St. Andrews University,* **which** *is the oldest university in Scotland, is the Scottish equivalent of Oxford.*

2 As object

> Alice asked Richard Gere, **who (whom)** she had immediately recognised, for his autograph.
> Mr James had been driving a brand-new car, **which** his father had given him for his birthday.

That can never be used in non-identifying clauses.

3 As possessive

> The author, **whose** latest novel is a bestseller, spent the afternoon signing copies of his book.
> The restaurant, **whose** name he could not remember, was one of the best he had ever eaten at.

Notes

1 In non-identifying relative clauses, *which* can refer to a whole clause.

> He climbed the mountain wearing only a T-shirt and trainers, **which** was a stupid thing to do.

2 In non-identifying relative clauses, after numbers and words like *many, most, neither, some,* we use *of* before *whom* and *which.*

> Dozens of people had been invited, most **of whom** I knew.

4 *Where, why* and *when*

Where, why and *when* can be used instead of a relative pronoun after a noun which refers to a place, a time or a reason.

A Identifying clauses

In identifying clauses *why* and *when* can be omitted.

> I'd like to live in a country **where** it's summer all year round.
> Do you know the reason **(why)** Kate's changed her mind?
> June is the month **(when)** many couples get married.

B Non-identifying clauses

In non-identifying relative clauses *when, where* and *why* cannot be omitted.

> Aileen was brought up in Scotland, **where** she was born, but she emigrated after her marriage.
> The town is quieter after lunch, **when** everyone is having a siesta.

5 Relative clauses and prepositions

A A preposition can either come before the relative pronoun (more usual in formal English) or at the end of the relative clause (more usual in informal English).

> The Hilton Hotel, **at which** we stayed while we were in New York, is expensive.
> The Hilton Hotel, **which** we stayed **at** while we were in New York, is expensive.

B Identifying relative clauses

	Formal	Informal
Person	*whom*	Ø
Thing	*which*	Ø

> The man **to whom I spoke** gave me different information.
> The man **I spoke to** gave me different information.
> The car **in which the robbers got away** had been stolen.
> The car **the robbers got away in** had been stolen.

C Non-identifying relative clauses

	Formal	Informal
Person	*whom*	*who*
Thing	*which*	*which*

> The hotel manager, **to whom I spoke** about my dissatisfaction, suggested I write to you.
> The hotel manager, **who I spoke to** about my dissatisfaction, suggested I call you.

Modifying adjectives and adverbs

A Some adjectives and adverbs can be used to intensify or reduce the strength of gradable adjectives and adverbs like *big* and *fast*. The most common modifying adverbs, in order of strength, are *very, rather, quite* and *fairly.*

> Norman did it **fairly** quickly.
> That book was **quite** interesting.

The following words can be used instead of *very* : *extremely, really, incredibly, terribly.* Of these, only *extremely* is used in formal English. *Pretty* can be used as an alternative to *rather.*

B The meaning of these words depends on the intonation.

1 *My dad's fairly **active** for a man of 60 .* (Weak stress on *fairly,* strong stress on *active*) = more active than you would expect a man that age to be.

2 *My dad's **fairly active** for a man of 60.* (Equal stress on both words) = reasonably active

3 *My dad's **fairly** active for a man of 60.* (Strong stress on *fairly*) = active but not especially so.

C *Rather* and *quite*

1 *Rather* has a similar meaning to *quite* and *fairly* but is often used with adjectives and adverbs which have the idea of something bad, or which the user disapproves of.

> Michael's **rather** old for her.

With approving adjectives and adverbs and rising intonation it means *better than expected.*

> I don't usually like Spielberg films, but his latest is **rather** good.

2 *Quite* can be used with ungradable adjectives like *enormous* and *incredible,* and strong gradable adjectives like *essential* to mean *absolutely* or *totally.*

> Edmund's journey was **quite** unnecessary.

3 *Rather* and *quite* can also be used with nouns.

> We had **quite** a good meal.

Unit 8

The passive

1 Verbs that can be used in the passive

Most transitive verbs can be used in the passive. A transitive verb is a verb which has an object, e.g. *catch.*

> The police **caught the thief.**

Intransitive verbs cannot be used in the passive. An intransitive verb is a verb which does not have an object, e.g. *fall.*

> Rodney **fell** and hurt his leg.

2 Form of the passive

The passive is formed with the verb *be* in the appropriate tense + the past participle of the main verb. In the case of modals, e.g. *could, must,* it is formed with the modal + *be* + past participle.

Tense	Subject	Verb 'be'	Past Participle
present simple	*Letters*	*are*	delivered twice a day.
present continuous	*Redmond*	*is being*	watched.
past simple	*The Loch Ness Monster*	*was (first)*	seen in 565 A.D.
past continuous	*Our hotel room*	*was being*	cleaned when we arrived.
present perfect	*Antiques worth over £10,000*	*have been*	stolen.
past perfect	*They*	*had been*	warned about the danger.
future	*You*	*will be*	paid on Friday.
modals	*Food*	*should be*	eaten before the sell-by date.

Note In informal English *get* can sometimes be used instead of *be* to form the passive. The agent is not generally mentioned.
> *Nigel **got stopped** for speeding.*

3 Choosing active or passive form

In an active sentence, the subject is the person or thing that does the action.
> ***Liverpool** beat Manchester United.*

In a passive sentence, the subject of the verb is the person or thing affected by the action.
> ***Manchester United** were beaten by Liverpool.*

When we want to focus on the person or thing **affected** by the action instead of the **doer** of the action (the agent) we use the passive.

4 Including the agent (doer)

When we use the passive we can choose to include the agent or not. The agent is the person or thing responsible for the action. We include the agent only if we consider it to be important.
> *The record is held **by Carl Lewis**.*

We do not include the agent:

a when the agent is not important.
> We do not say: *Trespassers will be prosecuted **by the landowner**.*

b when we do not know who the agent is and would have to use the words 'somebody' or 'a person'.
> We do not say: *My car has been stolen **by somebody**.*

c when the agent is obvious.
> We do not say: *The thief was sentenced to five years imprisonment **by the judge**.*

d when the agent has already been mentioned.
> We do not say: *Some of Stephen King's books have been written **by him** under the pseudonym Richard Bachman.*

5 Verbs with two objects

Some verbs can have two objects – a direct object (DO) and an indirect object (IO).
> *Lady Markham's late husband had given **the painting** (DO) **to the gallery** (IO).*
> *Lady Markham's late husband had given **the gallery** (IO) **the painting** (DO).*

Both objects can be the subject of the passive verb.
> ***The painting** had been given to the gallery by her late husband.*
> ***The gallery** had been given the painting by her late husband.*

When one of the objects is a person, it is more usual for this to be the subject.
> ***Bobby** was given a new bike for his birthday.*
> and not *A new bike was given to Bobby for his birthday.*

6 Passive constructions with the infinitive

When we want to pass on information but we do not know whether the information is true or not, or we do not want to say where the information came from, we can use the passive form of these verbs followed by the infinitive:
> *think, believe, report, consider, know, say, expect.*

When the information is about a present situation, we use the passive + infinitive.
> *The Queen **is believed to be** one of the richest people in the world.*
> *Mr Smith **is thought to be staying** with friends.*

When the information is about something in the past, we use the passive + the past infinitive (*to have* + past participle).
> *Cher is **said to have had** a face-lift.*

Unit 9

1 Making suggestions

Some common expressions used for making suggestions are:
> ***Why don't you** [1] / **we** [2] go to the USA for your / our holiday?*
> ***You** [1] / **we** [2] **could** visit New York while you're / we're there.*
> ***Let's** [2] go to the travel agent's this afternoon to book our ticket.*
> ***What / How** [3] **about** phoning first to see how much it is?*
> ***I suggest you** [1] / **we** [2] think about it a bit more first.*

Notes
1 These expressions do not include the speaker.
2 These expressions include the speaker.
3 These expressions could (but may not) include the speaker.

2 Giving advice

Here are some ways of expressing advice.
> ***I don't think you should** eat so much.*
> ***You ought to** eat less fast food.*
> ***You ought not to** eat so much fast food.*
> ***You shouldn't** drink so much – it's not good for you.*
> ***If I were you, I'd** go on a diet.*
> ***If I were in your position / shoes, I'd** do more exercise.*
> ***You'd better** be careful what you eat.*
> ***You'd better not** eat any more sweets. You'll be sick!*
> ***Whatever you do, don't** eat any more cake – it's very fattening.*

3 Giving warnings

1 Here are some expressions used for giving warnings.

> ***Don't*** *play around with fireworks,* ***or you might / could*** *be badly injured.*
>
> ***Look out! Be careful!***

2 *Otherwise* can be used instead of *or* to warn what will happen if advice is not followed.

> *Work hard* ***otherwise*** *you'll fail your exam.*

4 Use of should, ought to, could

A Should

1 Advice

> ***You should*** *go and see Casablanca – it's a brilliant old film.*

2 Obligations

> ***I should*** *get my father a card – it's his birthday tomorrow.*

3 Probability

> *If the train's on time,* ***we should*** *arrive at 3.30.*
>
> *(It is likely / probable that we will arrive at 3.30.)*

B Ought to

1 Advice

> ***You ought***[1] ***to*** *stop smoking – it's very bad for you.*

2 Obligations

> ***I really ought***[2] ***to*** *pay the telephone bill tomorrow.*

3 Theory

> ***John ought to*** *be here by now*[3] *– I hope he hasn't had an accident.*

Notes

1 *Ought to* expresses less personal advice than *should*.

2 *Ought to* here indicates that the speaker probably won't pay the bill tomorrow.

3 *Ought to* here means *was due to* or that it was expected.

C Could

1 Suggestions

> ***You could*** *call a taxi.*

2 Past ability

> *When I was five* ***I could*** *swim 500 metres.*

3 Possibility

> *My car* ***could*** *break down at any time – it's very old.*

4 Request for permission

> ***Could I*** *come in please?*

Contrasting ideas

Here are the most common ways of contrasting ideas.

A But

But is a conjunction which contrasts ideas in one sentence.

> *I want to leave school* ***but*** *my parents won't let me.*

B However

However contrasts ideas in different sentences.

> *My parents want me to go to college.* ***However***, *I have other ideas.*

However is most commonly used at the beginning of a sentence, but it can also come in the middle or at the end.

> ***However***, *I have other ideas.*
>
> *I,* ***however***, *have other ideas.*
>
> *I have other ideas,* ***however***.

C Despite / in spite of

Despite can be used to contrast ideas in one sentence.

a *Despite* + noun or gerund

> ***Despite*** *my headache, I took the exam.**
>
> ***Despite*** *feeling ill, I took the exam.*

b *Despite the fact (that)* + clause

> ***Despite*** *the fact that I felt ill, I took the exam.*

In all the above sentences, *despite* can be replaced by *in spite of*.

* **Note** It is only correct to use *despite* + *-ing* when the subject of the *-ing* form is the same as the subject of the verb in the main clause. You cannot say *Despite speaking more slowly, I still couldn't understand him.*

D Although

Although is a conjunction which is used to contrast ideas in one sentence. It can be used before or after the main clause.

> ***Although*** *it was raining hard, we took the dog for a walk.*
>
> *We took the dog for a walk,* ***although*** *it was raining hard.*

Even though is often used in informal speech instead of *although*. It puts greater emphasis on the contrast between the ideas.

Unit 10

Modal verbs

1 Obligation and necessity

A Must

Must + infinitive is used for strong obligations which express the authority of the speaker or writer. So, it is used:

a for formal rules or laws.

> *Passengers* ***must*** *fasten their seat belts for take-off.*

b for suggestions, advice or recommendations that the speaker or writer feels strongly about.

> *You* ***must*** *come to my party. Everyone's going to be there.*

B Have to

Have to + infinitive is used for strong obligations which express the authority of a third person, rather than the speaker or writer. So, it is used:

a when the speaker wants to show they are not responsible for imposing the obligation, or do not agree with it.

> *I'll be late home tonight. I* ***have to*** *work late. My boss said so.*

b when the speaker or writer is reminding someone about a rule or law.

> *I'm sorry, but you* ***have to*** *wear a seat belt in the back of cars now.*

C Have got to

Have got to is a more informal than *have to*. So, it is often used:

a for direct commands.

> *You've* ***got to*** *stop wasting your money.*

b for emphasis.

> *I don't care how hard I have to work, I've just* ***got to*** *pass this time.*

D *Need to*

Need to is used to express needs or necessities, rather than actual obligations.

> *If we're going to work together I **need to** know about your background and experience.*

E Negatives

1 *Mustn't* expresses prohibition (negative rules and laws or strong advice).

> *Drivers **must not** exceed the speed limit.*
> *You **mustn't** blame yourself. It's not your fault.*

2 *Do not have to / have not got to* express lack of obligation or necessity.

> *You **don't have to** wear school uniform, but you can if you want to.*

3 *Do not need to / needn't* + infinitive express lack of obligation or necessity and are similar in meaning to *do not have to*.

> *There are no lessons tomorrow, so I **don't need to** get up early.*
> *You **needn't** tell me your phone number if you don't want to.*

4 *Did not need to* + infinitive means 'It was not necessary, so we didn't do it'.

> *The train was delayed so we **didn't need to** hurry.*

5 *Needn't have* + past participle means 'It was not necessary, but we did it before we realized this'.

> *We had to wait for half an hour on the platform because the train was delayed. We **needn't have** hurried after all.*

2 Permission and prohibition

A *Can / can't*

This is one of the commonest ways of expressing permission and prohibition.

> *Can I use the phone, please?*
> *In Spain **you can't** leave school until the age of 16.*

Note

May I . . . ? means the same as *Can I . . . ?*, but is more formal and more polite.

B Other expressions of permission

> *You're allowed to buy cigarettes when you're 18.*
> *We were only permitted to take photographs in certain places.*
> *My parents let me stay up late at weekends.*

C Other expressions of prohibition

> *You aren't allowed to go abroad without a passport.*
> *Smoking is not permitted in most cinemas.*
> *You are not permitted to smoke in this theatre.*
> *People are forbidden from smoking on the Underground.*
> *The workers have been prohibited from striking.*
> *Nigel has been banned from driving for 6 months.*

Too, enough, very

1 *Too*

Too means *more than is needed or wanted* and is used in these ways:

a *Too* + adjective or adverb

> *It's **too hot** in here. Can I open a window?*
> *You're driving too fast. Slow down.*

b *Too* + adjective or adverb + *for*

> *This food is **too hot for** me. I can't eat it, I'm afraid.*
> *You're walking **too slowly for** me. Hurry up!*

c *Too* + adjective or adverb (+ *for* + object) + *to* + verb

> *My father was **too ill to look after** himself.*
> *That film was **too frightening for us to watch**. That's why we left before the end.*

d *Too* + quantifier (+ noun)

> *I ate **too much (food)** at lunchtime, so I don't feel hungry now.*
> *I'll never finish the exam. There's **too little time** left.*

2 *Enough*

Enough means *sufficient / as much as is needed* and is used in these ways:

a Adjective or adverb + *enough*

> *Holidays are never **long enough**.*
> *I didn't go to bed **early enough** last night.*

b Adjective or adverb + *enough* + *for* + noun or pronoun

> *My car isn't **big enough for the whole family**.*

c Adjective or adverb + *enough* + *to* + verb

> *My parents didn't think we were **old enough to get** married.*

3 *Very*

Very simply gives emphasis and is used in these ways:

a *Very* + adjective

> *Concorde is a **very fast** plane.*

b *Very* + adverb

> *I can walk **very quickly**.*

c *Very* + quantifier

> *I'm on a diet, so I'm eating **very little**.*

4 *Too, enough* or *very*

Compare these three sentences:

> *The holidays are **very long**. (We don't know how the speaker feels about this.)*
> *The holidays are **too long**. (The speaker doesn't like this.)*
> *The holidays are **long enough**. (This is just right.)*

Unit 11

Talking about ability

1 *Can, be able to*

Can and *be able to* are the verbs most commonly used to express ability. Sometimes it is possible to use either verb without changing the meaning of the sentence. Sometimes, however, we have to use *be able to* as there is no appropriate form of *can*.

Infinitive	—	*to be able to*
Present	*can*	*am / is / are able to*
Future	—	*will be able to*
Past	*could*	*was / were able to*
Present perfect	—	*have / has been able to*

See **4** below for uses of *could*.

2 Present ability

A To talk about a general ability in the present both forms are possible but *can* is more usual.

> Adrian **can** cook really well.
> (He **is able to** cook really well)

B To talk about a learned ability in the present *can* is more usual. *Know how to* can be used as an alternative to *can*.

> **Can** you play chess?
> Do you **know how to** play chess?

3 Future ability

To talk about an ability in the future we use the future form of *be able to*.

> **Will I be able to** play better after I've had some lessons?

4 Past ability

A To talk about a general ability in the past both forms are possible.

> Before his accident, Ben **could** run as fast as the best of them.
> Before his accident, Ben **was able to** run as fast as the best of them.

B To talk about an ability to do something in the past on one particular occasion, it is not possible to use *could*. We must use the past tense of *be able* or *manage* + infinitive or *succeed in* + -ing.

> Although she had lost a lot of blood, the doctors **were able to save** the girl's life.
> Despite the difficult conditions, the doctors **managed to perform** the operation successfully and **succeeded in saving** the man's leg.

Note If the event was unsuccessful, it is possible to use *couldn't* as well as the past tense forms of *be able to, manage to, succeed in*.

> Although he did his best, he **couldn't** finish it in time.

5 'Conditional' ability

A To talk about a hypothetical ability in the present or future we can use *could* or *would be able to*.

> I **could** probably jump higher if I had longer legs.
> I **would** probably **be able to** play better if I concentrated more.

B To talk about a hypothetical ability in the past we usually use *could* + *have* + past participle although we can also use *would have been able to*.

> Even if he'd got into the final, he **couldn't have beaten** Christie.
> Even if he'd run faster than he'd ever run, he **wouldn't have been able to beat** Christie.

6 Other structures used to talk about ability

A To talk about aptitude and capacity for doing something we can use *be capable of* + -ing.

> Eddie's certainly **capable of breaking** the world record.

B To talk about how well we do something we can use the structure *be good / bad at* + noun or gerund.

> I've never **been good at sports**.
> I was particularly **bad at running**.

Question tags

1 Form

A A question tag consists of the verb *be* or an auxiliary (*do, have*) or modal auxiliary (e.g. *can, should*) + subject pronoun. It is added to an affirmative or negative statement.

B As a general rule, if the statement is in the affirmative then the question tag goes in the negative and vice-versa.

> It**'s** 5 o'clock, **isn't** it?
> There **aren't** enough glasses, **are** there?

C If there is an auxiliary verb or a modal auxiliary verb or *be* in the statement, it is repeated in the question tag.

> You **haven't** seen Stuart, **have** you?
> You **can** come, **can't** you?
> I**'m** a bit early, **aren't** I? (Not *amn't I?*)

D If there is a full verb in the statement, the auxiliary verb *do* is used in the question tag.

> His plane **arrives** at 10 p.m., **doesn't** it?
> It **snowed** this time last year, **didn't** it?

Note When *have* is a full verb and not an auxiliary verb we use the auxiliary *do* in the question tag and not *have*.

> They **had** a good time, **didn't** they?

E After imperatives we can use the following forms: *will you? would you? can you? could you?*

> Take that to Mary, **will you?** (**would you?** is more formal)
> Speak up, **can you?** (**could you?** is more formal)
> The effect of the question tag here is similar to 'please'.

Note After a negative imperative only *will you?* is possible.

> Don't make a mess, **will you?**

F After statements containing negative words like *nothing, nobody, none*, we use an affirmative question tag.

> Nothing was stolen, **was it?**
> Nobody was hurt, **were they?**

Note With words like *nobody, somebody* we use the plural pronoun *they*.

2 Use and intonation

We usually use question tags:
a to ask for confirmation of something. This is like a real question, and the question tag is said with rising intonation.

> David's married, isn't he? (I think he is married but I want you to answer 'Yes he is' or 'No he isn't'.)
> He isn't arriving tomorrow, is he? (I didn't think he was arriving tomorrow but I'm not sure and I want confirmation of when he is arriving.)

b to ask other people if they agree with us. In this case the question tag is said with falling intonation.

> Alf's a good pianist, isn't he? (I expect you to say 'Yes'.)
> You don't know Tom, do you? (I expect you to say 'No')

Unit 12

Certainties and possibilities

1 Indicating attitudes to facts

If we are absolutely sure of our facts, we generally use a full verb to express this certainty.

> Craig **wasn't** at home yesterday afternoon.

If we are not absolutely sure of our facts, we can use the modal verbs *must, can't, may, might, could* to indicate how sure we are.

2 Expressing near certainty

If we are almost sure of our facts, and this certainty is based on evidence, we can make statements using *must* or *can't*. If we are talking about a present situation we use *must* or *can't +* infinitive without *to*.

> My doctor **must be** married. She wears a wedding ring. (I am almost certain she is married.)
>
> Angus **can't be** English. He's got a Scottish accent. (I am almost certain he isn't English.)

We can also use the continuous form of the verb.

> Virginia **must be going** to play tennis. She's carrying a racket. (I am almost certain she is going to play tennis.)

If we are talking about a past situation we use *must* or *can't +* *have* + past participle.

> Sandra **must have passed** her driving test because I saw her driving a car on her own. (I am almost certain she has passed her test.)
>
> Fiona and Neil **can't have enjoyed** their holiday because they haven't said anything about it. (I am almost certain they didn't enjoy their holiday.)

We can also use the continuous form of the verb.

> I'm sorry I'm late. You **must have been waiting** for ages!

Note   The negative of *must* in this case is *can't*, not *mustn't*.

3 Expressing possibility

If we are not sure of our facts but we think that they are possibilities, we can use the modals *could, may, might +* infinitive without *to* to talk about a present situation and *could, may, might + have + past participle* to talk about a past situation. It is also possible to use continuous forms. There is no real difference in meaning between the three forms.

> Paula **could be** on holiday. (Maybe she's on holiday.)
>
> Freda **might have overslept.** (It's possible that she's overslept.)
>
> The missing girl **may have been wearing** a blue skirt.
>
> Claude **may be** ill. (Perhaps he's ill.)

Note

The negative forms of *may* and *might* are *may not* and *might not*. It is not usual to use a contracted form.

> The defendant **may not be telling** the truth. (It's possible that he isn't telling the truth.)

The negative form is *couldn't*. It's meaning is similar to *can't*.

> He **couldn't be lying**. (I am almost certain he isn't lying.)

Wishes

1 Use

We use *wish* to talk about situations we would like to change but can't either because they are outside our control or because they are in the past.

2 Tenses

The tense of the verb after *wish* does not correspond to the time we are wishing about; it changes. The verb tense is one step back in time (as in reported speech. See page 192).

A   A wish about a present or future situation is expressed with a past tense.

Situation	Wish
I'm an only child	I wish I **wasn't** an only child.
I can't drive	I wish I **could** drive.
Rod isn't coming to the party	I wish Rod **was coming**.

Note   In formal English we say I / he / she / it *were* / *weren't*.

B   A wish about a past situation is expressed with a past perfect tense.

Situation	Wish
I've lost my best pen	I wish I **hadn't lost** it.
I didn't remember	I wish I**'d remembered**.

3 *Wish . . . would.*

We use *wish . . . would:*

a   when we want to complain about a present situation.

Situation	Wish
A dog is barking	I **wish** that dog **would** stop barking!
The road is icy	I **wish** you **wouldn't** drive so fast

Note We can't say I wish I would...

b   when we are impatient for an event outside our control to happen.

Situation	Wish
It's raining	I wish it **would stop** raining.
You're waiting for the bus	I wish the bus **would come**.

Notes

1   It is not possible to use *wish . . . would* with the verb *be*. We say *I wish it were Friday* and not *I wish it would be Friday*.

2   If we want a future event to happen or not happen, and this event is possible and not just a desire, we use the verb *hope +* *present simple*.

> I **hope I pass** my exams.

Unit 13

Speech

1 Direct speech

We can report what someone has said in two ways.
a We can report their actual words.
b We can report the idea they expressed.

When we report a person's actual words in writing, we put speech marks on either side of the words and use an appropriate verb, e.g. *say, tell, ask*.

> *'I'll be late home tomorrow,' Bob said.*

See the Terminology section on page 178 for notes on the use of punctuation in direct speech.

2 Reported speech

When we report the idea and not the actual words that a person says we often have to make certain changes. These changes are usually to verb tenses, pronouns, word order, and time and place references.

3 Reporting statements

A Changes in verb tenses

When the reporting verb is in the past tense, e.g. *said*, we usually move the tenses in the sentence we are reporting one step back in time.

Direct speech	Reported speech
Present simple ⟶	Past simple
'I'm a nurse,' she said.	*She said she was a nurse.*
Present continuous ⟶	Past continuous
'I'm not going,' he said.	*He said he wasn't going.*
Past simple ⟶	Past perfect
'Tony did it,' she said.	*She said Tony had done it.*
Present perfect ⟶	Past perfect
'I haven't read it,' she said.	*She said she hadn't read it.*
Past continuous ⟶	Past perfect continuous
'I was lying,' he said	*He said he'd been lying.*
'Will' future ⟶	Would
'I'll get it,' she said.	*She said she would get it.*
Can ⟶	Could
'I can speak French,' he said.	*He said he could speak French.*
May ⟶	Might
'I may be late,' she said.	*She said she might be late.*
Must ⟶	Had to
'I must go,' he said.	*He said he had to go.*

Note The past perfect and the modals *might, ought to, could, should* and *would* do not change in reported speech.

B No changes in verb tenses

1 When the reporting verb is in the present tense, e.g. *says*, we do not change the tense of the original verb. For example when we are reading what someone says in a newspaper or letter, e.g. *Darren says he's been too busy to write before*, or when we are passing on a message, e.g. *Lucy says she'll be late*.

2 When the reporting verb is in the past tense and we want to emphasize that the statement is still true we can keep the same tense if we wish.

> *'Bill is my cousin'* *She said Bill is her cousin.*

C Changes in time and place words

Some typical changes that may have to be made are:

Direct speech	Reported speech
today	**that day**
tomorrow	**the next day, the following day**
yesterday	**the previous day, the day before**
two days ago	**two days before, two days earlier**
now	**then**
here	**there**
come	**go**

Unless time and place words are reported at the same time and in the same place as they were originally said, they change.

> *'Marie phoned yesterday.'* (said on Monday) *He said (that) Marie had phoned two days ago / on Sunday.* (said on Tuesday)

D Other changes

1 Pronouns may change when we are reporting speech. This depends on who is reporting.
> *'**I**'ll give **you** a lift.'* (Jack to Barbara)
> *Jack said **he** would give **me** a lift.* (Barbara to Peter)

2 The determiners *this, that, these, those* may change to *the*.
> *'**These** jeans are too tight,' Cyril said.*
> *Cyril said **the** jeans were too tight.*

3 The pronouns *this* and *that* may change to *it*.
> *'Give me **that**!' Jayne said.*
> *Jayne told me to give **it** to her.*

E Reporting verbs

We can use the verbs *say* and *tell* to report statements. The structure after these verbs is *say (that)* + clause:
> *Richard **said (that) he would be late**.*

and *tell someone (that)* + clause:
> *Richard **told me (that) he would be late**.*

That is frequently omitted in spoken English.

4 Reporting questions

A Changes

We make the same changes to verb tenses, time and place words and pronouns as we do when we report statements. We also change the form of the original question into a statement and omit auxiliary verbs (*do, does, did*) and question marks.
> *'When are you arriving?'*
> *He asked me when I was arriving.*

If there is no question word in the original we must use *if* or *whether* (*if . . . or not*).
> *'Do you understand?'*
> *He asked her if / whether she understood.*

B Reporting verbs

To report questions we can use the verb *ask* or the structure *want to know*.
> *'Are you enjoying yourself?' Mr Jones asked.*
> *Mr Jones **wanted to know** if I was enjoying myself.*

5 Reporting other kinds of speech

A Reporting advice, commands, requests and warnings

We can report these kinds of speech using the verbs *advise, tell, ask* and *warn* + personal object pronoun + infinitive.

'You really should stop!' (advice)
*She **advised me to** stop.*
'Don't interrupt me!' (command)
*He **told me not to** interrupt him.*
'Could you close the door please?' (request)
*She **asked me to** close the door.*
'If you tell anyone, I'll ...!' (warning)
*She **warned me not to** tell anyone.*

Notes

1 The structure after *ask* is different when we are reporting a request or a question.

'Can you remind me please?' (request)
*He **asked me to** remind him.*
'Can you come tomorrow?' (question)
*She **asked me if I could** come the next day.*

2 The structure after *tell* is different when we are reporting a command or a statement.

'Come on! Hurry up!' (command)
*She **told us to** hurry up.*
'It doesn't start till 8.' (statement)
*He **told us (that)** it didn't start until 8.*

B Reporting suggestions

We can report suggestions with the verb *suggest* + clause
'Let's stay in.'
*She **suggested that** we (should) stay in.*
*She **suggested that** we stayed in.*
*She **suggested staying** in.*

Note You cannot use the infinitive in this structure.

Unit 14

Cause and effect

1 *Make*

The verb *make*, which means *to cause to (be)*, is used in two different ways.

a *Make* + object + adjective
*Going to bed late will **make you overtired**.*
*Exercise **makes you fit**.*
b *Make* + object + infinitive (without *to*)
*Aerobic exercise **makes your heart beat** faster.*
*Horror films **make me laugh**.*

Note If the subject of the verb is a person, *make* often means *to force* or *compel*.

*My father **made me finish** my homework.*
*The customs officer **made me empty** my suitcase.*

2 Other expressions of cause and effect

a *Bring about* + object
*Going to India **has brought about a complete change** in the way he looks at the world.*
b *Cause* + object / *cause* + object + *to* + verb
*Too much exercise **can cause** insomnia.*
*Seeing that terrible accident **has caused him to pay more attention** to his own driving.*
c *Result in* + noun
*Getting plenty of rest before an exam **can result in an improved performance**.*

Expressing purpose

Here are some common ways of talking about purpose.
1 *To* + infinitive
*People work **to earn money**.*
2 *In order to* + infinitive
*Nick went to Germany **in order to learn** the language.*
***In order not to be** recognized, Martin wore a disguise.*
3 *So as to* + infinitive
*William went into town by bus **so as to avoid** the usual parking problems.*
***So as not to wake** her parents, Juliet took her shoes off when she went upstairs.*
In order to and *so as to* are more formal than *to*.
4 *So that* + clause
*I turned the light on **so that I could see** what I was doing.*

Causative verbs

Have something done and *get something done* are both used to refer to actions which are done for the subject rather than by the subject. Causative verbs are used instead of passive verbs to show that the subject causes the action to be done.

1 *Have something done*
*I don't know how to repair cars, so I'm **having mine repaired** at the garage round the corner.*

2 *Get something done*
*I really must **get my eyes tested**. I'm sure I need glasses.*
***Get** your hair **cut**!*

Note The differences between *have* and *get something done* are that *have* is slightly more formal than *get*, and that *get* is more frequent than *have* in the imperative form.

3 Non-causative uses of *have* and *get*
Have and *get* are also used to refer to events which happened to someone, but were outside their control.
*After being late for work every day for two weeks, Billy **had his pay reduced**.*
*I stood so close to the fire that **I got my legs burnt**.*

Phrasal verbs

Introduction

A phrasal verb is a verb used with a particle (an adverb or a preposition). The meaning of the verb and the particle together is idiomatic – it means something different from the separate literal meanings of the verb and the particle. Phrasal verbs are very common, especially in informal English.

In addition to learning the meanings of phrasal verbs, you also need to know how to use them correctly. Most importantly, you need to know whether the verb and the particle have to stay together or whether they can be separated.

The grammar of phrasal verbs

From a grammatical point of view, there are four main types of phrasal verbs.

A Intransitive[1] verb + adverb

Examples *touch down*
set off

Verbs like these are always inseparable – the verb and the adverb always stay together and can never be separated by other words.
> The plane **touched down** at 6.25 precisely.
> We **set off** very early in the morning.

[1] An intransitive verb is a verb which cannot have an object.

B Transitive verb[2] + adverb + object
or transitive verb + object + adverb

Examples *make out*
pick up

Verbs like these are separable – the object of the verb can come between the verb and the adverb.
If the object is a noun, it may come before or after the particle.
If the object is a pronoun, it **must** come between the verb and the particle.
> I couldn't **make** the car number **out**.
> I couldn't **make out** the car number.
> I tried to see the car number, but I couldn't **make it out**.

[2] A transitive verb is a verb which can have an object.

C Verb + preposition + object

Examples *get at*
take after
cope with

Verbs like these are inseparable – the object of the verb cannot come between the verb and preposition.
> She really **takes after** her mother.
> I don't know how I'm going to **cope with** my new job.

This rule is still true when the object is a pronoun.
> Leave me alone! Just stop **getting at** me.

D Verb + adverb + preposition + object

Examples *run out of*
look forward to
put up with

Verbs like these are inseparable – the three parts of the verb always stay together, whether the object is a noun or a pronoun.
> When I was driving home last night, I **ran out of** petrol.
> I don't think I could **put up with** another hot summer.
> I'm really **looking forward to** it.

Meanings

Some phrasal verbs can have two meanings. This is sometimes the case when the particle can be used as an adverb *or* as a preposition. Here is an example with *get over*.
> I knew what I wanted to say, but I couldn't **get it over** to anybody else.

Here, *over* is an adverb, so **get over** meaning *communicate* or *convey* is a Type B phrasal verb.
> It took me about a week to **get over** the accident.

Here, *over* is a preposition, so **get over** meaning *recover from* is a Type C phrasal verb.

This table shows some more examples of verbs with two meanings.

	Verb Type B meaning	Verb Type C meaning
turn on	start something (e.g. *a light / the TV*)	attack suddenly and unexpectedly
make up	invent (e.g. *a story*)	constitute / form

Phrasal verbs used in this book

This includes all the useful phrasal verbs which appear in the reading texts and listening passages in this book and which are considered important for First Certificate.

Phrasal verbs which are part of a specific vocabulary exercise in the units, are printed in **bold** in this list. The number in brackets refers to the unit in which the verb first appears, and the letter (A–D) indicates the type of phrasal verb it is. Words in italics show the meaning of the verb in this particular context.

add up *make sense* (4) A
add up *calculate* (11) B
blow up (10) B
break down (6) A
break out (of) (6) A/D
break out *start* (7) A
break up (2) A
bring about (14) B
bring back (9) B
bring back (13) B
bring in (9) B
bring round (9) B
bring on (9) B
bring out (9) B
bring out (9) B
bring up (9) B
build up (12) A
burst into (8) C
care for (10) C
carry out *a threat* (10) B
carry out *research* (14) B
catch up with (14) D
clean up (8) B
come across (12) C
come out (12) A
come round *visit /regain consciousness* (12) A
come up (12) A
come up against (14) D
come up with (12) D
cut down (9) B
cut down on (14) D
drink up (8) B
drop off (8) A
eat up (8) B
fall into (14) C
fall over (11) A
fill up (8) B
find out (5) A/B

fit in (7) A
get away *escape* (8) A
get away from (1) D
get by (8) A
get down *depress* (8) B
get into (9) C
get off (9) C
get on *continue / manage* (8) A
get on with *have good relations with* (8) D
get on *board* (9) C
get out (of) *escape* (8) A/D
get over *recover from* (8) C
get up (6) A
give away (6) B
give in *surrender* (9) A
give up (2) B
go along with (14) D
go back to (13) D
go down to (1) D
go down with (14) D
go off *explode / go bad* (13) A
go on *happen* (1) A
go out *stop burning* (13) A
go over (13) C
go through (13) B
go with (13) C
grow up (1) A
hang on to (1) D
hang up (10) B
hold up *rob* (6) B
hurry up (1) A
keel over (13) A
keep at *persevere* (3) C
keep away from (2) D
keep to (10) C
keep up *maintain* (6) B
keep up with (14) D
jut out into (1) D

leave out (11) B
let down *disappoint* (6) B
load up (10) B
look after (10) C
look at (13) C
look for (5) C
look forward to (5) D
look out over (1) D
move in (10) A
move on to (9) D
move on (10) B
nod off (8) A
pass out (6) A
pay back (11) B
pay into (11) B
pay off (11) B
pep up (14) B
pick up *illnesses* (1) B
pick up *a person in a car* (5) B
point out (9) B
pop up (9) A
put down (9) B
put down (11) B
put off (3) B
put on (3) B
put towards (11) B
put up *build* (1) B
put up *increase* (2) B
put up with (2) D
read out (13) B
run away (10) A
run out (11) A
save up (11) A/B
set in (7) A
set off (5) A
set out *leave* (5) A
set out *have the intention* (13) A
settle down (1) A
show off (4) A/B
slow down (8) A
sort out (8) B
split up (6) A
switch off (3) B
switch on (10) B
take in *understand* (1) B
take after (4) C
take back *withdraw* (4) B
take down *write* (4) B
take off *remove* (3 / 10) B
take off *leave the ground* (5) A

take on (4) B
take out *withdraw* (11) B
take over (4) B
take round (5) B
take to (4) C
take up *start doing* (4) B
tear up (8) B
throw away (5) B
tidy up (8) B
tie in with (14) D
touch down (1) A
track down (2) B
try on (10) B
turn down *decrease / refuse* (7) B
turn into (1) C
turn to (7) C
turn off (3) B
turn out *come to see* (6) A
turn out *be discovered to be* (7) A
turn over (7) B
turn up *increase* (7) B
turn up *arrive* (10) A
wake up (5) A/B
watch out for (9) D
wear out (10) A/B
wipe out (12) B
work out (5) B
work out at (6) D
wrap up (8) B
write in (13) A

Vocabulary reference

This section comprises vocabulary related to the main topics in each unit. Most of the words listed are used in the book, but a few others have been added where they might be useful. Common words which students at this level should know by now have not been included. The following abbreviations are used:

n – noun   vb – verb   adj – adjective

Unit 1

Places

1 Buildings for living in
apartment
bedsit
block
  apartment block
  block of flats
bungalow
cottage
flat
floor
  on the ground /
  first / top floor
house
  detached house
  semi-detached
  house
  terraced house
storey
  a ten / multi-storey
  building

2 Other buildings and facilities
car park
castle
cathedral
church
office
  office block
park
post office
pub
shop
  baker's
  butcher's
  chemist's
  department store
  dry cleaner's
  fishmonger's
  fish-shop
  greengrocer's
  grocer's
  ironmonger's
stationer's
sweet shop
travel agent's
skyscraper
station
  bus station
  fire station
  police station
  railway station
town hall

3 Communities
city
  capital city
port
resort
  holiday resort
  seaside resort
  ski resort
town
village

4 Parts of communities
area
  country area
  residential area
  rural area
  urban area
centre
  city centre
  town centre
district
outskirts
  on the outskirts
region
residential area
suburbs
  in the suburbs
  suburban (adj)

5 Geographical features
bay
beach
coast
  on the coast
countryside
flat (adj)
forest
hill
  hilly (adj)
lake
mountain
  mountainous (adj)
plain (n)
river
sea
  by the sea
seaside
  at the seaside
shore
stream (n)
valley
wood
  woody / wooded
  (adjs.)

Unit 2

Jobs

accountant
air steward
architect
assistant
  personal assistant
  shop assistant
author
baker
barman / barmaid
  (bar person)
builder
businessman /
  woman / executive
butcher
caretaker
chef
civil servant
clerk
computer operator/
  programmer
cook
decorator
dentist
designer
director
  company director
  film director
doctor
driver
  bus / taxi / train
  driver
dustman (refuse
  collector)
economist
editor
electrician
engineer
farmer
fisherman
fishmonger
flight attendant
hairdresser
head teacher
jeweller
journalist
judge
lawyer
lecturer
manager
miner
musician
news reader / news
  presenter
nurse
optician
painter
photographer
pilot
police officer
politician
porter
printer
prison officer /
  warder
receptionist
sailor
salesman /
  saleswoman
scientist
secretary
soldier
solicitor
surgeon
tailor
teacher
telephonist
telephone operator
travel agent
TV cameraman
TV presenter
vet
waiter
writer

Unit 3

Entertainment & the Arts

1 Venues
art gallery
cinema
concert hall
exhibition centre
museum
opera house
stadium
theatre

2 People
actor
artist
audience
backing group
ballerina
choreographer
composer
conductor
dancer
director
drummer
guitarist (lead / bass)
magician
musician
orchestra
painter
pianist
playwright
producer
saxophonist
sculptor
singer
vocalist
violinist

3 Events
ballet
concert
exhibition
film
play
opera

4 Interiors and equipment
aisle
box
circle
curtain
footlight
gallery
lighting
microphone
orchestra pit
row
screen
scenery
set
speaker
stage
stalls
wings
workshop

5 Arts and crafts
carving
drawing
knitting
painting
pottery
sculpture
sewing

6 Materials
canvas
charcoal
clay
cloth
paint
papier-mâché
plaster
steel
stone
wood

7 Other related words
dubbed dialogue
encore
interval
lines
part
plot
photography
script
subtitles

8 Verbs
applaud
boo
conduct
exhibit
perform
play a part

Unit 4

Families and other relationships

1 Families
aunt
brother
  elder / older brother
cousin
father
grandchild
  granddaughter /
  son
  grandfather /
  mother
  grandparent(s)
husband
  ex-husband
in-laws
  son-in law, etc.
mother
niece
nephew
parents
sister
step-father
  step-daughter, etc.
twin
  twin-sister / brother
uncle
widow (woman)
widower (man)
wife
  ex-wife

2 Marital status
divorced
engaged
married / unmarried
separated
single
widowed

3 Other relationships
acquaintance
boss
colleague
employee
employer
fiancé / fiancée

friend
  best friend
  girlfriend /
  boyfriend
neighbour
partner

4 Verbs
get divorced (from) /
  engaged (to) /
  married (to)
get on (well) with
  someone
go out with someone
marry someone
start / end a
  relationship with
  someone

Unit 5

Sport

1 Sports
athletics (do)
badminton (play)
basketball (play)
boxing
cycling
diving
football (play)
golf (play)
gymnastics (do)
hockey (play)
horse-racing
ice-skating
motor-racing
riding
rugby (play)
skiing
snooker (play)
squash (play)
surfing
swimming
tennis (play)
volleyball (play)
weightlifting
windsurfing

2 People
athlete
badminton player
basketball player
boxer
cyclist
diver
footballer
golfer
gymnast
hockey player
jockey
ice-skater
racing driver
rider
rugby player
skater
skier

snooker player
squash player
surfer
swimmer
tennis player
volleyball player
weight-lifter

3 Equipment
ball
  football
  hockey ball
  golf ball
bat
cue
golf club
hockey stick
ice-skates
racing car
racket
saddle
sailboard
skis
shuttle cock
surfboard

4 Places
circuit
court
course
gym
pitch
ring
rink
stadium

5 Verbs
beat
box
catch
cycle
dive
draw
hit
kick
lose
miss
pass
pot
practise
race
ride
save
score (a point / a
  goal)
serve
shoot
skate
ski
swim
surf
tackle
train
throw
volley
win

6 Related words
amateur (adj / n)
ace

basket
captain
cup
game
goal
kit
match
medal
net
professional (adj / n)
race (n / vb)
record
referee
spectators
team
whistle

Unit 6

The body

**1 Head and
shoulders**
chin
cheek
ear
eye
  eyebrow
  eyelash(es)
forehead
hair
head
lip(s)
mouth
neck
nose
nostril
jaw
shoulder
tooth (teeth)
tongue
throat

2 Arms and hands
elbow
finger
  index finger
  middle finger
  little finger
  (finger)nail
fist
forearm
hand
  left / right hand
palm
thumb
wrist

3 Legs and feet
ankle
calf
foot (feet)
heel
hips
knee
leg
shin

thigh
toe
  big toe
  little toe
toenail

4 Trunk
bottom
chest
back
stomach (tummy)
waist

5 General words
bone
hair
muscle
skin

**6 Verbs with parts
of the body**
eyes
  blink
  glance
  stare
  wink
finger
  point
  scratch
foot
  kick
hands
  clap
  punch
  shake
  slap
  smack
head
  nod
  shake
lips
  kiss
mouth
  eat
  mutter
  talk
  whisper
nose
  breathe
  smell
  sniff
shoulders
  shrug
teeth
  bite
  chew
toe
  stub
tongue
  lick
throat
  swallow

Unit 7

Describing people

1 Age
Age categories
baby
toddler
child
teeny-bopper
teenager
young man / woman
youth *men only; often has negative associations;
  often used in connection with crime*
middle-aged (man / woman)
elderly (man / woman) *more polite word then
  'old'*
Precise ages
She is twenty-one (years old).
Imprecise ages
He's in his teens.
She's in her early / mid- / late twenties.
He's about thirty.   She's forty something.
He's fiftyish.   She's sixty odd.

2 Height
He's average height *average is a relative
  measurement*
She's above average height. *more common in
  formal or written language*
She's petite. *used for girls and women, it means
  short but dainty and feminine*
He's short.
She's tall(ish) / short(ish). *the suffix -ish means
  quite*
She's taller / shorter than average. *more
  common in spoken or informal language*

3 Build
Women and men
He's fat / overweight.
She's slim. *pleasingly thin*
He's thin. *often used in a negative way*
She's skinny. *too thin*
Women
She's got a good figure.
She's plump.
  pleasantly fat; more polite than 'fat'
Men
He's got a paunch. *a large, protruding stomach*
He's stocky. *short and strong*
He's well built.
  strong, largish but not fat

4 Hair
Length
long / short
medium-length / shoulder-length
  mainly used to describe women's hair
Colour
(jet) black
fair / dark
ginger / red
grey / going grey
light-brown / medium-brown / dark-brown
natural blond / dyed blond *written blonde for
  women*
white

Type

He's bald / going bald. / He's got a bald patch.
curly / spiky / straight / wavy
He's got a receding hairline. *more formal*
His hair's receding.
 less formal

Style (mainly women)

She's wearing her hair down / loose / up / in
 plaits / in a pony-tail.
She's got a fringe / side parting / centre
 parting.

Order of adjectives

The usual order is: length+colour+type
She's got short, blonde curly hair.
or (length)+type +colour
She's got wavy, blonde hair. *however, 'straight'
 usually comes before the colour.*

5 Complexion

She's got a fair /
 dark / olive / pale / tanned complexion.
He's got a clear / good / spotty complexion.
She's got freckles.

6 Distinguishing features

He's got a beard / moustache. He's clean-
 shaven.
He's got bushy eyebrows / a scar / a tattoo.
She wears glasses.

Unit 8

Food and drink

1 Types of meals
barbecue
buffet
four-course meal
picnic
snack
TV dinner

2 Condition of food
fresh
off
past its sell-by date
raw
ripe
rotten
stale
tender
tough
undercooked
unripe
overcooked

3 Taste and texture
bitter
bland
creamy
crisp
crunchy
hot
mild
salty
savoury
sickly
sour
spicy
stodgy
sweet
tasteless

4 Containers
bottle
box
can
carton
jar
packet
pot
tin

5 Quantities
bar
litre
loaf
lump
piece
pint
portion
slice
spoonful

6 Verbs
Cooking food
bake
boil
cook
fry
grill
heat
microwave
poach
roast
steam
stew
Preparing food
add
beat
blend
chop
dice
grate
melt
peel
shred
slice
spread
stir
whisk
Preparing drinks
add
fill
mix
pour
shake
stir
**Eating and
 drinking**
bite
chew
swallow
sip

7 Other words
crumbs
fast food
(non-)fattening
helping
pastry
slimming
sticky

Sleep

doze
dream
fast asleep
nap
nightmare
snore
stretch
toss and turn
wide awake
yawn

Celebrations and festivals

**1 Types of
 gathering**
barbecue
christening
family gathering
funeral
get-together
anniversary party
party
 birthday party
 cocktail party
 dinner party
 fancy dress party
wedding

2 Other words
band
banner
commemorate
costume
firework display
flag
float
parade
procession

Unit 9

Travel

1 Air
airport
check-in (n) / check
 in (vb)
land (vb)
landing (n)
plane
take-off (n) / take
 off (vb)

2 Land
bicycle (bike)
bus
 bus station
car
coach
 coach station
lane
motorbike
motorway
rail
 go by rail
railway
 railway station
road
 main road
 minor road
taxi
traffic
train
 express train
 stopping train
tube
underground

3 Sea
boat
crossing
ferry
port
sea
ship
voyage

4 Verbs
board (boat / plane)
go by (boat, train,
 etc.)
go on board
hitch-hike (vb)
 go hitch-hiking
set off
set sail

5 General
destination
journey
passenger
route
travel
travel agent
trip

Holidays

camp (vb)
 go camping
charter flight
cruise
excursion
(youth) hostel
hotel
luggage
motel
package holiday
self-catering holiday
sightseeing
 go sightseeing
(suit)case
tour
 tourism
 tourist

Unit 10

Clothes

1 General
anorak
belt
blouse
cardigan
dress
gloves
jacket
jeans
jumper
mac(k) / mackintosh
overcoat
pullover
raincoat
scarf
shirt
 sweat-shirt
 T-shirt
skirt
shorts
socks
suit
sweater

2 Headgear
beret
cap
hat
helmet

3 Footwear
boots
plimsolls
sandals
slippers
shoes
trainers

4 Underwear
bra
knickers
pants
tights
vest

5 Night-wear
dressing-gown
night-dress / nightie
pyjamas

**6 Sports-wear and
 swim-wear**
bikini
swimming costume /
 swim-suit (women)
swimming trunks
 (men)
jogging suit
tracksuit

Materials

1 Artificial
plastic
nylon
polyester

2 Natural
cotton
denim
leather
linen
rubber
silk
suede
wool (n)
 woollen (adj)

Patterns

check (n / adj)
 checked (adj)
flowery (adj)
patterned (adj)
plain (adj)
spot (n)
 spotted (adj)
stripe (n)
 striped (adj)
tartan (n / adj)

Unit 11

Money

1 Banking and investing
(traveller's) cheques
account
bank statement
bankrupt
borrow
budget (n / vb)
cash
cashier
credit (card)
currency
debt
deposit (n / vb)
exchange rate
interest (rate)
invest
investment
lend
loan
mortgage (n / vb)
owe
pay
save
savings
shares
withdraw

2 Earning
bonus
earn
earnings
income
 net
 gross
rise
salary
wage

3 Buying and spending
bargain
bill
cost (n / vb)
expense
instalments
price
purchase (n / vb)
purse
receipt
reduction
refund (n / vb)
spend
wallet

4 Giving, receiving and paying
collection
donation
fee
fine (n / vb)
grant
income tax
inherit

inheritance
pension
pocket money
rent (n/vb)
tip (n / vb)
winnings

5 Related adjectives
affluent
broke
generous
hard-up
mean
poor
prosperous
rich
stingy
wealthy
well off

6 Verbs and expressions
add up
go up / down
make ends meet
pay back
pay into
put down
put towards
run out
save up
take out

7 Other words
valuable
value
wealth
worth
worthless

Unit 12

Science and technology

1 Machinery (general terms)
appliance
engine
gadget
machine

2 People
inventor
researcher
scientist
technician

3 Adjectives
battery- / mains-
 operated
high-tech
remote control
portable
scientific
technical

4 Inventions
computer
communications
 satellite
microchip

The mind

1 Adjectives
articulate
brainy
bright
gifted
imaginative
intelligent

2 Verbs
analyse
calculate
infer
memorize
realize
recognize
work out

3 Other words
brain
emotion
genius
idea
intellect
knowledge
logic
memory
mind
skill
thought
virtuoso

The senses

1 Senses
hearing
sight
smell
taste
touch

2 Verbs
catch a glimpse
glance
glimpse
hear
listen
look at
notice
observe
scan
see
stare

3 Other words
(colour) blind
deaf
eyesight
hard of hearing
short- / long-sighted

microscope
microwave
robot
speedometer
thermometer

5 Verbs
discover
experiment
invent
research

6 Other words
fax (facsimile copy)
 (n / vb)
lab (laboratory)

The environment

1 Natural disasters
drought
earthquake
flood
tidal wave
typhoon
volcanic eruption

2 Environmental issues
acid rain
aerosol
bottle-bank
carbon monoxide
climate
conservation
endangered species
energy
 nuclear
 solar
exhaust fumes
fertilizers
forest fires
global warming
greenhouse effect
(non)-renewable
 resources
nuclear
 fallout
 reactor
oil-slick
ozone layer
pesticide
pollution
protected animal
rain forest
unleaded petrol
waste
 nuclear
 radio-active
wildlife

3 Politics
environmental
 group
green issues
pressure group

4 Verbs
cut down
destroy
dispose (of)
dump
protect
pollute
recycle
save
throw away
use up

Unit 13

Crime

1 Crimes
arson
assault
blackmail
burglary
fraud
hijacking
hooliganism
kidnapping
mugging
murder
(armed) robbery
shoplifting
smuggling
terrorism
theft
vandalism

2 Criminals
arsonist
blackmailer
burglar
hijacker
hooligan
kidnapper
mugger
murderer
robber
shoplifter
smuggler
terrorist
thief
vandal

3 Justice and punishment
appeal
barrister
cell
corporal punishment
capital punishment
court
court case
death penalty
defence
gaol (Br) jail (US)
guilty
(life) imprisonment
innocent
judge
jury

justice
lawyer
offence
(life) sentence
prison
probation
prosecution
remand home
solicitor
trial
verdict
witness

4 Verbs
arrest
ban
break in
break out
break the law
burgle
charge
commit a crime
escape
get away
get away with
hold up
investigate
rob
steal

5 Other words
armed
burglar / car alarm
legal (illegal)
store detective
weapon

Unit 14

Education

1 Subjects
art
business studies
dance
drama
economics
games (sport)
geography
geology
history
home economics
foreign (modern)
 languages
maths
music
physical education
religious education
science
 biology
 chemistry
 physics
sociology
technology

2 People
head-teacher

infant
lecturer
pupil
schoolboy
schoolgirl
student
teacher

3 Types of school
boarding school
  a boarder
day school
primary school
  infant school
  junior school
  nursery school
secondary school
(sixth form) college
university

4 Exams
cheat
fail
pass
take / sit an exam
  retake / re-sit
revise for
test (n / vb)

5 Qualifications
certificate
degree
  BA / MA / BSc /
  MSc / PhD
diploma

Health

1 People
dentist
doctor
general practitioner
midwife
nurse
patient
specialist
surgeon

2 Places
hospital
operating theatre
surgery (doctor's /
  dental)
waiting room
ward

3 Treatment
bandage
a check-up
a dose (of medicine)
drugs
injection
  give someone an
  injection
medicine
  take medicine
operation
pain-killer
pill

plaster
tablet
tranquillizer

4 Illnesses
ache
  headache
  stomach ache
  ear ache
  toothache
cancer
cold
cough
flu
heart disease
heart attack
infection
  infectious (disease)
pain
virus

5 Minor injuries
bruise
cut
graze (n / vb)
wound

6 Verbs
catch
  catch flu
cure
heal
hurt
injure
operate on
prescribe
  prescription (n)
treat
  treatment (n)

7 Adjectives
fit
ill
sick
  feel sick
  be sick (vomit)
healthy
  unhealthy
painful

Other words
ambulance
emergency
first aid
health insurance

Irregular verbs

Infinitive	Past simple	Past participle
be	was / were	been
beat	beat	beaten
become	became	become
begin	began	begun
bend	bent	bent
bite	bit	bitten
bleed	bled	bled
blow	blew	blown
break	broke	broken
bring	brought	brought
build	built	built
burn	burnt, burned	burnt, burned
burst	burst	burst
buy	bought	bought
catch	caught	caught
choose	chose	chosen
come	came	come
cost	cost	cost
cut	cut	cut
deal	dealt	dealt
do	did	done
draw	drew	drawn
dream	dreamt, dreamed	dreamt, dreamed
drink	drank	drunk
drive	drove	driven
eat	ate	eaten
fall	fell	fallen
feed	fed	fed
feel	felt	felt
fight	fought	fought
find	found	found
fly	flew	flown
forbid	forbade	forbidden
forget	forgot	forgotten
forgive	forgave	forgiven
freeze	froze	frozen
get	got	got; (US) gotten
give	gave	given
go	went	gone
grow	grew	grown
hang	hung, hanged	hung, hanged
have	had	had
hear	heard	heard
hide	hid	hidden
hit	hit	hit
hold	held	held
hurt	hurt	hurt
keep	kept	kept
know	knew	known
lay	laid	laid
lead	led	led
lean	leant, leaned	leant, leaned
learn	learnt, learned	learnt, learned
leave	left	left
lend	lent	lent
let	let	let
lie	lay	lain
light	lit	lit
lose	lost	lost
make	made	made

Infinitive	Past simple	Past participle
mean	meant	meant
meet	met	met
pay	paid	paid
put	put	put
read	read	read
ride	rode	ridden
ring	rang	rung
rise	rose	risen
run	ran	run
say	said	said
see	saw	seen
sell	sold	sold
send	sent	sent
set	set	set
shake	shook	shaken
shine	shone	shone
shoot	shot	shot
show	showed	shown, showed
shrink	shrank, shrunk	shrunk
shut	shut	shut
sing	sang	sung
sink	sank	sunk
sit	sat	sat
sleep	slept	slept
smell	smelt, smelled	smelt, smelled
speak	spoke	spoken
spell	spelt, spelled	spelt, spelled
spend	spent	spent
spill	spilt, spilled	spilt, spilled
spin	spun	spun
spoil	spoilt, spoiled	spoilt, spoiled
spread	spread	spread
stand	stood	stood
steal	stole	stolen
stick	stuck	stuck
sting	stung	stung
strike	struck	struck
sweep	swept	swept
swell	swelled	swollen, swelled
swim	swam	swum
swing	swung	swung
take	took	taken
teach	taught	taught
tear	tore	torn
tell	told	told
think	thought	thought
throw	threw	thrown
wake	woke	woken
wear	wore	worn
win	won	won
wind	wound	wound
write	wrote	written

Index

Page numbers in roman refer to the units; numbers in **bold** refer to the Grammar reference.

Acknowledgements

The authors and publisher are grateful to those who have given permission to reproduce the following extracts and adaptations of copyright material:

p.2 adapted from Fiona Malcolm: 'For my next trick', photograph by David Secombe, in *Sunday Times Magazine*, © Times Newspapers Ltd, 1992, by permission. p.7 extract from Molly Parkin: 'Bad Habits' reproduced from *Marie Claire*/European Magazines 1989/Robert Harding Syndication. p.26 adapted from Brendan Martin: 'Talking to . . . Elton John', in *Woman's Realm*, by permission of the author. p.38 adapted from Mandy Bruce: 'Whose finger is on the button in your house?', illustration by Graham Thompson, reproduced from *Woman*, © Woman/Solo Synidcation, by permission. p.52 adaptation of 'It happened to me . . .' reproduced from *Woman*, © Woman/Solo Syndication, by permisison. pp.64–5 adapted from Terence Brady: 'The festival of hope that reminds us we are human' in *The Mail on Sunday*, © Mail on Sunday/Solo Syndication, and adapted table, 'The twelve ways of Christmas', from *The Daily Mail*, © Daily Mail/Solo Syndication, both by permission. p.91 extracts from 'Lowdown of Friday the 13th', in the *Observer Magazine*, by permission of The Observer ©. p.101 extract from Sandy Sulaiman: 'Toys for the grown-up boys', © The Guardian, by permission. pp.102–3 (on cassette) adapted from Alison Leigh Jones: 'Are your kids playing with danger?' in *Woman*, © Woman/Solo Syndication, by permission. pp.106–7 abridged from Katie Wood: 'Eurorailing', first published in National Student Extra, January 1992, by permission of the author. p.121 adapted from Duncan Campbell: 'TV killer of council planner gets life', and 'Obsession that led to gun murder', © The Guardian, by permission. p.125 extract from Barry Hugill: 'The four-year-old undergraduate', in *The Observer*, by permission of The Observer ©. pp.142–3 extract from article by Nigel Hawkes in *World Magazine* (BBC), by permission of the author. p.150 adapted from Martin Wainwright: 'Cardboard patrols cut out speeding', © The Guardian, by permission. p.165 'Exam Factsheets for *Getting Physical*' by Dr Aric Sigman, by permission of the author, written for the BBC's *Going Live* (BBC1, 28.3.92). pp.167–8 (on cassette) adapted from Liz Hodgkinson: 'Play it again, Doc', in *You* magazine, by permission of the author.

Although every effort has been made to trace and contact copyright holders before publication, this has not been possible in these cases. We apologize for any apparent infringement of copyright and if notified, the publisher will be pleased to rectify any errors or omissions at the earliest opportunity. p.18 adapted article by Jan Vijg in *Plus Magazine*. p.42 (on cassette) from an article by Catherine Charnaud in *The Indy*. p.76 article by Genevieve Muinzer. p.88 article by Paul Haddlesey in *Scoop*. p.100 python article, source unknown. p.101 letter from *She*, writer unknown. p.126 article by Louise Hidalgo in *The Indy*. p.152 (on cassette) from an article in *Early Times*. p.156 article from *The Indy*. p.173 article on pets, source unknown.

Illustrations by: David Austin: p.158 (left). Richard Deverell: pp.17, 34 (top), 114. Nicki Elson: p.56. Simon Fell/Universal Pictures: p.101. Sophie Grillet: 5, 11 (bottom), pp.21, 27, 35, 45, 61, 71, 85, 95, 109, 123, 133, 144, 162 (bottom), 170. Sue Hillwood-Harris: pp.40, 52, 53, 120, 145. John Holder: p.67. Sian Leetham: pp.28, 29, 55, 66, 166. David Loftus: pp.20, 132. Fiona MacVicar: pp.7, 32, 57, 88, 94, 119, 155, 162 (top). Margaret Morgan: p.44. Oxford Illustrators: pp.60, 87 (graph), 91, 169. Punch Library: p.103. Stuart Robertson: pp.80, 81, 165. Colin Salmon: pp.58, 98, 146. Susan Scott: pp.10, 11 (top). Graham Thomas/Woman: p.38
Handwriting by: Kathy Baxendale
Studio photography by: Philip Dunn: p.90 (centre)
Mark Mason: paper backgrounds
Location photography by: Philip Dunn: pp.13, 14, 16, 69 (top), 82, 84, 105. J. L. Poulmarc'h: p.12

The publishers would like to thank the following for their permission to reproduce photographs and other copyright material:
Sam Abell: p.47 (left). Action Plus: Glyn Kirk p.30 (bottom), Chris Barry p.40 (soccer), p.114 (rugby), Mike Hewitt p.122 (bottom), p.152 (bottom right), Peter Tarry p.152 (bottom left), Richard Francis p.152 (top right). Allsport: Gerard Planchenault p.5 (background), Pascal Tournaire p.5 (foreground), Bob Martin p.31 (top, centre and right), Howard Boylan p.79 (bottom), Chris Cole pp.113 and 115 (Sumo wrestlers), Adrian Murrell p.152 (top left). Amnesty International: p.156. Aquarius Picture Library: pp.130 (right), 131 (centre and bottom). Ardea: John Daniels p.40 (bottom right), P. Morris p.161 (right). Art Directors: pp.25 (top left), 87 (bottom left). BBC: p.42 (Turnabout). Beken of Cowes: p.13 (top). Brabantia: p.137 (bottom left). Brainwaves/Design Marketing: p.137 (top centre left and right, and bottom centre). Clarks Shoes: p.90 (bottom left). Collections: Anthea Sieveking pp.4 (main picture), 75 (top left), 125 (top centre), Brian Shuel p.113 (schoolboys), Nigel Hawkins p.167 (top centre left). Colorific: John Moss p.4 (main picture), p.97, Henning Christoph p.8 (centre), Patrick Ward p.122 (centre), Carol Lee p.142 (bottom). Cunard: p.15. James Davis: pp.9 (bottom), 37 (bottom), 40 (River Amazon), 91 (left and right), 113 (Ceremonial guards), 167 (top centre right, and bottom left). East Anglian Daily Times: p.54. Robert Estall: p.113 (Heads of state). Diego Andres Gomez: p.79 (top). The Guardian: Denis Thorpe p.141 (top), Guglielmo Galvin p.141 (bottom). The Ronald Grant Archive: p.40 (top centre and right), pp.41, 130 (left and centre), 131 (top). Sally and Richard Greenhill Photo Library: pp.37 (top), 75 (top centre). Robert Harding Photo Library: p.23, Geoff Renner p.51 (top left), p.114 (right). Hitachi: p.137 (bottom right).

Hulton-Deutsch: p.139. Image Bank: p.63. Images: p.1 (right). Impact: Piers Cavendish p.21, John Cole pp.106, 113 (top fashion models), Bruce Stephens p.114 (left), Peter Arkell p.114 (centre left). Tony Lees: p.158. Life File: Cluny Macpherson p.8 (bottom), Alan Gordon p.19, Nicola Sutton p.70, Bill Webster p.92 (right), Emma Lee p.92 (top left), Tim Fisher p.96, Ian Lochhead p.151 (top right). Magnum Photos: Richard Kalvar p.47 (right), Jean Gaumy p.125 (top left), Erich Lessing p.151 (left centre), Stuart Franklin p.163 (top left). Mars Confectionery: p.90 (bottom right). Mercury Press Agency: p.46. Network: Mike Goldwater pp.48 (left), 64 (left), 134 (top left), Gideon Mendel p.92 (top centre), John Sturrock p.134 (top right), Martin Mayer p.151 (top left), Barry Lewis pp.163 (bottom right), 167 (top right). Gavin Newman: p.58. Nintendo: p.102. North of England Newspapers: p.121. Photofusion: Sarah Saunders p.69 (bottom), p.Gino Glover pp.75 (bottom centre), 163 (bottom left), Sally Lancaster pp.138, 151 (right centre). Popperfoto: Limberger pp.25 (bottom right), 142 (centre). Philippa Rampling: p.32 (left and right). Claire Redwood: p.32 (centre). Retna Pictures: Neal Preston p.26. Rex Features: pp.18 (top left), 76, 129 (bottom), Richard Young p.25 (top right), The Sun p.25 (bottom left), Nils Jorgensen pp.36 (top), 161 (left), Cyntilia Carris p.36 (bottom), Eugene Adebari p.40 (bottom left), David Hartley p.44, The Sunday Times p.64 (bottom right), Vanystadt-Fury p.75 (top right), Francoise de Mulder p.75 (bottom left), Stuart Clarke p.129 (top), Chat p.159, Eddie Boldizsar p.163 (top right), Tony Larkin/Mike Daines p.126. Science Photo Library: Phillippe Plailly p.87 (top), James Holmes p.87 (bottom right), Peter Menzel p.142 (top), E. R. Degginger p.143. Scottish and Newcastle Breweries: p.90 (top right). Gavin Smith: p.125 (bottom left). Sony: p.48 (bottom). Frank Spooner: J. Budge 2, p.40 (top left). The Sunday Times: David Secombe p.1 (left). Svenskt Pressfoto: Jansson p.92 (bottom left). Syndication International: pp.8 (top), 51 (bottom), 77, 151 (bottom right), 167 (bottom right). Telegraph Colour Library: p.9 (top), G. Marche, p.18 (right), p.51 (top right), M. Krasowitz p.113 (Doctors), p.113 (Professional ballet dancers), p.113 (Monks), p.122 (top). Times Newspapers: Peter Trievnor p.128. Trip: Eye Ubiquitous p.90 (top left), Bob Turner p.151 (bottom left). Universal Pictorial Press Agency: p.75 (bottom left). John Walmsley: pp.125 (top right), 134 (bottom left and right), 167 (top left). Zanussi: pp.90 (centre left), 137 (top right)

The authors are grateful to the following people for their help:
Tony Kidd, Beverley Maltby, Pete and Chris Proctor, Madame Rivière (le Gai Logis), Maison Urwin.

The authors and publisher would like to thank all the teachers and students who contributed to the research and development of the course. The following people and institutions who piloted and reported on the material deserve special thanks:
Kerry Allen; Ann Ayton, ILA; Simone Aronsohn; Deborah and Sarah Boodt; Elizabeth Curry, Frontisterio Papoutsi-Mitta; Raquel Reyes Delgado; Mrs Detsika; Carolyn Frenzel, Nick Love and Helen Gialias, Anglo-Continental; Tony Gill and Lorraine Kelly, Language Studies Ltd; Jesus Gimeniz and Joaquim Silos, Today School; Jill Grimshaw; Clare Hindley, Central School; Tim Hoggard; David Jones, ETC (UK); Mrs Katsianou; Mr Kontogeorgis; Mrs Koumatou; Clare McGinn, King Street College; Rita Misaelidou; Maria Moumtzi and Mrs Angelaki; Rhian Owen, Esade; Mr and Mrs Papageorgiou; Mr Papalexiou; Athina Papasotiriou, Frontisterio Haralambidis; Lilly Sell and Susan Barber, Lake School; Mrs Sigizi; Costas Sotiriou; Pete Staboglis and George Trigas; Gisela Szpytko, Anglo World; George Tavridis, Nikos Avramides, Melinda Tsagarouli, Kelly Webb, Fany Antoniou, Helen Konstantinidi, Kathy Kontogianni and Iraklis Papadopoulos, Strategakis Central School; Lesley Thompson; Tony Triggs; Deborah Watson; Louise Webb and Margie Johnson, Eurocentres; Clare West; Saraita Whan and Imogen Arnold, Godmer House; Peter Wilson, Dickens School; Stephen Yeats; Mrs Zazani.

Oxford University Press   Walton Street, Oxford OX2 6DP

Oxford   New York   Toronto   Madrid   Delhi   Bombay
Calcutta   Madras   Karachi   Kuala Lumpur
Singapore   Hong Kong   Nairobi   Dar es Salaam
Cape Town   Melbourne   Auckland

and associated companies in   Berlin   Ibadan

OXFORD and OXFORD ENGLISH are trade marks of Oxford University Press

ISBN 0 19 4328198

© Oxford University Press 1994

First published 1994
Second impression 1994

No unauthorized photocopying

All rights reserved. No part of this publication may be reproduced, stored in a retrieval system, or transmitted, in any form or by any means, electronic, mechanical, photocopying, recording or otherwise, without the prior written permission of Oxford University Press.

This book is sold subject to the conditions that it shall not, by way of trade or otherwise, be lent, re-sold, hired out, or otherwise circulated without the publisher's prior consent in any form of binding or cover other than that in which it is published and without a similar condition including this condition being imposed on the subsequent purchaser.

Printed in Hong Kong